# PORTUGUESE STUDIES

VOLUME 33 NUMBER 1
2017

*Founding Editor*
HELDER MACEDO

*Editors*
CATARINA FOUTO
TOBY GREEN
TORI HOLMES
PAULO DE MEDEIROS
PAUL MELO E CASTRO
HILARY OWEN
CLAIRE WILLIAMS

*Editorial Assistant*
RICHARD CORRELL

*Production Editor*
GRAHAM NELSON

MODERN HUMANITIES RESEARCH ASSOCIATION

# PORTUGUESE STUDIES

*A peer-reviewed biannual multi-disciplinary journal devoted to research on the cultures, literatures, history and societies of the Lusophone world*

International Advisory Board

DAVID BROOKSHAW
JOÃO DE PINA CABRAL
IVO JOSÉ DE CASTRO
THOMAS F. EARLE
JOHN GLEDSON
ANNA KLOBUCKA

MARIA MANUEL LISBOA
KENNETH MAXWELL
LAURA DE MELLO E SOUZA
MARIA IRENE RAMALHO
SILVIANO SANTIAGO

*Portuguese Studies* and other journals published by the MHRA may be ordered from JSTOR (http://about.jstor.org/csp).

The **Modern Humanities Research Association** was founded in Cambridge in 1918 and has become an international organization with members in all parts of the world. It is a registered charity number 1064670, and a company limited by guarantee, registered in England number 3446016. Its main object is to encourage advanced study and research in modern and medieval European languages, literatures, and cultures by its publication of journals, book series, and its Style Guide. Further information about the activities of the Association and individual membership may be obtained from the Membership Secretary, email membership@mhra.org.uk, or from the website at: **www.mhra.org.uk**

Disclaimer: Statements of fact and opinion in the content of *Portuguese Studies* are those of the respective authors and contributors and not of the journal editors or of the Modern Humanities Research Association (MHRA). MHRA makes no representation, express or implied, in respect of the accuracy of the material in this journal and cannot accept any legal responsibility or liability for any errors or omissions that may be made.

Parts of this work may be reproduced as permitted under legal provisions for fair dealing (or fair use) for the purposes of research, private study, criticism, or review, or when a relevant collective licensing agreement is in place. All other reproduction requires the written permission of the copyright holder who may be contacted at rights@mhra.org.uk.

ISSN 0267–5315 (print)   ISSN 2222–4270 (online)
ISBN 978-1-78188-600-7

© 2017 The Modern Humanities Research Association
Salisbury House, Station Road, Cambridge CB1 2LA, United Kingdom

# Portuguese Studies vol. 33 no. 1

## CONTENTS

| | |
|---|---|
| Preface | 5 |
| 'Oh, what words can do!': Rhetoric and the Moral Ambiguities of António Ferreira's *Castro*<br>SIMON PARK | 7 |
| The *Papel Volante*: A Marginalized Genre in Eighteenth-Century Portuguese Culture?<br>PEDRO MARQUES | 22 |
| Landscapes of Portugal in Two Hundred Years of Narratives<br>ANA ISABEL QUEIROZ | 39 |
| How to Construct a Master: Pessoa and Caeiro<br>JERÓNIMO PIZARRO | 56 |
| A Life Framed: Serafim Alves de Carvalho's *Emigrar... Emigrar: as contas do meu rosário* (1986)<br>CARMEN RAMOS VILLAR | 70 |
| Writing on Behalf of Those Women 'Que Não [?] Têm Escrita': Gendered Boundaries inside and outside the Fiction of Mia Couto<br>TOM STENNETT | 85 |

*Archive material in translation*

| | |
|---|---|
| Six *Crônicas* on Slavery and Abolition<br>JOAQUIM MARIA MACHADO DE ASSIS<br>Translated and introduced by ROBERT PATRICK NEWCOMB | 105 |
| Reviews | 123 |
| Abstracts | 131 |

# NOTES FOR CONTRIBUTORS

Articles to be considered for publication may be on any subject within the field but must not exceed 7,500 words, and should be submitted in a form ready for publication in English, sent as an email attachment to the Editorial Assistant at portuguese@mhra.org.uk.

Contributions whose standard of English is inadequate will be returned. Any quotations in Portuguese must be accompanied by an English translation. Submissions in Portuguese may be considered, but publication will be conditional on provision of a satisfactory translation at the author's expense. The Editorial Assistant may undertake translations on request for a reasonable charge.

Text and references should conform precisely to the conventions of the *MHRA Style Guide*, 3rd edn, 2013 (978-1-78188-009-8), £9.50, $19.00, €12.00, obtainable in print or online version from www.style.mhra.org.uk. All articles are subject to independent, anonymous peer review by experts in the field; authors receive written feedback on the editors' decision and guidance on any revisions required. *Portuguese Studies* regrets it must charge contributors for the cost of corrections in proof deemed excessive.

It is a condition of publication in this journal that authors of articles and reviews assign copyright, including electronic copyright, to the MHRA. Inter alia, this allows the General Editor to deal efficiently and consistently with requests from third parties for permission to reproduce material. The journal has been published simultaneously in printed and electronic form since January 2001. Permission, without fee, for authors to use their own material in other publications, after a reasonable period of time has elapsed, is not normally withheld. Authors may make closed-access deposit of accepted manuscripts in their academic institution's digital repository upon acceptance. Full open access to the accepted manuscript is permitted no sooner than 12 months following publication of the Contribution by the MHRA. Contributions may also be republished on authors' personal websites without seeking further permission from the Association, but no earlier than 24 months after publication by the MHRA.

Books for review should be sent to: Reviews Editor, *Portuguese Studies*, Dr Paul Melo e Castro, School of Modern Languages and Cultures, University of Leeds, Leeds LS2 9JT.

# Preface

This issue of *Portuguese Studies* covers an unusually wide range of topics, time periods and geographic locations across the Lusophone world. The thought-provoking and inventive articles appear in chronological order ranging from a new reading of Antonio Ferreira's classic verse tragedy *Castro* (1598) to a study of some of the latest novels by Mozambican Mia Couto (2012 and 2015).

The issue opens with **Simon Park**'s analysis of the rhetorical strategies deployed by Ferreira's characters in the light of Seneca's *De clementia* and Renaissance treatises on kingship. The words spoken by the kings and their counsellors in the play are considered with special emphasis on the ways they may have been interpreted by early modern audiences. The role of the eighteenth-century genre of popular pamphlets known as the *papel volante* is re-evaluated by **Pedro Marques**. He argues that rather than being dismissed for their lack of literary quality, they should be recognized as often subversive publications which exploited their means of production and circulation in order to disseminate new and provocative topics.

**Ana Isabel Queiroz** tackles the portrayal of the natural environment in works by canonical Portuguese authors including Eça de Queiroz, Miguel Torga and Lídia Jorge. Whereas some authors have described man-made threats to the natural world, such as deforestation and poaching, others have focused on the sweeping changes to the Portuguese landscape over the last few decades and raised concerns about damage to the environment. The construction of master poet and heteronym Alberto Caeiro by Fernando Pessoa is studied by **Jerónimo Pizarro**, who takes a diachronic approach and pieces together evidence from Pessoa's letters and early publications in order to compile a genetic dossier charting Caeiro's evolution. Pizarro argues that a full picture can only be achieved when all the existing evidence, including handwritten notes and fragments, is taken into account.

**Carmen Ramos Villar**'s article proposes a close reading of Serafim Alves de Carvalho's *Emigrar… Emigrar: as contas do meu rosário* (1986) in order to ascertain how the author's identity is constructed alongside his experiences as a migrant to the United States in the early twentieth century. She goes on to analyse the specific historical context in which the autobiography was commissioned and published, showing it can be read as a discourse of national as well as individual identity. **Tom Stennett** addresses the relationship between gender and boundaries in three recent novels by Mia Couto — *Jesusalém* (2009), *A Confissão da Leoa* (2012) and *Mulheres de Cinza* (2015) — discussing not only the narrative strategies within the texts, but also the potential repercussions of Couto's 'gender-ambiguous identity' on women writers, who have limited access to a literary scene which he dominates.

In accordance with our practice of occasionally publishing translations of significant Portuguese texts, this issue ends with **Robert Newcomb**'s English versions of six newspaper *crônicas* by Machado de Assis which deal directly with slavery and abolition, plus a short critical introduction. There has been much debate about the apparent lack of engagement with the situation of slavery in Machado's literary work but there is no doubt that it is there in his journalism, presented as a logical outgrowth of society's underlying brutality.

Finally, the Reviews Section contains four reviews of books covering migration in Lusophone cinema, an eighteenth-century confraternity of painters, Fernando Pessoa's intertextual relationship with Shakespeare and a volume of essays on the streets of Renaissance Lisbon.

THE EDITORS

# 'Oh, what words can do!': Rhetoric and the Moral Ambiguities of António Ferreira's *Castro*

SIMON PARK

*University of Oxford*

António Ferreira's verse tragedy, *Castro* (1598), is a play full of conflict: almost every character has a battle to fight, a fight to win. Yet, as Barthes said of Racine's tragedies, in *Castro*, too, 'parler, c'est faire'; the play's battles are waged in words, but no character can be sure that they have had — or even heard — the final word.[1] Characters invest in language to settle the meaning of actions and to determine which actions should be taken, but words betray those who wield them and slip out of their control. Rather than with bloodshed, *Castro* enthrals by sending our intellectual and emotional allegiances ricocheting between the characters, sometimes in unison, sometimes at divergent angles.

*Castro* draws on Portuguese history for its plot, telling the story of the judicial murder of Inês de Castro in 1355, the events leading up to this incident, and the beginnings of its catastrophic aftermath. Inês was a Galician noblewoman who accompanied her mistress, Constança of Castile, to the Portuguese court when the latter married Prince Pedro, heir to the Portuguese throne, then occupied by his father Afonso IV. Despite the marriage, Pedro and Inês fell deeply in love. The Castilian influence of Inês and her brothers on the prince, however, perturbed the king and the Portuguese nobility. When Constança suddenly died in 1345, Pedro refused to take anyone but Inês as his wife, regardless of his father's wishes. The strength of their love and the political implications of the liaison (which had resulted in two children by this point) had Pedro's father, Afonso IV, increasingly worried and eventually his advisors declared that something drastic must be done to end the relationship. This is where the play begins. In Act I, Inês revels in her love affair, sharing her thoughts with her nurse, who is full of ominous foresight. The women leave the stage and the audience witness a fierce argument between Pedro and his secretary, who urges Pedro to end things with Inês. He refuses. The next act introduces us to King Afonso and his advisors, Pacheco and Coelho. Afonso's instinct is to be lenient with Inês, but his counsellors levy strong arguments in favour of killing Inês in order to safeguard the nation. In Act III Inês recounts a premonitory dream to

---

[1] Roland Barthes, *Sur Racine* (Paris: Seuil, 1960), p. 66.

the Ama just before the news of Afonso's decision reaches her. The following act features Inês confronting Afonso and his advisors. Inês's passionate speech in IV. 2. persuades Afonso and he decides to let her go free. Her reprieve is short, however, as the counsellors urge Afonso to reconsider; he eventually leaves Inês's fate in their hands and they set out to kill her. In the final act, Pedro returns to the stage to hear the news of his lover's death and he declares vengeance on his father, initiating the conflict that would, historically speaking, envelop the country in civil war.

The play was written during the 1550s whilst Ferreira was a student, and later *lente* [Reader], at the University of Coimbra.[2] At this time, the theme of dynastic crisis — embodied in the figure of Inês as a mother of Castilian lineage — must have struck a chord with the play's Portuguese audience. In 1554, Prince João, heir to the Portuguese throne, died to widespread mourning. He was the ninth child of the unfortunate parents, D. João III and D. Catarina, to die and this series of misfortunes meant that the political climate in Portugal during the latter years of D. João III's reign was marked by anxiety and despair.[3] Given the play's relevance to the political situation of its time, early readers/ spectators likely sought out a moral lesson in it. Indeed, theoretical discussions about tragedy written and read in the period prescribed that drama should teach such a lesson by giving a moral portrait of a character to be emulated or avoided.[4] Inês seems to have been that figure. Diogo Bernardes, for instance, a contemporary and friend of Ferreira's, suggests in a verse epistle to Ferreira that the play's heroine offers lessons on how to be Stoically constant in the face of disaster; lessons relevant to the need to remain calm and composed in the face of the tragedy and potential political turmoil resulting from so many royal deaths.[5] Indeed, another play of the period, Diogo de Teive's *Ioannes princeps* (a tragedy written in 1554, printed in 1558, and precisely concerned with the death of the young Prince João), offers a vision of D. João III as a paragon of Stoic calm when confronted with the death of his son and heir.[6]

---

[2] T. F. Earle, 'António Ferreira's Castro: Tragedy at the Cross-Roads', in *Portuguese Humanism and the Republic of Letters*, ed. by Maria Berbara and Karl A. E. Enenkel (Leiden: Brill, 2012), pp. 289–318 (pp. 289–90).
[3] Anthony Disney, *A History of Portugal and the Portuguese Empire*, 2 vols (Cambridge: Cambridge University Press, 2009), I, 172–73.
[4] See Catarina Fouto, 'The Reinvention of Classical Comedy and Tragedy in Portugal', in *The Reinvention of Theatre in Sixteenth-Century Europe*, ed. by T. F. Earle and Catarina Fouto (Oxford: Legenda, 2015), pp. 89–114 (p. 99).
[5] Carta II, 'Ao doutor António Ferreira', ll. 37–45, in Diogo Bernardes, *O Lima*, ed. by J. Cândido Martins (Porto: Caixotim, 2009).
[6] Nair de Nazaré Castro Soares, 'A *Tragédia do Príncipe João* (1554) de Diogo de Teive, primeiro dramaturgo neolatino português', in *Teatro neolatino em Portugal no contexto da Europa: 450 anos de Diogo de Teive*, ed. by Sebastião de Pinho (Coimbra: Imprensa da Universidade de Coimbra, 2006), pp. 183–214 (p. 213 n. 65). For an edition of the play with a translation into Portuguese, see: Diogo de Teive, *Tragédia do Príncipe João*, ed. and trans. by Nair de Nazaré Castro Soares (Coimbra: Universidade de Coimbra, 1977).

When considered as a whole, though, it is striking for a play that spends so much time talking about morality that a clear moral victor never emerges in *Castro*. Inês might be Stoic, but the key moral questions of the play are discussed in some scenes where Inês is not even present and the king, prince, and their advisors are the ones to thrash out many of the plays ethical quandaries. To draw out further the moral ambiguities of *Castro*, then, this essay re-examines the characters of Prince Pedro and the counsellors, Pacheco and Coelho, and reassesses critical judgements of their actions and arguments by paying particular attention to the relationship between rhetoric, ethics and emotion. This study also adds to our understanding of Ferreira's play by identifying echoes of Seneca's influential treatise, *De clementia*, in *Castro* that have not been recognized to date.[7] Through an exploration of this Senecan intertext, I cast the debate between the King and his counsellors in Act II in a new light and argue that their stichomythic exchange dramatizes the clash of two equally legitimate moral schemes, rather than simply portraying the scheming of corrupt, Machiavellian advisors. Whilst stichomythia tends to be seen as little more than a stylistic feature that early modern authors inherited from their classical forebears, I demonstrate that it provides Ferreira with a formal tool for exploring the political dilemmas of the historical events behind the play and for generating ethical doubts amongst his readers/audience.[8] I argue that Ferreira stages the Renaissance the crisis of language and meaning in the stichomythic battles of the play: definitions of key terms for moral evaluation end up as 'stipulative description[s]', wriggling out of the semantic confines that characters attempt to set up.[9]

In addition to this reappraisal of stichomythia, a renewed focus on rhetoric in the play affords us insights into the mindset of the characters. Critics tend to go soft on Prince Pedro, but a close reading of the closing scenes of the play brings to light how terrifying Act V really is: Pedro transforms into an angry tyrant and this is displayed through his excessive and confused way of speaking. From the perspective of *De clementia* and other early modern treatises on kingship, Pedro's actions here are far from reasonable and thus I suggest that Ferreira's contemporaries might have judged him the most harshly. This adds to the moral ambiguity of the play as, up to this point, the audience have probably been on his side because they have heard from Inês, the Chorus, Pedro himself, and even his father, Afonso, a series of arguments that explain

---

[7] Several scholars have sought to identify the sources of Ferreira's play, and have pointed to other Senecan intertexts, but *De clementia* has not been paid any attention to my knowledge. See: J. Wickersham Crawford, 'The Influence of Seneca's Tragedies on Ferreira's "Castro" and Bermúdez' "Nise lastimosa" and "Nise laureada"', *Modern Philology*, 12.3 (1914), 171–86; António Ferreira, *La Tragédie 'Castro' d'António Ferreira*, ed. by Adrien Roig (Paris: Centro Cultural Português, 1971); and Nair de Nazaré Castro Soares, 'A Castro à luz das suas fontes', *Humanitas*, 35–36 (1983–84), 271–348.
[8] Soares points to Ferreira's skill at using stichomythia, but only goes so far as to say that it enlivens his text, 'A Castro', p. 290.
[9] Ian Maclean, *Interpretation and Meaning in the Renaissance: The Case of Law* (Cambridge: Cambridge University Press, 1992), p. 177.

Pedro's love affair with Inês, presenting his actions as understandable because they are those of a lover. Fear for what Pedro's threats in Act v portend tempers the sympathies that the audience has developed for him throughout the play and render him a more dubious figure at its close.

Before I turn my attention to Pedro in more detail, I shall zero in on one of the most misunderstood debates staged in the play: that between Pacheco, Coelho, and Afonso. Discussion of Pacheco and Coelho's arguments centre on the 'reason of state' argument put forward in II. 1 (ll. 696–700), where Pacheco and Coelho urge their king to consider the greater good and suggest that ends can justify means.[10] Their arguments, however, also belong to a tradition that stretches back to ancient political philosophy; Seneca's *De clementia*, for example, argues that it is reasonable for kings to kill in the name of the common good.[11] Traditionally, these characters have been seen, in the scathing words of John R. C. Martyn, as the 'sinister proponents of an unjust murder'.[12] In the Chorus's words, they convince the king by the power of their words alone, a statement that plays into widespread fears about the power of counsellors should they turn to flatter their prince rather than give him true moral advice: 'Ah, quanto podem | palavras, e razões em peito brando!' [What power | Words and arguments have over a feeble heart!].[13]

Nonetheless, ambiguities flicker in the Chorus's moral judgements, as I will explore later in this essay. Indeed, as T. F. Earle has said, critics have often been unfair in assessing the advisors' moral character: the counsellors 'are not wicked, and are willing to take personal responsibility for their actions [...]. It is the political situation following Pedro's refusal in Act I to abandon Inês that makes it impossible for them to give any other advice.'[14] More than this, a closer inspection of the terms used to support the counsellor's arguments suggests that these characters construct a plausible case for the killing of Inês, one based on a moral scheme that stretches back at least as far as Seneca and which would have been familiar to Ferreira's audience. Once we begin to take their

---

[10] See António José Saraiva and Oscar Lopes, *História da literatura portuguesa*, 4th edn (Porto: Porto Editora, n.d.), pp. 291–92; and Martim de Albuquerque, *Maquiavel e Portugal* (Lisbon: Alêtheia, 2007), p. 52.
[11] *De clementia* in Seneca, *Moral Essays*, ed. and trans. by John W. Basore, 3 vols (London: Heinemann, 1970), I, 1.12.1. Further citations are to this edition. For a discussion of the topic of 'reason of state' in the Renaissance, see Peter Burke, 'Tacitism, Scepticism and Reason of State', in *The Cambridge History of Political Thought, 1450–1700*, ed. by J. H. Burns and Mark Goldie (Cambridge: Cambridge University Press, 1991), pp. 477–98.
[12] António Ferreira, *The Tragedy of Ines de Castro*, ed. and trans. by John R. C. Martyn (Coimbra: Universidade de Coimbra, 1987), p. 134.
[13] 'Castro' in António Ferreira, *Poemas Lusitanos*, ed. by T. F. Earle, 2nd edn (Lisbon: Fundação Calouste Gulbenkian, 2008), pp. 379–460, ll. 1504–05. The translation is from Ferreira, *The Tragedy of Ines de Castro*, ed. by Martyn, IV. 3. 290–91. Further references to the play follow in the text and are from these editions. For a discussion of early modern worries around the rhetorical power of counsellors, see Joanne Paul, 'The Best Counsellors are the Dead: Counsel and Shakespeare's Hamlet', *Renaissance Studies*, 30.5 (2016), 646–65 (pp. 650–52).
[14] T. F. Earle, 'António Ferreira, Castro', in *A Companion to Portuguese Literature*, ed. by T. F. Earle, Stephen Parkinson and Cláudia Pazos Alonso (Woodbridge: Tamesis, 2009), pp. 68–71 (pp. 69–70).

arguments seriously and explain their sources, then, the moral conundrums of the play appear even more insoluble.

Consider the following speech made by Pacheco in II. 1, the first scene in which the counsellors try to persuade Afonso to kill Inês for the good of Portugal's continued sovereignty:

> A clemência por certo é grã virtude,
> e dina mais dos reis que outras virtudes,
> polo perigo grande que há na ira
> em quem tão livremente assi a executa.
> Mas com esta o rigor é necessário,
> por não vir em desprezo tal virtude.
> Este é o que se chamou severidade,
> de que tantos exemplos nos deixaram
> os famosos romãos em paz, e guerra.
> Estas colunas ambas são tão fortes:
> que bemaventurado este teu reino,
> que nelas por ti só está tão fundado!
> De tal modo, senhor, hás-de usar delas,
> que ũa vá sempre d'outra acompanhada.
> Exemplos tens mostrado de clemência.
> Mostra agora, que é bem, severidade. (ll. 729–44)

[Certainly, clemency is a great virtue, | More worthy of kings than other virtues, | Because of the great peril inherent in anger | In one who can gratify it so freely. | But as well as clemency, toughness is necessary, | So that this virtue does not fall into contempt. | This is what has been called severity, | Of which the famous Romans have left us | So many examples in times of peace and war. | These two columns are so strong | That your kingdom is truly fortunate | To have been founded on them by you alone. | Sire, you should use them in such a way | That one is always accompanied by the other. | You have given examples of clemency; | Now show severity, for it is right to do so.] (II. 1. 131–50)[15]

Without proper contextualization, it can seem as though the counsellors warp the language of virtue by a very crooked logic indeed. The 'harshness', 'toughness', and 'severity' that they prescribe, however, form not euphemistic packaging for evil intentions, but rather pertain to the virtue of *severitas* [strictness]. The argument made here finds parallels in various ancient and Renaissance treatises on kingship that considered strictness a virtue that rulers needed to show on particular occasions. Although the allusions are somewhat indirect, one can see elements of Seneca's *De clementia* in Pacheco's speech, as he tries to demonstrate that both clemency and strictness are virtues for a king, citing 'the famous Romans' as his example for the need to demonstrate both leniency and rigour, as the situation demands. In this way, he makes Afonso aware that cruelty and strictness are quite different, as Seneca also

---

[15] The translation has been slightly altered here because Martyn translates 'aspereza', 'rigor' and 'severidade' all as 'severity'.

does: 'The ill-informed think that its [i.e. clemency's] opposite is strictness; but no virtue is the opposite of a virtue. What then is set over against mercy? It is cruelty, which is nothing else than harshness of mind in exacting punishment' (*De clementia*, II. 4. 1). *De clementia* became something of a reference work in early modern political thought, filtering into many treatises and manuals on how best to rule.[16] As a Humanist poet educated at the University of Coimbra, Ferreira in all likelihood knew Seneca's moral essay and possibly read it in the complete works compiled by Erasmus, of which there are several copies in Portuguese libraries.[17] But it is not necessary to find a direct citation of Seneca's essay in the play to be able to argue that Pacheco's argument had legitimacy at the time. Cicero advocated *severitas* as a suitable course of action in his letters to Brutus where he recommends that strictness was required to put a stop to the civil wars.[18] Petrarch also suggests, in a text with both Senecan and Ciceronian inflections, that too much leniency could end up being very cruel.[19] The Humanist, Jerónimo Osório also cites in his *De nobilitate* (first published in 1542) a number of biblical figures, including Moses and Christ himself, who succeed in blending kindness with strictness.[20]

That is not to say that strictness was always preferred to clemency. In Seneca's eyes, pity and cruelty were the vicious extremes of the virtues of clemency and strictness respectively; excessive clemency would devolve into pity (a vice) and excessive strictness into cruelty (also a vice). Indeed, as Afonso says in line 1462, Seneca suggests that it is better to err on the side of clemency, because cruelty (as the extreme form of strictness) has more destructive consequences (*De clementia* II. 4. 4.).[21] These ideas were certainly circulating in Ferreira's time as Diogo de Teive shares a similar opinion in one of his *sententiae* addressed to the young D. Sebastião in *Epodon siue Iabicorum* [sic] *carminum libri tres* (first printed in 1565 with parallel Latin and Portuguese text): 'Severidade muito poucas vezes | Se louva ou se busca ou se deseja, | Quasi sempre a clemência é desejada' [Severity is rarely praised or sought out or desired; almost always clemency is desired].[22]

---

[16] For a discussion of how extensive the influence of this essay was in early modern Europe, see Peter Stacey, *Roman Monarchy and the Renaissance Prince* (Cambridge: Cambridge University Press, 2007), p. 208.
[17] For a general discussion of the dissemination of Erasmus's printed works in Portugal during the sixteenth century, see Catarina Barceló Fouto, 'Diogo de Teive's *Institutio Sebastiani Primi* and the Reception of Erasmus' Works in Portugal', in *Portuguese Humanism and the Republic of Letters*, ed. by Maria Berbara and Karl A. E. Enenkel (Leiden: Brill, 2012), pp. 128-49.
[18] For examples, see To Brutus in Marcus Tulius Cicero, *The Letters to His Friends*, ed. by W. Glynn Williams (Cambridge, MA: Harvard University Press, 1954), III, 615-738 (I. 2a. 2 and II. 5. 5). See also Melissa Barden Dowling, *Clemency and Cruelty in the Roman World* (Ann Arbor: University of Michigan Press, 2006), pp. 34-37.
[19] See Stacey, p. 155.
[20] Jerónimo Osório, *Tratados da nobreza civil e cristã*, trans. by António Guimarães Pinto (Lisbon: Imprensa Nacional — Casa da Moeda, 1976), pp. 209-10.
[21] Lapsing into vice is possible because pity and cruelty are close to clemency and strictness, see: *De clementia*, II. 4. 4.
[22] Diogo de Teive, *Obra completa*, ed. and trans. by António Guimarães Pinto (Lisbon: Esfera do

What the counsellors propose, then, coheres with *modi operandi* that various classical and early modern theorists deemed virtuous. Though many writers would side with Teive and Seneca himself when it came to *clementia* and *severitas*, there was no single viewpoint on kingly behaviour that was universally accepted, as is shown by the numerous examples of texts that cite *severitas* as a necessary virtue in a ruler. Unlike critics such as Martyn, I think that Ferreira did not intend to make the audience side only with Afonso, but to stop and think whether — under the extremely difficult circumstances of the play — the actions promoted by the counsellors could be seen as valid.

This clash between clemency and strictness sends shockwaves through the terms of ethical evaluation deployed in the play, dislodging them from solid, unambiguous meanings. What is — or is not — 'just' becomes dependent upon the moral scheme to which one subscribes. In order to explore this in more detail, let us turn to one of the tensest moments of the play (IV. 2) when Pacheco and Coelho fight to change the King's mind after Inês has talked him round in the preceding scene:

> *Rei*: Não vejo culpa que mereça pena.
> *Pacheco*: Inda hoje a viste. Quem ta esconde agora?
> *Rei*: Mais quero perdoar que ser injusto.
> *Coelho*: Injusto é quem perdoa a pena justa.
> *Rei*: Peque antes ness'estremo que em crueza.
> *Coelho*: Não se consente o rei pecar em nada.
> *Rei*: Sou homem.
> *Coelho*:              Porém rei.
> *Rei*:                             O rei perdoa.
> *Pacheco*: Nem sempre perdoar é piadade. (ll. 1458–65)

[*King*: I do not see a fault which deserves punishment. *Pacheco*: You saw it only today; who hides it from you now? *King*: I prefer pardon to injustice. *Coelho*: Unjust is he who does not inflict a just penalty. *King*: Rather might I sin in this excess, than in cruelty. *Coelho*: A King is not allowed to sin at all. *King*: I am human. *Coelho*: But a King. *King*: A King pardons. *Pacheco*: To pardon is not always merciful.] (IV. 2. 244–51)

Here, Ferreira exploits the dramatic potential of stichomythia to the fullest, demonstrating the stalemate between two lines of moral thinking. In stichomythia, where speakers alternate in quick succession, the flow of the dialogue depends upon each speaker picking up where another left off. Speakers thus appropriate the language of their interlocutor and 'aggressively wrap' this in their own world-view.[23] This hostile takeover of another person's words renders this dialogue fraught and uncomfortable because neither side is able to settle the meaning of the words they use: the concepts one speaker uses to promote their own ideas are wielded, in turn, against them. The tension builds

---

Caos, 2012), p. 827.
[23] Simon Goldhill, *Sophocles and the Language of Tragedy* (New York: Oxford University Press, 2012), p. 51.

as two different moral frameworks push against each other: one in which it is better to be too clement than to risk being unjust and another that sees granting pardons too easily as the route to injustice.

A dimension of Ferreira's play that is often neglected, because of the scanty information available about its performance history, is how a scene like the one cited above would be staged. When asked about this issue, undergraduate students are remarkable in the consistency of their imagination: they have Pacheco and Coelho hounding Afonso on stage, stalking him as he tries to get away from their crafty replies. In other words, they bring their ideas about staging in line with conventional views of the two counsellors, suggesting they are snarling Machiavels in advisor's clothing. But the debate is a deadlock, as neither side manages to bring the other round to their way of thinking. The counsellors seek the assent of their king for their proposed actions and do not assume the power simply to compel their king to act in the way they see fit, they challenge the king, as good counsellors should, but are waiting for the king's permission ('licença', l. 1501) before they act. Indeed, the discussion continues for another thirty lines after the passage cited above, suggesting that the argument is one not easily won. If we see the advisors as acting with some moral legitimacy in the play, it would be preferable to see this scene as a series of verbal lunges, parries, and ripostes, where king and counsellors both hold their own and face each other down without giving ground on the stage. Viewing this as a scene of aggression, then, derives from the harsh judgements of the counsellors made by critics and students who have not recognized the moral validity of their arguments and the fact that they had currency and weight in the period. The challenge for a director who wants to embrace the true ambivalence of the play is to make Pacheco and Coelho appear less wicked than students sometimes imagine them to be, affording their words the moral authority that they might once have possessed and which renders Afonso's decision all the more impossible.

The fact that the arguments on both sides of the debate have recourse to the same evaluative terms unsettles the meaning of key words in the play. A verbal tug of war ensues where both sides try to get the firmer grip on a word like justice (*justiça*) and drag it in the direction they want. The same is true of another morally evaluative term, central to *De clementia* and to medieval and early modern political theory at large: cruelty. When someone hurls the word 'crueza' [cruelty] — or its related words 'cruel' [cruel], 'cru(a)' [cruel], 'crueldade' [cruelty], 'cruamente'/'cruelmente' [cruelly] — at someone else, they challenge a ruler's moral (and political) authority.[24] But the play shows that — at least in theory — one person's cruelty can be another person's justice, as Pacheco states:

---

[24] Daniel Baraz, *Medieval Cruelty* (Ithaca, NY: Cornell University Press, 2003), pp. 10, 88, 124.

> Se te parece em parte isto crueza,
> não é crueza aquela, mas justiça,
> quando de cruel ânimo não nasce. (ll. 722-24)

[If to you there seems to be some cruelty in this, | It is not at all an act of cruelty, but of justice, | For it does not stem from a cruel heart] (II. 1. 128-30)

Here, as elsewhere, we see the characters in *Castro* wage a battle of words over what they should — or should not — deem cruel; in other words, over who has the moral high ground. 'Crueza' [cruelty] and its related noun, adjectives, and adverbs appear sixty-seven times in the play and are shot at particular actions as a rhetorical way of delegitimizing them: no one wants to be called cruel and, therefore, to be placed in a long line of tyrannical figures from myth and history.

It is Inês and her ally, the Chorus, who use these words most frequently. In Inês's plea for mercy, in IV. 1, cruelty becomes a critical term in dissuading Afonso from acting the way he intends. It is important, though, to recognize that the Chorus is not a disinterested party in the events of the play; when they intervene in the action of the play, they usually support Inês, rather than acting as an impartial 'voice of reason'.[25] In IV. 1, for instance, Inês calls the Chorus her 'friends' (l. 1222) and asks them to assist her in asking for mercy from the Afonso (l. 1224).

Once Inês has been killed, the Chorus becomes Inês's principal champion, though their attribution of cruelty to Afonso's actions does not remain uncontested:

> *Coro*: Enfim venceu a ira, cruel imiga
> de todo bom conselho. Ah, quanto podem
> palavras, e razões em peito brando!
> Eu vejo teu esprito combatido
> de mil ondas, ó Rei. Bom é teu zelo;
> o conselho leal; cruel a obra.
> *Rei*: Por crueza julgais o que é justiça?
> *Coro*: Crueza a chamará tod'outra idade.
> *Rei*: Minh'alma inocente é, conselho sigo. (ll. 1503-11)

[*Chorus*: Finally anger has triumphed, cruel enemy | Of all good counsel. Ah! What power | Words and argument have over a feeble heart! | I see your spirit tossed | On a thousand waves, O King. Your zeal is good; | Your counsel, loyal; your action, cruel. *King*: You judge as cruel what is just? *Chorus*: Posterity will call it cruelty. *King*: My soul is innocent; I have followed counsel.] (IV. 3. 289-97, translation modified)

J. Wickersham Crawford dismisses line 1509 as a weak defence against the Chorus's accusations and considers it further evidence of the King's hopeless

---

[25] For further discussion of the Chorus and especially the ambiguous odes that close four of the play's five acts, see Earle, 'Tragedy at the Cross-Roads', pp. 297-309.

vacillating in the play as a whole, because Afonso soon after changes his attitude from defensiveness to regret.[26] In contrast, I think that these lines show Ferreira's staging of the difficulty of moral judgement. Part of the ambiguity of *Castro* is the way in which words can be used (with equal legitimacy) for startlingly different purposes. As Quentin Skinner and Michael Moriarty have argued, vices and virtues could, in the early modern period, be dressed up in language to look remarkably like one another, causing a great deal of moral anxiety.[27] In Portuguese literature, one only has to look at the *velho de Restelo* in *Os Lusíadas* for the way in which events can be re-described in surprising ways. For the old man of Restelo, fame is a euphemistic *paradiastole* of greed, the real motivation behind the Portuguese voyages to India.[28] Here, in *Castro*, the verbs 'julgar' and 'chamar' draw attention to the game of re-description at play: actions are 'judged' or 'named' cruel rather than being inherently so.

To add to the moral complexities of the play, the Chorus's denouncements of Pacheco, Coelho and Afonso come with equivocations. In the lines cited above, the Chorus suggests that anger prevails, threatening 'bom conselho' [good counsel], yet then assert that the advice given was 'leal' [loyal]: a positive judgement of it, as loyalty was the most important quality in a counsellor.[29] Manuals about how to behave as a king all warned against self-interested advisors more focused on winning favour for themselves than on helping their prince make good decisions.[30] Pacheco and Coelho do not pursue their own ambitions, but aim to secure Portugal from the threat of loss of independence represented by Inês and her connections to Castile. It is in this way that their advice can be called 'loyal' and, ultimately, good. The description of their advice as 'leal' seems at odds with other moments when the Chorus is very clear about its condemnation of Pacheco and Coelho (e.g. ll. 1096–1100). I think, though, it is important to keep both the positive and the negative in mind. Ferreira valued the counsel of friends or royal advisors as a necessary part of toeing a moral line in life. His poems are populated by figures who need advice and those who give it. Indeed, in the passage above, Afonso defends himself against the charges of the Chorus by referring to the fact that he follows advice: 'Minh'alma inocente é, conselho sigo' (l. 1511) [My soul is innocent; I have followed counsel (IV. 3. 297)]. In other words, advice is what is supposed to save him. Were it not for the Chorus and the actions of Pedro at the end of the play, we might even think that Afonso took a tragic, but justifiable decision.

---

[26] Crawford, p. 179.
[27] Quentin Skinner, *Visions of Politics* (Cambridge: Cambridge University Press, 2002); Michael Moriarty, *Disguised Vices* (Oxford: Oxford University Press, 2011).
[28] For a discussion of *paradiastole* in Camões's epic, see Hélio J. S. Alves, *Camões, Corte-Real e o sistema da epopeia quinhentista* (Coimbra: Universidade de Coimbra 2001), pp. 513–23.
[29] See also ll. 1514–16 where the Chorus, too, fails to extract a moral lesson from the play's events.
[30] See, for example, Jerónimo Osório *Da instituição real e sua disciplina*, trans. by António Jotta da Cruz Figueiredo (Lisbon: Pro Domo, 1944), pp. 125, 400; Desiderius Erasmus, *The Education of a Christian Prince*, ed. and trans. by Lester Kruger Born (New York: Norton, 1968), pp. 193–94.

In Ferreira's eyes, poets and kings require counsellors to assure their moral wellbeing, especially in trying situations. In his other works, Ferreira suggests that he has his friends, like Manuel de Sampaio, to reel him in and that kings have their advisors and humanist poets, such as Ferreira himself, to offer them the advice they need to rule virtuously.[31] It would thus be strange to think that Ferreira would want to make counsellors in *Castro* come across as the bad guys. In light of the moral basis for the counsellors' arguments, the Chorus's half-praise for them, and the view of advisors propagated in Ferreira's wider work, we should not be too heavy-handed in our treatment of these characters, because, in spite of their persistence, it is clear that they do allow Afonso to make the final call. Plenty of good advice is given in Ferreira's tragedy: problems arise more frequently when characters do not listen to it. The Ama, for example, gives good Stoic advice to Inês. One might even say that it is because of her that such an amazing transformation takes place during the play, as Inês changes from love-struck lady into Stoic heroine. The Secretário also explicitly declares himself Pedro's adviser, there to temper his anger and to keep the impetuous prince in check (see ll. 282–87).

If his father sees himself trapped between his fears of being cruel and a compulsion to follow the advice he has been given, weak because he could not make up his mind (ll. 773–77), Pedro completely ignores his wise advisor. In the case of Pacheco and Coelho there is some doubt as to whether their advice should have been followed, but there is little doubt that the Secretário has a point in I. 3 when he tells Pedro to quell his anger. From the perspective of the *speculum principis* tradition, Pedro emerges as particularly morally wayward — worse perhaps than his father — because he refuses to listen to advice at all:

> *Ifante*: Sigue minha razão, minha vontade.
> *Secretário*: Não te vejo razão, vejo vontade.
> *Ifante*: Sigue a vontade, que forçar não podes.
> *Secretário*: Manda-me o que te devo que a não siga.
> *Ifante*: Queres mandar teu príncipe?
> *Secretário*:                    Mas sirvo.
> *Ifante*: Obedece ao que quero.
> *Secretário*:                    Manda o justo. (ll. 408–13)

[*Pedro*: Follow my reason, my desire. *Secretary*: In you I see no reason, but just desire. *Pedro*: Follow that desire, against which you can do nothing. *Secretary*: My duty to you commands me not to follow this desire. *Pedro*: Do [you] want to command your Prince? *Secretary*: Rather, serve him. *Pedro*: Be obedient to my wishes. *Secretary*: Order what is just.] (I. 3. 408–13)

Words relating to power and ruling crowd these lines ('vontade', 'servir', 'mandar', 'forçar', 'obedecer', 'poder' [desire, to serve, to order, to force, to obey, to be able]). Once again, however, the characters contest the definition of key terms. The Secretário challenges what Pedro understands by ordering and

---

[31] See Ode I. 4 and 7, and Cartas II. 1 and 2 in Ferreira's *Poemas Lusitanos*.

serving: he makes it clear that should the prince not order what is right, serving him would not mean doing his bidding, but disobeying him. This echoes a long line of political thinkers who argued that rulers could rightfully be deposed if they overstepped the mark and descended into cruelty; a viewpoint re-iterated by contemporaries of Ferreira, such as Camões.[32] The Secretário also confronts how Pedro conflates 'razão' [reason] with 'vontade' [desire] in the opening line of this passage. The syntax of line 408 suggests a certain synonymity between 'razão' and 'vontade' by the repetition of 'minha' [my] and the absence of a conjunction. This is possible because both 'reason' and 'will' have to do with orders: 'razão' refers to Pedro's reasoning (i.e. what he has decided to do) and 'vontade' more straightforwardly to his wishes. The Secretário, however, disturbs the suggested relationship between these two words by implying that he sees only one in Pedro's behaviour. He thus highlights the difference in the semantic range of the two words; namely, the associations of 'reason' with *rational* thought and 'desire' with *irrational, emotional* thinking. There is a proleptic dimension to this passage too, as it signals that Pedro has some tyrannical character traits: he lacks reason and wishes to subjugate everyone to his will.[33] Indeed, earlier even Pedro himself points to his hot-headedness, saying that his anger is growing against those who challenge him and indicating that it is the Secretário who can (and must) calm him down (ll. 203–04).

All this suggests that Pedro has some worrying characteristics, which erupt in Act v when he transforms into a furious, Senecan tyrant.[34] This early scene between the secretary and Pedro gives us an indication of how his anger will ignite civil war in Portugal after Inês's death. Interestingly, the counsellors and Afonso are also accused of being overcome by anger. But when we compare their behaviour with that of Pedro, there is little comparison to be made. Pacheco, Coelho and Afonso speak in a measured way and they put forward careful (and justifiable) arguments.

As I have explored, for the majority of the play, the Chorus, Inês, Pacheco, Coelho and the King make concerted efforts to lift the label of 'cruel' from their actions or affix it to the course of action promoted by another character. It is startling, then, that, at the end of the play, Pedro claims cruelty for himself:

> Mas eu me matarei mais cruelmente
> do que te a ti mataram, se não vingo
> com novas crueldades tua morte. (ll. 1750–52)

[But I shall kill myself more cruelly | Than they killed you, if I do not avenge | Your death with new cruelties.] (v. 2. 148–50; translation modified)

Beyond *what* he says, Pedro's rhetoric in Act v bears the mark of anger. As

---

[32] Clive Willis explores this tradition in relation to *Os Lusíadas* in his *Camões: Prince of Poets* (Bristol: HiPLAM, 2010), pp. 132–34.
[33] For the fact that savagery and cruelty distinguish the tyrant from the king, see *De clementia* I. 12. 1.
[34] Earle, 'Tragedy at the Cross-Roads', p. 291.

Peter Stacey has argued, 'tyrants have a distinctive rhetoric: their lack of *ratio* is manifested in their *oratio*'.[35] We can detect Pedro's unreasoned, tyrannical thinking, then, in the way he speaks. Indeed, rhetorical manuals of the period emphasize the need for rhetorical tropes to match the emotional state of the speaker. For example, Cypriano Soarez, a Spanish rhetorician who taught and printed his work in Portugal, suggests in his *De arte rhetorica* (1562): 'when brutality, hatred, and pity are the weapons of debate, who will endure a speaker who expresses his anger, sorrow, or entreaties in figures of antithesis, in balanced cadences, and in correspondences in word terminations?'[36] As much as rhetoric is a way of writing, then, it can be also used as a way of reading: rhetorical analysis can expose the emotions a writer intended a character to display. In Pedro's case, this kind of diagnosis by rhetorical analysis proves illuminating especially when we contrast the way Pedro speaks to the manners of speaking of the other characters in *Castro*. Pedro's speech once he hears the news of Inês's death is rhetorically excessive; exclamations and rhetorical questions abound, suggesting that Pedro does not know what to do as grief takes over:[37]

> Que direi? Que farei? Que clamarei?
> Ó fortuna! Ó crueza! Ó mal tamanho!
> Ó minha Dona Inês, ó alma minha,
> morta m'és tu? Morte houve tão ousada
> que contra ti podesse? Ouço-o, e vivo?
> Eu vivo, e tu és morta? Ó morte crua!
> [...]
> Ah, minha Dona Inês, ah, ah, minha alma! (ll. 1673–78, 1684)

[What shall I say? What shall I do? What shall I cry? | Oh, fortune! Oh, cruelty! Oh, terrible evil! | Oh, my Lady Ines, Oh my soul, | Are you dead? Was death bold enough to exercise | Its power against you? Do I hear this, and live? | How am I alive if you are dead? O cruel death! | [...] | Ah! My Lady Ines! Ah, ah! You, my soul!] (v. 2. 71–75, 82)

The density of devices typically used to evoke intense emotions suggests that his reason has fully evaporated. In the rhetorical treatise, *Ad Herennium*, the figure of *exclamatio* [apostrophe] is connected with grief and indignation, both of which are at play here.[38] By line 1684 his speech descends into a slew of exclamations: the syntax breaks down like his reason. Anger then slowly comes to replace grief and Pedro transforms into a tyrant who delights in gore:

> Abra eu com minhas mãos aqueles peitos.
> Arranque deles uns corações feros,
> que tal crueza ousaram. (ll. 1754–56)

---

[35] Stacey, p. 60.
[36] Lawrence J. Flynn, *The 'De Arte Rhetorica' (1568) by Cyprian Soarez: A Translation with Introduction and Notes* (unpublished PhD dissertation, University of Florida, 1955), p. 334.
[37] For a list of the tropes of anger, see Juvenal, *Satires: Book 1*, ed. by Susanna Morton Braund (Cambridge: Cambridge University Press, 1996), p. 18.
[38] *Rhetorica ad Herennium*, ed. and trans. by Harry Caplan (London: Heinemann, 1954), IV. 15. 22.

[May I be able to open their chests with my hands, | May I be able to tear out such cruel hearts | Which dared commit such a cruelty] (v. 2. 152–54)

Pedro's irrationality is brought further into relief by the Stoic words of the Messageiro, who attempts to get Pedro to control his grief and to occupy himself with what is his duty:

> Senhor, pera chorar fica assaz tempo.
> Mas lágrimas que fazem contr'a morte?
> Vai ver aquele corpo, vai fazer-lhe
> as honras que lhe deves. (ll. 1714–17)

[Sire, enough time remains for weeping, | But what power do tears have against death? | Go and see this body, go and render to it | The honours which you owe to her.] (v. 2. 112–15)

The intervention of the messenger suggests that a more controlled response is possible, highlighting that Pedro is lost to reason. This also might remind readers of Teive's play *Ioannes princeps* where the King's Stoic response to calamity is praised by Eubularchus and Philanax in Act v. Pedro is certainly not the same kind of character.

Ferreira insists on the king as the head of the body politic (ll. 715–16) and this is why Afonso's vacillations are so worrying: a king should not dither, but be constant and resolute, otherwise, like Agamemnon, he becomes unfit for his responsibilities.[39] It is also because of the king's status as the head of the country's political body that anger is particularly dangerous in Pedro and Afonso. As Peter Stacey says, 'the *res publica* risks losing its mind if the ruler loses his temper'.[40]

A reader well-versed in Seneca's moral ideas and in the 'mirror for princes' genre might well view Pedro particularly harshly, then, because anger is viewed in these treatises as the foulest of all passions: his judgement clouded in a hot-blooded haze, the angry prince is unable to act according to the Stoic precepts that should guide him and thrusts himself and his state into jeopardy. Seneca is clear about this when he declares 'cruel and inexorable anger is not seemly for a king' (*De clementia* I. 5. 6) and this is a thought echoed by Diogo de Teive in his *sentenças*: 'Conselheira malíssima é a ira: | Má certamente a todo homem é sempre | Mas pior conselheira é ao príncipe' [Anger is a terrible advisor: it is always bad for everyone, but worse still for the prince].[41] Ferreira himself in a verse epistle to Simão da Silveira highlights the perils of anger: 'Ira a guerra pariu, ira armas gera | ira chamou à boa razão fraqueza' [Anger spawned war, anger fathers arms, anger brought weakness to good reason].[42] In light of this, I

---

[39] See Earle, 'Tragedy at the Cross-Roads', pp. 314–15.
[40] Stacey, p. 35.
[41] Teive, p. 816.
[42] Ferreira, Carta 'a D. Simão da Silveira', Book II. 10. 52–54. See also Seneca's *De ira* in Seneca, *Anger, Mercy, Revenge*, ed. and trans. by Robert A. Kaster (Chicago, IL: University of Chicago Press, 2010), pp. 3–13.

think it is possible that Pedro — because he is angry and because he dismisses good counsel — could have been viewed as the worst character in the play by Ferreira and his early modern readers. Yet, Ferreira's play admits so many readings that it is difficult to be too assured in any single interpretation. Indeed, the play does offer two mitigating factors in defence (or, rather, in explanation) of Pedro's actions: the implacable force of love and the family history that sets a bad example for the young prince, suggesting that he belongs to one of those inescapably destructive dynasties that regularly feature in ancient and early modern drama. In the end, though, I think that appreciating the heat of Pedro's anger adds rather than takes away from the moral ambiguities of the play, because his anger only erupts at the end, once the Chorus have provided a whole series of arguments to excuse his behaviour.

Unlike in many Senecan imitations of the early modern period, Ferreira avoids adding a moralistic ending to *Castro*: Pedro declares his intentions unambiguously, but no punishment ensues in the play or, for that matter, in history, as Portuguese readers familiar with the historical events would be all too aware.[43] No other character shines as a paragon of virtue, though. Let us not forget that even Inês has been involved with a married man...

So, what is cruelty? What is justice? What can or should a state do in the name of its self-preservation? *Castro* offers no clear-cut answers. Rather, the play throws the meaning of key terms of moral evaluation into doubt. As I have shown, the counsellors, Pacheco and Coelho, have Seneca on their side when suggesting that Afonso kill Inês, so we need to rethink our assumptions about how 'evil' we take these characters to be. The excessive rhetoric of Pedro suggests that he is out of control and might have been considered the most terrifying character of them all by early modern audiences. Ultimately, though, Ferreira tangles the audience in a Gordian knot of conflicting emotions and moral perspectives. They are left with the difficult task of deciding what is cruel or just for themselves.

---

[43] A. J. Boyle, *Tragic Seneca: An Essay in the Theatrical Tradition* (London: Routledge, 1997), pp. 183–84.

# The *Papel Volante*: A Marginalized Genre in Eighteenth-Century Portuguese Culture?

PEDRO MARQUES

*Instituto Camões, London*

In 1975, essayist Arnaldo Saraiva applied his concept of marginal/ized literature to what is commonly designated as *literatura de cordel*, a typical eighteenth-century publication associated with the field of popular culture.[1] His definition of marginal/ized literature replaced the label *popular* with 'ignorada, esquecida, censurada, marginal/izada pelos poderes literários, ou culturais, ou políticos, por razões de linguagem ou de produção e circulação no mercado' [ignored, forgotten, censured and marginal/ized by the literary, cultural and political powers because of questions of production and market circulation].[2] Saraiva's concept suggests a way of addressing and analysing *literatura de cordel* that is intuitively correct. On the one hand, it renders the popular/erudite distinction forged by Romanticism obsolete; on the other, it reassesses the problem in terms of a subversion of values that assign *literatura de cordel* a self-fashioned or imposed marginal position within eighteenth-century Portuguese print culture.

Saraiva used the designation warily because it encompasses a series of misconceptions, and does not provide any information on what *literatura de cordel* actually is, that is, its most common topics and discursive resources. Saraiva argued that with the use of this term he did not intend to draw a simplistic association with the wider field of popular literature but instead to put forward the hypothesis that the notion of marginalization is, in fact, a very effective way of describing the genre.[3] In 2007, Saraiva reiterated that the term marginal/ized literature is useful because it points out examples of bias and exclusion, and takes as its subject matter any literary production, regardless of historical period, complexity, erudition, length or medium.[4]

The aim of this article is to investigate the bias introduced by the designation *literatura de cordel*, and assess the validity of the defining principle behind it, namely that this particular form of literature existed at the margins of eighteenth-century Portuguese print culture. The term is, therefore, replaced

---

[1] Arnaldo Saraiva, 'Literatura marginal/izada (a propósito da literatura de cordel)', in *Literatura marginal/izada* (Porto: Árvore, 1975) pp. 109–21 (p. 166).
[2] Saraiva, p. 118.
[3] Saraiva, p. 116.
[4] Arnaldo Saraiva, 'A crise da literatura e a literatura marginal ou marginalizada', *Santa Barbara Portuguese Studies*, 9 (2007), 5–15 (p. 14).

here by the name used at the time — *papel volante* [literally, flying pamphlet; chapbook] — and the multitude of meanings associated with the notion of marginal/ized forms of expression[5] is narrowed down to authorship, target audience, and content. These elements will be useful in assessing how *papéis volantes* resolve the tension between marginality and legitimization. A reading of two publications that provide a discussion on the nature of the genre, *Eco de Diferentes Vozes* [The Echo of Different Voices] and *Monstruoso Parto da Famosa Giganta de Coimbra* [The Monstrous Birth of the Famous Giantess from Coimbra], will enable me to characterize the dynamics between authorship and target audience. Furthermore, the content of *papéis volantes* will be debated in relation to three cases: the examples of utopian narratives, the subversive politics of anti-Napoleonic pamphlets in the early 1800s, and, in greater detail, the series of polemical *papéis* on the Woman Question published throughout the eighteenth century.

Usually, the term *literatura de cordel* is illustrated by or traced back to Nicolau Tolentino's poem 'O Bilhar',[6] which features a brief reference to the sale of printed pamphlets in the streets, displayed hanging from strings (*cordéis*). The term was most probably created and popularized in the 1800s as a by-product of Romantic interest in the subject and comes across as an attempt to define a variety of literary products by equating the marketing and selling of booklets directly to the public with a popular authorship and readership.

The phrase *de cordel* refers, then, to a mode of print circulation. Far from being a neutral label, it is closely linked to the Romantic ethnographic tradition which sees this kind of production as a genuine or picturesque repository of popular sensibilities. In 1885, Teófilo Braga emphasized that the popular and, to a greater extent, the traditional origins of the *cordel* provided a textual insight into the aesthetic sensibilities and inner life of the Portuguese people.[7] The distinction between popular and traditional forms of literary production enabled him to tell novelty texts, usually by a single author, apart from genuine expressions of popular culture, created by a collective author (the Portuguese people) or by individuals with an in-depth knowledge of real popular sensibilities. To illustrate the latter, Braga highlights Gil Vicente and Bandarra, but he fails to recognize the complex processes of authorship and intertextuality, and the politically motivated trajectories of texts that may be seen to fall within the realm of *literatura de cordel*.[8]

---

[5] Arnaldo Saraiva, 'A literatura marginal', in *Anais da UTAD, Fórum de literatura e teoria literária* (Vila Real: Universidade de Trás-os-Montes e Alto Douro, 1992), pp. 341–46.
[6] Luísa de Paiva Boléo, 'Mulheres de cordel: breve abordagem aos folhetos de cordel do séc. XVIII', in *Estudos sobre as mulheres*, ed. by Maria Beatriz Nizza da Silva and Anne Cova (Lisbon: Universidade Aberta and Centro de Estudos das Migrações e das Relações Interculturais, 1998), pp. 113–43 (p. 113); Carlos Nogueira, *O essencial sobre a literatura de cordel portuguesa* (Lisbon: Imprensa Nacional–Casa da Moeda, 2004), pp. 7–9.
[7] Teófilo Braga, *O povo português nos seus costumes, crenças e tradições*, 2 vols (Lisbon: Dom Quixote, 1994), II, 317–19.
[8] See Diogo Ramada Curto, 'Littérature de large circulation au Portugal (XVI-XVIII siècles)', in

In a series of articles on eighteenth-century print culture, Violeta Crespo Figueiredo adopted a term that avoids the ideological pitfalls of the Romantic search for popular expression. The name used at the time, *papel volante*, signalled a lowest common denominator relating to the mode of production — the print format — and drew Figueiredo's attention to identifying the topics and genres typical of this great variety of texts: narratives about monsters, exoticism, chivalry, the Woman Question, and humour.[9] Furthermore, it acknowledged that there was an institutional and political dimension to the material.[10]

The designation was used to cover a number of different sub-classifications, ranging from terms pertaining to the material structure of the publication, to terms that described its textual content. Similar to the book format today, *papel volante* was a broad designation that allowed for a degree of flexibility in relation to the status of different topics, genres, and modes of distribution. Indeed, the *papel volante* embraced texts on medicine, practical advice, agriculture, or history, as well as accommodating a breadth of genres as varied as polemics, journalism, epistolary writing, narrative and drama. Furthermore, it could be distributed through different channels by agents with overlapping interests and target audiences: printers and bookbinders, booksellers, members of the *Irmandade do Menino Jesus dos Homens Cegos* [Corporation of Blind Men], and street vendors.[11] Therefore, to an extent, one common denominator seems to be the object itself: a short booklet of around eight to thirty-two pages, made from low-quality paper and printed using large typographic characters.[12] However, even a purely bibliographic definition[13] cannot encompass the wider range of *papéis*, since many were printed on high-quality paper (in fact, most existing specimens are in relatively good condition), especially eulogies and sermons.

*Papel* was, therefore, an umbrella designation that accommodated a number of variables. This is the solution advocated by Márcia Abreu in a study that challenges the idea that the eighteenth-century Portuguese *papel volante* was a forerunner of the Brazilian *literatura de cordel*. According to Abreu, Portuguese and Brazilian literary forms, just as in many other countries, obeyed a common

*Colportage et lecture populaire: imprimés de large circulation en Europe, XVI-XIX siècles*, ed. by Roger Chartier and H.-J. Lüsebrink (Paris: IMEC, 1996), pp. 299-329 (pp. 314-15).
[9] Violeta Crespo Figueiredo, 'Papéis volantes do século XVIII 1. O mundo lugar de perigo (monstros e calamidades)', *História*, November 1978, pp. 54-63; 'Papéis volantes do século XVIII 2. O exotismo no tempo de D. João V', *História*, December 1978, pp. 66-72; 'Papéis volantes do século XVIII 3. O exotismo no tempo de D. João V (anos de 1750 a 1768)', *História*, January 1979, pp. 60-69; 'Papéis volantes do século XVIII 4. Histórias (autos e novelas de cavalaria e amores)', *História*, February 1979, pp. 70-78; 'Papéis volantes do século XVIII 5. Mulher', *História*, March 1979, pp. 54-64; 'Papéis volantes do século XVIII 6. Riso', *História*, April 1979, pp. 71-76.
[10] Violeta Crespo Figueiredo, 'Papéis volantes do século XVIII 7. Público, política e censura', *História*, June 1979, pp. 70-78.
[11] Manuela Domingos, *Livreiros de setecentos* (Lisbon: Biblioteca Nacional, 2000), pp. 58-59; Fernando Guedes, *O livro e a leitura em Portugal, subsídios para a sua história, séculos XVIII-XIX* (Lisbon and São Paulo: Verbo, 1987), pp. 259-75.
[12] Figueiredo, 'Papéis volantes do século XVIII 7. Público, política e censura', p. 71.
[13] Albino Forjaz de Sampaio, *Teatro de cordel (catálogo da colecção do autor)* (Lisbon: Academia das Ciências de Lisboa and Imprensa Nacional de Lisboa, 1922), p. 9.

editorial strategy, since publishers catered to an audience that wished to become acquainted with texts that circulated amongst the educated elite, as long as the price was affordable. Therefore, both form and content catered to the target audience.[14]

The research programme suggested by Saraiva's concept of marginal/ized literature is deemed by Abreu a useful tool in the understanding of both Brazilian *cordel* and Portuguese *papéis* because it eliminates the straightforward association with the idea of popular origins and replaces it with the idea of a literature produced at the margins of the literary, cultural and political establishments, with its own distinctive linguistic or editorial format.[15] Abreu makes the case for a separate genesis of the Brazilian *cordel*, and focuses on how its specific context independently created the need for a similar publication, characterized by its inexpensive booklets, accessible content adapted to local contexts, and a large target audience[16] — a set of features that position the genre at the margins of elite forms of textual production and publishing practices.

Crucially, for Abreu, the strategy common to both forms is not enough to prove the existence of a relationship between them because the Brazilian *cordel* is more unified in terms of topics and textual formats (there is a set of fixed rules for rhyme and metrics), whereas Portuguese *papéis* show no such homogeneity.[17] The 1763-66 conflict between the *Irmandade* and the corporation of booksellers suggests that the diversified nature of the Portuguese *papéis* was due to the fact that the target audience crossed different social classes. The dispute developed over the fact that the blind men were selling publications different from the short booklets one might associate with *literatura de cordel*, and ended with the authorities taking the side of the blind men, favouring the greater availability of a range of texts to a bigger audience.[18] This has been variously referred to as 'door-to-door culture' and a market for objects of 'mass consumption'.[19] The publishing of *papéis* did take place at the margins of elite print production patterns but it also took advantage of a favourable institutional climate provided by the emerging publishing industry under the rule of D. João V.[20] Whereas elite print production took the form of sizeable scholarly projects on theology, history or literature, sponsored by the royal house or the Academia Real da História Portuguesa, such as *Vocabulário Português e Latino* (1712-28) by Bluteau or *Biblioteca Lusitana* (1741-59) by Diogo Barbosa

---

[14] Márcia Abreu, *Histórias de cordéis e folhetos* (Campinas: ALB and Mercado de Letras, 1999), pp. 24-25.
[15] Abreu, pp. 22-23.
[16] Abreu, p. 134.
[17] Abreu, p. 108.
[18] Guedes, pp. 259-75.
[19] Maria José Moutinho Santos, 'O folheto de cordel: mulher, família e sociedade no Portugal do século XVIII' (unpublished master's thesis, Faculdade de Letras da Universidade do Porto, 1987), p. 9; João Luís Lisboa, 'Papéis de larga circulação no século XVIII', *Revista de história das ideias*, 20 (1999), 131-47 (p. 132).
[20] Artur Anselmo, *Estudos de história do livro* (Lisbon: Guimarães Editores, 1997), p. 89.

Machado,[21] the production of *papéis volantes*, as elsewhere in Europe, ran parallel, addressing a fragmented audience with diverse and conflicting interests.[22] Indeed, *papéis volantes* do not claim a straightforward popular identity (in terms of authorship and content); instead, they offer a discussion on how the large target audience and the concession to popular literary tastes affect its status.

*Eco de Diferentes Vozes* is an undated *papel* that ascribes a lowly status to the *papel volante* genre precisely because of its popularity. Its supposed author, a student, acquiesces to a request by a friend to pen a publication for the amusement of the populace. The reason for the request was that most of the many printed texts in circulation were deemed degrading.[23] The response becomes a pretext for an assessment of the *papel volante* as a literary genre, and an exercise in pastiche targeting two of its subcategories, the chivalric romance and the fantasy narrative. *Eco de Diferentes Vozes* sums up the reasons why the genre came to be seen as popular and in bad taste. Both content and form are criticized for not abiding by a certain standard of scholarly erudition. However, the lack of erudition is not the ultimate criterion for a negative assessment of the genre because the student acknowledges that most authors show a degree of ingenious artistry. The argument develops in a circular format so that the responsibility for judgement falls on the reader. On the one hand, readers fail to be entertained by the philosophical writings of erudite authors; on the other, catering to their preferences is the sole objective of clever authors who bypass quality.[24]

The student then goes on to urge his friend to prepare the printing press and apply for a publishing licence while he quickly writes a work that he simultaneously describes as only worth the price readers are prepared to pay for it, and as a skilfully constructed miscellany aimed at pleasing the average curious reader by means of a 'modo cômum, de agradar a todos' [common method that will please everyone].[25] If it is met with dissatisfaction, the student argues, it shall be by those readers looking for low-brow satire, which is not likely to be approved by the censors in any case.[26] In fact, what the student mainly objects to is the fact that *papéis* are subjected to the judgement of learned and ignorant readers alike.[27]

---

[21] Anselmo, pp. 96–97.
[22] Roger Chartier, 'Introduction: librairie de colportage et lecteurs "populaires"', in *Colportage et lecture populaire: imprimés de large circulation en Europe, XVI–XIX siècles*, ed. by Roger Chartier and H.-J. Lüsebrink (Paris: IMEC, 1996), pp. 11–18 (pp. 16–17).
[23] *Ecco de Differentes Vozes; com que hum Estudante do Barreiro, Satisfaz a hum seu Amigo de Lisboa, que o Persuadio a que Fizesse alguns Papeis Curiozos, para Divertimento do Povo* (Lisbon: n.pub., n.d.), p. 1.
[24] *Ecco de Differentes Vozes*, p. 1.
[25] Translation mine.
[26] *Ecco de Differentes Vozes*, p. 4.
[27] *Ecco de Differentes Vozes*, p. 8.

In *Monstruoso Parto da Famosa Giganta de Coimbra* (1741), a poverty-stricken and starving student from Coimbra is urged by an old man to make use of his talents and write a *papel* that, once sold in town or in Lisbon, by the blind, would rescue him from his dire situation.[28] As in *Eco de Diferentes Vozes*, there is a simulation of different genres, a poetic description of Coimbra, and the transcription of a newspaper article from the imaginary kingdom of Scholacia. The giantess in the title is a trick. The author admits on the last page that he had no intention of including a monster in his narrative.[29] Narratives about monsters were tolerated by the censors because of the moral and political message they represented, based on the superiority of the Catholic faith.[30] However, in *Monstruoso Parto*, the monster's only redeeming feature was to attract as many readers as possible, and become one of the many fake fantastic creatures that fuelled everyday conversations. The aim was to feed an industry that depended on a constant stream of new texts, and generate a profit, regardless of any criticism of the writing style, which, according to the old man's advice, should not concern the student as long as the text sold well.[31]

Despite being fictional accounts of the origins of *papéis*, *Eco de Diferentes Vozes* and *Monstruoso Parto* do provide a fairly realistic picture. In a case study of one prospective sponsor of a *papel volante* and its author, Olímpia Loureiro shows how *papéis* could, in principle, include contributions that really were of popular origin, usually through the mediation of an educated agent — which might explain the recurrent figure of the student. Loureiro shows that the process was met with severe obstruction. A student writes a dialogue on the art of courtship that achieves great success among the customers of Lourenço Afonso's barber's shop. Lourenço, believing he has a chance of making a profit, requests a publishing licence from the *Real Mesa Censória* [Royal Board of Censorship], which regards the *papel* as improper, and arrests and interrogates both Lourenço and the student. The episode comes to an end with a reprimand and both are eventually set free. As a conclusion, Loureiro puts forward the hypothesis that there was a split between the popular patterns of textual production and consumption, and the surveillance and repression exerted by a restricted elite.[32]

In these examples, the *papel volante* is defined not only as a genre that adapts its texts to the local context and market (either popular or erudite), but also one that cannot hand-pick its readership and must therefore cater to a variety of readers (of various degrees of literacy). At the opposite end of the spectrum,

---

[28] *Monstruoso Parto da Famosa Giganta de Coimbra* (Coimbra: Officina de Antonio Simoens Ferreyra, Impressor da Universidade, 1741), pp. 2–3.
[29] *Monstruoso Parto*, p. 8.
[30] P. Fontes da Costa, 'Between Fact and Fiction: Narratives of Monsters in Eighteenth-Century Portugal', *Portuguese Studies*, 20 (2004), 63–72 (p. 72).
[31] *Monstruoso Parto*, pp. 2–3.
[32] Olímpia Loureiro, 'Espaços defesos da escrita no Portugal setecentista', *Revista de história das ideias*, 20 (1999), 31–46.

elite texts strove to circumscribe the range of legitimate readings. In the first instalment of his *Suplemento ao Vocabulário Português e Latino* [Supplement to the Portuguese and Latin Vocabulary], Rafael Bluteau listed those readers he acknowledged as competent or incompetent to pronounce a judgement of value on his dictionary. One of Bluteau's addressees, the malevolent reader, is dubbed insignificant and lacking in authority, and, crucially, does not appear on the list of those who are qualified to read the dictionary: scholars, patrons, politicians, noblemen, clergymen and censors.[33]

Since the underlying aim of the genre is to reach out to as large an audience as possible, *Eco de Diferentes Vozes* depicts a virtual entity, the average curious reader, in turn presupposing an average mode of expression, and thereby representing a compromise between an erudite but exclusive discourse and vulgar diatribes unlikely to pass censorship. Rather than being an accurate portrayal of the editorial dynamics of the genre, the figure of the average curious reader shows a concern for the lack of a degree of hierarchical order brought about by the seemingly ubiquitous *papel volante*, and yet at the same time an awareness of its subversive potential, reined in by a conciliatory average mode of expression and a benign censor.

In this context, the *papel volante* is indeed a marginal genre, not in the sense that it exists outside an institutional setting (censorship is a tangible presence), but in the sense that it manages to exist according to a different set of rules that tend to democratize access to the written word. It is not a learned text, it is not legitimized by being accessible to an elite, but it targets a wider public/market, and it uses outmoded topics and discursive formulations deemed worthy of ridicule, such as the medieval-inspired chivalric novel in *Eco de Diferentes Vozes*, or the narratives about monsters in *Monstruoso Parto*.

The choice of the student as author is not arbitrary because he brings a degree of scholarly knowledge to the *papéis*. Furthermore, it shifts the burden of the marginal cultural value of the genre towards the audience, represented as an undiscerning mass of customers looking for outrageous topics of conversation and light entertainment. However, there is an acknowledgement here of the audience as integral to the *papel*'s existence and function. On one hand, it is the audience who determines whether or not a *papel* becomes a successful enterprise in terms of sales and reach; on the other, the audience provides a useful contrast to the writer of *papéis*, who manages to display flourishes of erudition and technique. The last paragraph in *Monstruoso Parto* is both a tribute to its own author and a criticism of the reader. The student not only congratulates himself on having created a grandiose title able to rouse the curiosity of the audience, thus mastering the craft of writing a *papel*, but also on restricting the deceit to the title.[34] In this way he manages to retain the moral high ground over the

---

[33] Raphael Bluteau, *Supplemento ao Vocabulário Portuguez e Latino*, 2 vols (Lisbon: Officina de Joseph da Sylva, 1727), I, 9–38.
[34] *Monstruoso Parto*, p. 10.

reader, who is told to look for monsters and giants in philosophers elsewhere, in the story of Charlemagne, and in *Don Quijote*, to which, as the initiated would have recognized, the title alludes.

The *papel volante* organizes the relationship between author and audience in such a way that the former has a higher status than the latter. Authors condescend to lower their standards in terms of style, erudition, and subject matter to accommodate a mass audience. The inclusion of derogatory simulations of subgenres such as the chivalric novel and the narrative about monsters shows how, very early on, the genre was seen as a repository of tried and tested discursive routines, devoid of any innovation, existing on the margins of erudite literary production which had moved away from subjects that remained popular throughout the eighteenth century.[35] The rehabilitation of the genre during the Romantic period drew upon this representation, and failed to realize that the popularity of certain subgenres did not necessarily mean they were of popular origin. This, in turn, led to the perception of the *papel volante* as the vehicle for formulaic topics and rhetorical forms popular among the uneducated classes.[36]

The focus on genre, seen either as a formulaic or a traditional form of cultural expression, ignores topics and discourses that deviate from the mainstream production of both *papéis volantes* and higher-status printed texts. An examination of such cases can help us understand how the genre was actually used to disseminate alternative or even subversive discourses.

In 2004, Jorge Miguel Bastos da Silva published an anthology of utopian texts that counteracts the idea that, with the exception of Sebastianism and millenarism, there is no tradition of utopian thinking in Portugal; this apparent absence has historically been explained as resulting from a lack of a critical citizenship able to reinvent social structures.[37] While recognizing the difficulties inherent in generalizing about cultural phenomena, Silva still manages to collect a number of examples: from Antero de Quental's negative diagnosis of the cultural dynamics of the peninsular nationalities to Eduardo Lourenço's assessment of the legacy of the Portuguese maritime expansion. Silva argues that utopian writing does exist in Portugal and its vehicle in the eighteenth century was the *papel volante*. He emphasizes a number of features of the genre: the diversity of topics that, in addition to developments in education and society, would lead to the advent of the periodical press, the existence of erudite forms of expression such as the sermon, the wide social reach, and what he calls the 'degree of redundancy' of the *papel volante*, which takes the form

---

[35] See Figueiredo, 'Papéis volantes do século XVIII 4. Histórias (autos e novelas de cavalaria e amores)', p. 72.
[36] See Robert Scholes, *The Crafty Reader* (New Haven, CT, and London: Yale University Press, 2001), p. 141.
[37] Jorge Miguel Bastos da Silva, *Utopias de cordel e textos afins, uma antologia* (Vila Nova de Famalicão: Quasi, 2004), pp. 13–26.

of frequent adaptations, imitations and collages of different works.[38] These features enable Silva to see the *papel volante* not as a genre limited by any orthodoxy but as one that fully manages the external constraints (audience and censorship) to display a subtle openness to new ideas.[39]

In António Pedro Vicente's study of the anti-Napoleonic literature of the early 1800s, the starting point is the lack of an established public opinion underpinned by a politically and culturally engaged periodical press. The French invasion was soon to change the situation, provoking the publication of hundreds of passionate pamphlets with sizeable print runs that circulated in the most densely populated Portuguese cities.[40] These pamphlets were typical of the *papel volante* genre, in other words they were short anecdotal texts in the form of satire, theatre and poetry, but they also incorporated more erudite texts on history, philosophy and religion.[41] However, erudite and entertainment texts alike were endorsed by the authorities and printed by official publishing houses in Lisbon and Coimbra,[42] and both were notably topical.[43] Vicente argues that the authorities allowed authors a period of freedom so as to facilitate a surge in publishing activity that could instigate rebellion. This situation also inadvertently triggered the creation of an emergent public opinion, which was promptly repressed by the same elite who had encouraged its growth when it proved useful against the French invader. Vicente explains that the dissemination of anti-Napoleonic pamphlets enabled the development of a new kind of reader and a new form of public participation, whereby the struggle against Napoleon equated to the creation of a wider political awareness that was to extend beyond the context of the Peninsular Wars, and eventually question the sustainability of the Absolutist regime.[44]

These examples suggest that the *papel volante* was not just a repository of discursive formulae intended to elicit the reader's recognition of well-known topics and genres. Silva identifies a chaotic openness to different influences, and Vicente draws a direct link to social and political reality.

A third example is a number of texts that debated the Woman Question from a markedly positive perspective, in opposition to the mainstream misogyny of most *papéis volantes*. The debate was laid out in a series of thirteen *papéis* (totalling twenty-two editions), from 1715 to the first half of the 1800s. Its misogynistic counterpart amounts to eleven texts spread out across thirty editions during the eighteenth and nineteenth centuries. However, the total number of misogynous texts greatly outnumbers the examples of pro-woman

---

[38] Silva, pp. 28–31.
[39] Silva, pp. 32–33.
[40] António Pedro Vicente, 'Panfletos anti-napoleónicos durante a guerra peninsular, actividade editorial da Real Imprensa da Universidade', *Revista de história das ideias*, 20 (1999), 101–30 (pp. 108–09).
[41] Vicente, pp. 115–17.
[42] Vicente, p. 109.
[43] Vicente, pp. 116–17.
[44] Vicente, pp. 120–25.

literature. Indeed, one of the most popular misogynous invectives, *Malícia das Mulheres* [Women's Maliciousness] by Baltazar Dias (1640),[45] saw a total of eighteen editions.

The first *papel* to tackle the Woman Question in a combative way, along the lines of a *querelle des femmes*,[46] was Paula da Graça's *Bondade das Mulheres Vindicada* [Woman's Goodness Vindicated] (1715).[47] This pamphlet set out to address the long-standing positive reception of Dias's *Malícia das Mulheres* by telling the truth about women. The author's foremost concern was to divert the public away from an unthinking and unquestioning acceptance of misogynous mockery and towards an awareness of its iniquity. Her proposal employed a similar entertaining approach underpinned by a more honest attitude; honest both in terms of maintaining the boundaries of decency and in its commitment to a truthful viewpoint: '[o] papel, que impugnamos, cujos motivos me persuadiram a dar este à luz, [...] servindo para diversão do povo, sem se opor à observância do honesto' [the *papel* we impugn awakened in me the urge to write a response that would provide amusement for the people with no impediment to observing the limits of honesty].[48] Indeed, elsewhere in the pamphlet she defended a reading of the classical authors and the Bible based on a different 'mirror', that is, based on the presupposition that souls are not intrinsically male or female.[49] Despite the final appeal being directed to readers in general, the author first addressed female readers, postulating the existence of a female audience predisposed to understand her arguments.[50] While there is a substantial departure from the depiction of the audience in *Eco de Diferentes Vozes* and *Monstruoso Parto*, the existence of a diverse public is necessary for the *papel* to have the desired effect. Instead of regarding the audience as a necessary evil, here the author is inviting a community to share her beliefs in order to legitimize a view on a topic previously controlled by misogynous discourse.

*Bondade das Mulheres* signals some of the key features of the series of *papéis* that would follow suit. They employ a female (or at least pro-woman) voice that addresses an audience that is expected to convert to a standard of civility and reason, they contrast the misogynous anecdotes about female flaws with the reality of women's lives and education, and they use the same pool of resources

---

[45] [Baltasar Dias], *Malicia das Mulheres. Obra Novamente Feita, na qual se Tratão muitas Sentenças, e Authoridades acerca da Malicia que Ha em algumas dellas, e assim Trata como duas Mulheres Enganaraõ seus Maridos Graciosamente* (Lisbon: Officina de Francisco Borges de Sousa, 1759).
[46] Literary dispute about the nature and status of women that took place during the fifteenth and sixteenth centuries.
[47] Paula da Graça, *Bondade das Mulheres Vindicada, e Malicia dos Homens Manifesta. Papel Metrico, e Apologetico, em que se defende a Femenina Innocencia, contra outro em que Injustamente se argúe a sua Maldade, com o Titulo de Malicia das Mulheres* (Lisbon: Officina de António Gomes, 1793).
[48] *Bondade das Mulheres Vindicada*, p. 2. In Bluteau's dictionary, *honesto* means 'pudico' [prudish] and 'conforme a boa razão' [faithful to reason] (Raphael Bluteau, *Vocabulario Portuguez & Latino*, 8 vols (Coimbra: Collegio das Artes da Companhia de Jesus, 1712–28), VIII (1728), p. 50.
[49] *Bondade das Mulheres Vindicada*, p. 6.
[50] *Bondade das Mulheres Vindicada*, p. 2.

of misogynous texts, whether the jocular register of Baltazar Dias or more erudite rhetorical devices, such as *auctoritates* and *exempla*.[51]

Arguably, the 'marginalizing' element of this series of pro-woman *papéis* is not so much the topic itself, but the combative mindset, and the degree of authority that the author constructs, which matches or prevails over those of the misogynous texts. Indeed, authors of pro-woman *papéis volantes* source their material from an established corpus of user-friendly material (biographies of exemplary women and works of the Enlightenment), but they also refer to earlier misogynistic works (matrimonial treatises, for example). The *papéis volantes* depart from these erudite sources in the way that they make calculated choices and subtle rearrangements of the original material, and disseminate their ideas via a genre whose readership crossed social classes.

Along with *Bondade das Mulheres Vindicada*, the two instalments of Gertrudes Margarida de Jesus's *Carta[s] Apologética[s]* [Apologetic Letter/s] (1761),[52] which respond to a misogynous text entitled *Espelho Crítico* [Critical Mirror], have been highlighted as the most antagonistic examples in the series. In the 1761 pamphlets Maria Antónia Lopes has identified an appeal for readers to develop a critical ability to deconstruct misogynous discourse.[53] Elias Torres Feijó has read the *Carta[s]* as a transgressive dissemination of a set of erudite references by means of a model of public intervention usually reserved for men: the *carta apologética*. Torres Feijó argues that that genre was the most effective for the dissemination of new ideas because, besides its long tradition in Iberian cultural life, it functioned as an intermediate step between a mixed personal/collective form of communication and decidedly public forms of intervention in the periodical press.[54] Most recently, Vanda Anastácio has highlighted the rhetorical structure of the pamphlets. According to Anastácio, the use of *auctoritates, exempla* and historical and literary references amounts to an 'overwhelming display of erudition' that, despite its traditional main arguments, conceals the real innovation: the introduction of contemporary references.[55]

[51] *Auctoritates* is the use of quotations from authoritative writers who pass on knowledge and truth. The *exemplum* is an example or model of behaviour based on history, mythology or literature that illustrates a moral point.
[52] Gertrudes Margarida de Jesus, *Primeira Carta Apologetica em Favor e Defensa das Mulheres, Escrita por Dona Gertrudes Margarida de Jesus ao Irmaõ Amador do Dezengano, com a qual destróe toda a Fabrica do seu Espelho Critico* (Lisbon: Offic. de Antonio Gomes, 1791); *Segunda Carta Apologética, Favor, e Defensa das Mulheres, Escrita por Dona Gertrudes Margarida de Jesus, ao Irmaõ Amador do Dezengano, com a qual destroe toda a Fabrica do seu Espelho Critico. E se responde ao Terceiro Defeito, que nelle comtemplou* (Lisbon: Officina de Francisco Borges de Sousa, 1761).
[53] Maria Antónia Lopes, *Mulheres Espaço e Sociabilidade: A Transformação dos Papéis Femininos em Portugal à Luz de Fontes Literárias (Segunda Metade do Século XVIII)* (Lisbon: Livros Horizonte, 1989), p. 32.
[54] Elias Torres Feijó, 'Cartas apologéticas, cartas polemistas. As cartas apologéticas de Gertrudes Margarida de Jesus. Argumentaçom e inovaçom', in *Correspondências. Usos da carta no século XVIII*, ed. by Vanda Anastácio (Lisbon: Edições Colibri, 2005), pp. 223–53 (pp. 225, 251–52).
[55] Vanda Anastácio, 'Notes on the *Querelle des femmes* in Eighteenth-Century Portugal', *Portuguese Studies*, 31.1 (2015), 50–63 (p. 60).

The misogynous text *Espelho Crítico* was published in 1761.[56] Its aim was to draw attention to perceived flaws in women (ignorance, inconstancy and beauty) with the help of classical authors and experience (evidence). The pamphlet is a collage of aphorisms on the nature of women and short narratives to which the author adds his own comments, either to clarify or reinforce the meaning. For example, the author expands upon D. Francisco Manuel de Melo's anecdote about women's intelligence being limited to organizing the linen chest[57] by concluding that he would be impressed if a woman could do even as much as tying up a bundle of linen.[58] However, the disparaging tone has a pedagogical objective, which is to invite women to refrain from dressing ostentatiously, and to become eloquent in speaking the truth, rather than lying and slandering.[59] The licences to print *Espelho Crítico* were requested by a Manuel Ribeiro in December 1760.[60] The text was published in January 1761 or soon thereafter, and resurfaced[61] that same year as the second part of an earlier publication, *Método Prático* [Practical Method] (1760), which suggests that this second edition sought to capitalize on the success of *Método* (two editions in 1760).

The two-part response to *Espelho Crítico* was also published in 1761, with a further edition in 1791. Gertrudes Margarida de Jesus ignored the moral message of the misogynous text and took the attribution of flaws as an insult to all women. The author subscribes to reason as the best weapon against the brute force used by men to impose their will and perspective on women, a tactic which, in her opinion, lacks discernment. The premise of reason paves the way towards a more socially attuned understanding of female ignorance, which she explains as a consequence of the lack of formal education available to them, rather than a congenital defect. The same premise allows for a consideration of *exempla* that reach beyond those conforming to a misogynous viewpoint (the opposites of infamous and motherly/saintly women), by analysing the cases of women trained in the arts, the sciences or warcraft.[62]

---

[56] *Espelho Critico, no qual Claramente se Vem alguns Defeitos das Mulheres*, Fabricado na Loja da Verdade pelo Irmaõ Amador do Dezengano, que Pode Servir de Estimulo para a Reforma dos mesmos Defeitos (Lisbon: Offic. de António Vicente da Silva, 1761).
[57] 'I cannot but admire at a Saying of that so much quoted Bishop of ours D. Affonso, which was, The most knowing Woman, only knows how to lay up a Chest of Linnen. Nor can I forget Another who said, The most knowing Woman, knows as much as two Women.' D. Francisco Manuel [de Melo], *The Government of a Wife or, Wholsom and Pleasant Advice for Married men: in a Letter to a Friend*, trans. by John Stevens (London: Jacob Tonson, 1697), p. 83.
[58] *Espelho Critico*, pp. 4-5.
[59] *Espelho Critico*, p. 5.
[60] I.A.N.T.T., Inquisição-Conselho Geral, Livro 357 (2 and 23 December 1760); licences in the appendix.
[61] Maria José Moutinho Santos, 'Perspectivas sobre a situação da mulher no século XVIII', *Revista de história*, 4 (1981), 35–48 (p. 39).
[62] The unacknowledged core source of the publication is Benito Jerónimo Feijó's 'Defensa de las Mujeres' (1726), part of his *Teatro Crítico Universal* [Universal Critical Theatre]. *Exempla* are explicitly attributed to the *Dictionnaire Historique-Portatif* [Portable Historical Dictionary] (1752) by Jean-Baptiste Ladvocat, and *Teatro Heroíno* (1736 and 1740) by Damião de Froes Perim, pseudonym of Fray João de São Pedro. Other passages are drawn from *Imagens da Vida Cristã* [Images of Christian Life]

While both sides of the controversy build upon a collage of references and quotations in order to develop an argument, they differ in how effectively they construct an authoritative voice. The female voice displays a higher degree of agency in defining the terms of the discussion, and the way the collage is constructed in both misogynous and pro-woman texts suggests that they were written contiguously so as to strengthen the arguments of the latter. For example, a reference to Euripides in *Primeira Carta* [First Letter], translated from Feijó's 'Defensa de las Mujeres' [Defence of Women],[63] is included in the sequence of arguments as a response to a reference to the same classical author in *Espelho Crítico*.[64] In order to explain the apparent integration, Torres Feijó has put forward the hypothesis that *Espelho Crítico* and the *Carta[s]* were created in tandem to disseminate a more contemporary cultural repertoire,[65] notably the Enlightenment thinking of Benito Jerónimo Feijó.

The parallel creation of these publications becomes more evident when we consider Feijó in juxtaposition with the core source of the misogynous text *Nova Floresta* [New Forest] (1706–28) by Manuel Bernardes. The opening precept in *Espelho Crítico*, 'A mulher é naufrágio do homem, tempestade da casa, cativeiro da vida, leoa abraçando, animal malicioso e mal necessário' [Women are the shipwreck of men, their domestic storm, the captivity of life, the embrace of a lioness, a malicious animal and a necessary evil],[66] borrowed from a section of *Nova Floresta*,[67] is an example of Bernardes's overall negative attitude, which was based on traditional misogynous notions of women being an instrument of the devil. Moreover, the more positive instances of Bernardes's view on women do not stray away from the frame of reference of religious or matrimonial life, which is informed by *Jardim de Portugal* [The Garden of Portugal], the collection of exemplary women compiled by Fray Luís dos Anjos.[68] Crucially, the source of Portuguese *exempla* in *Segunda Carta Apologética* is not *Jardim de Portugal* but *Teatro Heroíno* [Theatre of Heroines], which cites Feijó as a precursor, and acknowledges female achievements in literature, the arts, and the sciences to a greater degree. As well as choosing a modern reference rather than a more established one, *Segunda Carta* also makes a careful selection from the contents provided by the source. While Fray Luís dos Anjos's entry on the Infanta Maria, the Princess of Parma, emphasizes virtue and devoutness with a

---

(1563) by Fray Heitor Pinto.
[63] *Primeira Carta Apologetica*, p. 6; Benito Jerónimo Feijoo, 'Defensa de las Mujeres', in *Teatro Crítico Universal*, 8 vols (Madrid: Real Compañía de Impresores y Libreros, 1778), I, 325–98 (p. 327).
[64] *Espelho Critico*, p. 3.
[65] Torres Feijó, pp. 251–52.
[66] *Espelho Critico*, p. 4.
[67] Manuel Bernardes, *Nova Floresta, ou Sylva de Varios Apophthegmas*, 5 vols (Lisbon: Officina de Valentim da Costa Deslandes, 1708), II, 67.
[68] See William de Souza Martins, 'Representações femininas na obra do padre Manuel Bernardes (1644-1710)', *Lócus: revista de história*, 17.02 (2011), 35–55 (pp. 35–38) and Maria de Lurdes Correia Fernandes, 'Introdução', in Frei Luís dos Anjos, *Jardim de Portugal* (Porto: Campo das Letras, 1999), pp. 9–26 (p. 26).

brief mention of her studies,[69] *Teatro Heroíno* provides a more balanced picture since it refers to the princess's talents in the study of languages, mathematics and the scriptures.[70] In its turn, *Segunda Carta* ignores the information about the virtuous matriarch altogether and elects to present information on her learning.[71]

Furthermore, the opposition between Bernardes and Feijó is also developed in the unbalanced way that *Espelho Crítico* and *Carta[s] Apologética[s]* share their core sources to reinforce the pro-woman arguments. *Espelho Crítico* uses a passage from Feijó's 'Defensa de las Mujeres' on Helen of Troy and Princess Caba[72] to argue that beauty is the cause of unfortunate consequences; however, this was written in the knowledge that the source did provide the tools to dismantle the traditional misogynous argument. Indeed, *Segunda Carta* picks up Feijó's argument and uses it as he had originally intended, explaining that Helen's or Caba's beauty, contrary to the claim in *Espelho Crítico*, did not cause the Trojan War or the defeat of Rodrigo, king of the Goths, by the Muslims.[73] When the author of *Primeira Carta* uses the moral teachings of Bernardes's apologue of the wolf and the lamb to accuse men of deliberately looking for guilt in innocence (women),[74] it is Bernardes who is being criticized for not abiding by his own principles when dealing with the Woman Question. The strategy in the *Primeira Carta* of defending women with the same weapons as those used by its adversary *Espelho Crítico* is not just a general comment on the use of the same discursive resources or a similar emotional investment by two writers who disagree fundamentally about a topic. Instead, it is a warning that the audience is about to read a public critique of the inconsistencies of a stronghold of traditional misogynous thinking against more innovative references.

While it is true that both misogynous and pro-woman literature use standard discursive resources, the highlighting of this fact sometimes overshadows the existence of more nuanced messages.[75] The dialogue between *Espelho Crítico* and the *Carta[s] Apologética[s]* plays out the confrontation between two distinct ideological repertoires not only by carefully selecting and juxtaposing passages, but also by subtly moving the discussion in directions not fully supported by the Portuguese discursive tradition, notably the relevance given to female achievements in the arts and sciences. In 1734, the licences of *Portugal Ilustrado pelo Sexo Feminino* [Portugal Illustrated by the Female Sex], which is the basis

---

[69] Anjos, pp. 263–70.
[70] Damião de Froes Perym, *Theatro Heroino*, 2 vols (Lisboa: Regia Officina Sylviana, e da Academia Real, 1740), II, 122.
[71] *Segunda Carta Apologetica*, pp. 7–8.
[72] *Espelho Critico*, p. 11; Feijoo, p. 333.
[73] *Segunda Carta Apologetica*, p. 6.
[74] *Primeira Carta Apologetica*, p. 4.
[75] Maria José Moutinho Santos argues that pro-woman literature lacks factual information, and that misogynous texts, due to their insight into daily life, are more useful in the construction of a social history of the eighteeth-century woman (Santos, 'O Folheto de cordel: mulher, família e sociedade no Portugal do século XVIII', p. 5).

for much of *Teatro Heroíno*, gently reprimanded the author for not having paid more attention to religious women, who constitute the bulk of the collection of *exempla*.[76] In the licences appended to the *Carta[s]*, the censor Bento Cardoso praises the use of Fray Heitor Pinto's religious platonistic definition of beauty but ignores the attack on the misogynistic views inspired by Bernardes.[77] In the context of the controversies raised, the *Carta[s] Apologética[s]* emerge as the most compelling texts: an autonomous[78] and authoritative example of the *querelle des femmes* in eighteenth-century Portugal.

The *papel volante* provided a relatively safe vehicle for fairly aggressive discursive strategies and veiled erudite ideological wars. Since there was potential for a hostile reception, the authors found a safety net in the wider reading public as opposed to the elite who had the power to veto publication and thereby prevent the circulation of such ideas. Such an understanding of *papéis volantes* does become possible if one discounts the bias introduced by the designation *de cordel*, which regards literary products such as the series of controversial *papéis* on the Woman Question as merely a picturesque altercation with an apolitical stance, effectively denying that they engaged in public discussion of ideological questions. The works of Saraiva, Figueiredo and Abreu provide the cues calling for a reassessment of the *papel volante* as a politically engaged genre of publishing that carved out its own unique position at the margins of elite publishing practices in terms of authorship, target audience and content. Abreu's criticism of the idea of the Portuguese form as a precursor of Brazilian *literatura de cordel* is especially useful as it highlights the wider cross-society target audience of the Portuguese *papéis*. The *papel volante* was indeed a popular genre in the sense that it had a greater readership than more erudite texts, complicating the relationship between the two.

The gap between a popular publication and a prestigious one was not just measured in terms of subject since they often overlapped in terms of topics and genres. The difference between a prestigious/learned publication such as Bluteau's *Vocabulário*, and the non-prestigious/popular *papéis*, such as *Eco de Diferentes Vozes* and *Monstruoso Parto*, was more complex. Whereas the carefully selected audience of prestigious works is trusted to perform a legitimate reading of the work, less prestigious publications show a distrust of the wider audience and the potential for subversive readings. In *Eco de Diferentes Vozes* and *Monstruoso Parto* the audience is represented as numerous, undifferentiated, and, for the most part, uneducated and used to

---

[76] Diogo Manuel Aires de Azevedo, *Portugal Illustrado pelo Sexo Feminino*, 2 vols (Lisbon: Officina de Pedro Ferreira, 1734), pp. 9-10.
[77] *Segunda Carta Apologetica*, p. 4 and licences.
[78] The topic tends not to be articulated in independent texts in early modern Iberia. Tobias Brandenberger, 'Malas hembras und virtuosas mujeres: Querelles in der spätmittelalterlichen und frühneuzeitlichen Iberoromania', in *Die europäische Querelle des Femmes. Geschlechterdebatten seit dem 15. Jahrhundert*, ed. by Gisela Bock, Margarete Zimmermann and Monika Kopyczinski (Stuttgart: J. B. Metzler, 1997), pp. 183-202 (p. 195).

commonplace discursive formulae. This is one way of disregarding the validity of readings and their possible outcomes. The self-professed lowly status of the *papel volante* can be seen as a pre-emptive strike against any effects it may have. The dramatic difference in size of the readership especially when compared to those who would read a prestigious publication such as Bluteau's *Vocabulário*, entailed the adoption of complex modes of expression that, in addition to the challenges of a diverse audience, had to deal with the discursive tradition and a vigilant censorship. This explains why in *Eco de Diferentes Vozes* the author expresses perplexity at the need to use a standard mode of expression, which must reach a compromise between the discourse routinely associated with popular literary productions and resources of a distinctly erudite nature. The clash came between a select group of elite individuals and a mass audience.

The drawback in losing a select elite readership could have been the lack of control over the reading process, diluted as it was among a faceless mass audience. It was this apparent lack of a well-defined hierarchical order between production and reception that led Lourenço Afonso, a mere barber, to entertain the idea of publishing a *papel* but, as Loureiro has suggested, the patterns of popular textual production at the time simply did not meet the requirements of the elite. The lack of a hierarchical order went as far as allowing for a growth in readership. The constraints were much more palpable in the area of production, where authors had to demonstrate an ability to manipulate the legitimate discursive resources and authorities in order to access the print medium. However, the representations of the situation in *Eco de Diferentes Vozes* and *Monstruoso Parto* signal an insightful consideration of the power and the subversive potential of the *papel volante*. Since this genre reached out to a wider range of readers, at different stages of literacy, it can lead to different layers of interpretation. Discourses were experienced by the audience through their diverse reading strategies, which were more or less dependent on the recognition of formulaic topics and genres, more or less sophisticated and informed, and more or less attuned to the ideological stance of the work, depending on the position of individual readers within the cross-society audience of the *papel volante*.

The dissemination of anti-Napoleonic literature is a good example of how the subversive potential of the genre developed. The pamphlets were not meant in the first instance to encourage a broader political awareness that would question the absolutist regime and precipitate the liberal revolution. It could be argued that utopian literature did not realize its potential as a tool for reinventing social structures. Nevertheless, the fact that utopianism found its way to an eighteenth-century readership through the *papel volante* highlights the virtues of the genre as a place for experimentation in bringing together relatively marginal ideas, rhetorical patterns, genres, authors and audiences.

The series of pamphlets on the Woman Question (or the combined effect of misogynous and pro-woman texts) is an example of how effective the *papel volante* was as a medium for testing out a compelling mode of expression within the constraints of eighteenth-century patterns of production and dissemination of discourses. The chosen formula in *Espelho Crítico* and *Carta[s] Apologética[s]* was to recreate the opposition between the misogynous tradition of Bernardes and the Enlightenment thinking of Feijó as an audience-friendly polemic between a cleric and an educated woman. The content was repackaged to attend to the needs of a diverse audience (sparking off lively public discussion) and the obstacle of censorship (with the inclusion of Fray Heitor Pinto, a staple of theological literature). It is true that pro-woman literature used established and accepted discursive traditions (it was required reading if one wished to access the discussion) but it was not taken for granted that the topic, especially in the way it was reformulated in the *Carta[s] Apologética[s]*, was going to meet the expectations of most of its audience. This is why a presumably well-informed reader like Fray Bento Cardoso eagerly claimed ownership of the Fray Heitor Pinto reference to divert readers from the more controversial issues in the *Carta[s]*, and encourage the misleading understanding that the pamphlets were a religious discussion on beauty as a reflection of God. The attempt to prevent undesired readings suggests an awareness that the *papel volante* was a genre that provoked unpredictable outcomes. In the case of *Espelho Crítico* and *Carta[s] Apologética[s]*, the genre was reinvented as an up-to-date *querelle des femmes* in an autonomous text, and advanced the discussion into territory not fully served by either the misogynous or the non-misogynous tradition.

Fully aware of the political and ideological implications of their choices, authors of *papéis volantes* carefully articulated credited and uncredited sources, references, and original content to negotiate the furthering of new ideas in the context of a tight control of discourse practices. Authors and publishers of *papéis volantes* used their in-depth knowledge of eighteenth-century patterns of production and dissemination of discourses to subvert its rules. It was the ability to manipulate the core of rules and expectations that enabled the *papel volante* to function as a platform where the relative lack of a hierarchical order allowed the publication of texts on marginal topics and genres.

The genre did not fully comply with the orthodoxy of elite publishing practices. Indeed, it subtly reshaped the dynamics between authorship, content and target audience. The *papel volante* was a blank canvas for the experimental merging of genres and controversial topics for a mass audience, including topics commonly thought to be absent from early modern Portuguese intellectual production (whether a politically engaged press, examples of utopian writing or autonomous reflections on the role of women). The flexibility of the *papel volante* enabled it to act as a pivotal repository of various modes of expression and content that made it a relatively safe medium for the sparking of controversy on marginal topics in eighteenth-century Portuguese culture.

# Landscapes of Portugal in Two Hundred Years of Narratives

ANA ISABEL QUEIROZ

*IHC-FCSH and IELT-FCSH, Universidade Nova de Lisboa*

Years ago, a colleague told me of an episode that happened while she was working on the identification of landscape units. During her field work, she talked to a local shepherd in a rural area, in the border country of southern Portugal. While looking after his flock of sheep on top of a hill, with a view over a broad valley of prairies and bushes, he told her that there was no such thing as a landscape to be found there. The shepherd proceeded to apologize to her, assuming that the place he inhabited was somehow flawed, and advised her to look elsewhere for a landscape. The story reminds me of an excerpt from Miguel Torga (1907–1995), in which the writer describes a similar situation:

> Hoje à tarde, quando visitava as penedias do Sirol — uma maravilha que a erosão das águas ali fez — e pasmava diante de uma inacreditável fachada romântica natural, o bandido de um moleiro, a quem perguntei se aquilo não lhe dizia nada lá por dentro, respondeu-me tal e qual:
> — Para quem nunca viu pedras...
>
> [This afternoon, when I was visiting the rocky region of Sirol — a wonder created by water erosion — and was admiring an extraordinary natural Romanic façade, a rascally miller to whom I asked if that didn't appeal to his inner feelings, gave me this exact answer:
> — If you have never seen rocks before...].[1]

These two situations mark a starting point for the understanding of the relationship between the referent and the representation, how landscape appreciation is determined by perception and which processes and elements converge for the identification and understanding of landscapes, by common people, writers and those who care about the enhancement and preservation of landscape.

The shepherd and the miller knew the components of their surrounding environments but they did not recognize how remarkable they were. Used to those places, they could not interpret, nor could they value, the natural and cultural elements of their everyday landscape. The writer and my colleague, on the other hand, who had just arrived at these places, besides appreciating the aesthetic and sensory experience, were able to find significance there.

---

[1] Miguel Torga, 'Leiria, 25 de Novembro de 1940', Diário I, in *Diário*, vols I–IV (Lisbon: Dom Quixote, 2010), p. 94. Note: unless otherwise indicated, translations into English are my own.

With the same subject in mind, Michel Collot created the compound word *pensée-paysage*, which he defines as 'la relation qu'établit l'expérience du paysage entre une étendue de pays et celui qui l'observe' [the relationship that the experience of landscape establishes between a stretch of country and the person who observes it].[2] In the 1980s, the geographer Denis Cosgrove had already emphasized landscape as a cultural construct and identified the role of perception in this process. He suggested that the landscape could not exist without interpretation because it was both space and meaning. Cosgrove, then, understood landscape as 'a way of seeing',[3] explaining that there were many ways of seeing the same reality. As such, the same reality could be presented and represented in different ways, and the distance from its referential could vary.

José Sánchez de Muniain reflected on the relationship between the writer's personal experience and the content of his literary works regarding landscape.[4] He stated that Virgil, Camões, Cervantes, San Juan de la Cruz and Shakespeare (and one could add many others) said what they wanted to say with great strength because they had a first-hand knowledge of the matters they were talking about. Likewise the British naturalist Richard Jefferies also wrote of landscape: 'It is necessary to stay in it like the oaks to know it'.[5] David Lowental stated that conceptions of space resulted from a combination of perception, memory, logic, faith, learning and imagination, which vary from person to person.[6] Neil Evernden suggested that a person's vision of Nature (and its representation) was based on their own experience, on the ideas and knowledge of their age, on their occupation and the surrounding components of their environment.[7] More recently, José Manuel Marrero Henríquez concluded that 'la literatura también dice del mundo e que al decir del mundo decide sus formulaciones' [literature also describes the world and on describing the world it decides its formulations]. Thus, the literary landscape's values arise 'de la cualidad poética que late en la capacidad representativa del lenguaje' [from the poetical quality that lies in the representative capacity of language].[8]

Without denying the cultural character of representations, ecocriticism studies the relationship between people and the environment, analysing the

---

[2] Michel Collot, *La Pensée-paysage* (Arles: Actes du Sud, 2011), p. 20.
[3] Denis Cosgrove, 'Prospect, Perspective and the Evolution of the Landscape Idea', *Transactions of the Institute of British Geographers*, 10.1 (1985), 45–62 (p. 46).
[4] José María Sánchez de Muniain, *Estética del paisaje natural* (Madrid: Publicaciones Arbor, Consejo Superior de Investigaciones Científicas, 1945).
[5] From the essay, 'Meadow Thoughts', first published in the *Graphic*, 5 April 1884. Quoted by J. Hooker, *Writers in a Landscape* (Cardiff: University of Wales Press, 1996), p. 19.
[6] David Lowental, 'Geography, Experience, and Imagination: Towards a Geographical Epistemology', *Annals of the Association of American Geographers*, 51.3 (September 1961), 241–60.
[7] Derrick Jensen, *Listening to the Land: Conversations about Nature, Culture and Eros* (San Francisco: Sierra Club Books, 1995), pp. 112–21.
[8] José Manuel Marrero Henríquez, 'Introducción. Sobre lecturas del paisaje', in *Lecturas del paisaje*, ed. by José Manuel Marrero Henríquez (Las Palmas: Universidad de Las Palmas de Gran Canaria, 2009), pp. 9–15 (p. 11); idem, 'La crítica como refugio: animales, plantas y enclaves literarios en peligro de extinción', in idem, pp. 17–32 (p. 20).

forms of artistic expression (literary and others) in which this relationship is evident, arguing in favour of a return to referentiality in literary criticism. In this regard, Lawrence Buell wrote: '[s]uch disposition to take the word–world linkage seriously at a time when privileging literature's capacity for mimesis and referentiality remains unfashionable has given rise to considerable anxiety and division'.[9] For the ecocritical analysis, the question is not *whether* the creators composed their works, but *how* and *why*.[10] This analysis values the presence of the elements the author summoned from the reality that served as his referent. It assumes that texts, drawings, paintings, photographs, movies or other formats are directly connected with the world. In line with other holistic attempts to understand culture and nature, some ecocritics are in favour of bringing the humanities and sciences together in the context of studying specific landscapes and regions.[11]

Almost three decades ago, the American landscape architect Ervin Zube presented the 'transactional model of human/landscape relationship' to explain the process of perceiving (based on information and experience) and responding to environmental change (based on the 'personal utility function' and socio-cultural context):

> Land form and land use patterns are important sources of information in this process. The distribution of fields, woodlots, hedgerows, water features and buildings and changes in these distributional patterns are perceived differently over time by different individuals. Together with the individuals' range of experiences they shape individual perceptions. And perceptions — mediated by the socio-cultural context in which the person exists and his or her personal utility functions — influence responses to the landscape.[12]

In the universe of meanings from which literature is built, the ability to interpret comes as much from the sensorial and emotional experience as from a botanical, zoological, geological or cultural knowledge. Despite that, information about the landscape's natural elements is essential, for it defines the way in which it will be mentioned or described: a tree might be depicted as just a 'tree' or it might have a more specific designation and description. It might be an oak, a chestnut or a pine tree, it might be an evergreen species or it might be leafless during winter, its leaves might be large or narrow, soft or hard, smooth or stiff. The same can be said about 'birds', generically named so or otherwise called

---

[9] Lawrence Buell, *The Future of Environmental Criticism: Environmental Crisis and Literary Imagination* (Malden, MA: Blackwell, 2005), p. 31.
[10] Isaiah Smithson, 'Thoreau, Thomas Cole, and Asher Durand: Composing the American Landscape', in *Thoreau's Sense of Place: Essays in American Environmental Writing*, ed. by Richard J. Schneider (Iowa City: University of Iowa Press, 2000), pp. 93–114.
[11] e.g. William Howarth, 'Some Principles of Ecocriticism', in *The Ecocriticism Reader: Landmarks in Literary Ecology*, ed. by Cheryll Glotfelty and Harold Fromm (Athens: University of Georgia Press, 1996), pp. 69–91.
[12] Ervin H. Zube, 'Perceived Land Use Patterns and Landscape Values', *Landscape Ecology*, 1.1 (1987), 37–45 (pp. 39–40).

by their specific names: sparrows, blackbirds, nightingales, larks, bee-eaters and many others. And how about shape and size, plumage, singing, nesting, migration, etc.? Will the writer master this kind of knowledge?

From their own perception of, and response to a place, the writer generates a new and specific entity embedded in meaning and symbolism, which is then presented to the reader in the form of a text. Cultural geographers have praised these literary descriptions of landscape and drawn on realistic fiction for evidentiary support.[13] Historians also read literary works on political crises, conflicts, wars and revolutions to find descriptions of real events in the fictional plot, and to discover if they were set in actual geographical places. Axel Goodbody wrote about the collective experiences subsumed in prose fiction, drama and poetry:

> [W]orks of literature are characteristically structured by symbolic figurations of memory. The term 'figurations of memory' was introduced by the Assmanns to denote a constantly evolving archive of narratives and images deriving from the Bible, Greek myth, fairy tales, history, world literature, etc. These structures, which crystallize meaning around events, people and places, blend factual and textual recall with imagination.[14]

Any landscape summons up intellect, emotion, memories, knowledge and a sensorial experience. To feel a landscape, to think about it, and to interpret it one should look not only at extraordinary landscapes but also at ordinary landscapes, those that Meinig defined as a continuous surface created by and through the 'routine lives of ordinary people',[15] and in which the human element is not only a driver but an intrinsic part of it.

The increasing acknowledgment of the need to preserve landscape values has led to an operational definition, used in regulations, that gathers the subjective and objective dimensions of landscape, and the inherent mechanisms of appreciation and understanding. According to the European Landscape Convention, 'landscape is part of the land, as perceived by local people or visitors, which evolves through time as a result of being acted upon by natural forces and human beings. [...] Each landscape forms a blend of components and structures: types of territories, social perceptions and ever-changing natural, social and economic forces.'[16] Despite not being universally accepted, this concept of landscape includes urban and rural, ordinary and extraordinary, preserved and degraded landscapes: any landscape is an entity with intrinsic

---

[13] At least since J. K. Wright who called for the need to teach geosophy in the universities or colleges; J. K. Wright, 'Terrae Incognitae: The Place of Imagination in Geography', *Annals of the Association of American Geographers*, 37 (1947), 1–15.
[14] Axel Goodbody, 'Sense of Place and Lieu de Mémoire: A Cultural Memory Approach to Environmental Texts', in *Ecocritical Theory: New European Approaches*, ed. by Axel Goodbody and Kate Rigby (Charlottesville: University of Virginia Press, 2011), pp. 55–70 (pp. 59).
[15] Donald W. Meinig, *The Interpretation of Ordinary Landscapes: Geographical Essays* (New York and Oxford: Oxford University Press, 1979), p. 6.
[16] <http://www.coe.int/en/web/landscape/the-european-landscape-convention>.

value, regardless of the elements composing it or the extent to which it is recognized. Likewise, today, the ecocritical analysis devotes itself to the study of contemporary texts, practising so-called 'second-wave ecocriticism',[17] which, as Michael Bennett strongly advocates, includes as its objects of study all kinds of literary landscapes.[18]

This article addresses the literary landscape in a broad corpus of Portuguese literature, from Romanticism to the present. Over this period of almost two hundred years, landscape representations, mediated by individual perception and the creative process, remained present in the literary narratives.

A broad sample of landscape writers and their landscape writings are presented here. This article constitutes an overview of the landscape in Portuguese literature and aims to present the evolution of representations, in terms of the form, content and scale in which they are described, and to identify the issues that may alter its constituent elements. Three periods of analysis were established, in which different aesthetical and ideological trends were followed.

This exercise explores the literary excerpts of landscape descriptions compiled by the collective project LITESCAPE.PT — Atlas of Literary Landscapes of mainland Portugal <https://ielt.fcsh.unl.pt/paisagensliterarias/>. Making a general review, it runs the same risks as all other samplings, as it tries to be comprehensive without being exhaustive, selective without being discriminatory, and illustrative without being misleading. Inevitably, more writers and works will be left out than will find a space in this text.

### The Nineteenth Century

At a time when the appreciation of rural life reappears as a reaction against urban and industrial development — a classic topic of several Portuguese thinkers — Alexandre Herculano (1810-1877) emerges as one of the most acclaimed exponents of Romanticism in Portugal. On a trip up the River Tagus, 'in a slow-moving ship', the author described the surrounding pastures of the marshy lands as if they were a work of art:

> As manadas de touros, parados gravemente pela margem, ou metidos na água por entre os caniços e juncais, pareciam observar o movimento do rio, [...] nos seus meneios lentos [...] ninguém lhes adivinhava a nativa ferocidade. Na limpidez do céu, nas tintas cambiantes das terras calvas, nos verdes variados da vegetação, no murmúrio do vento havia uma harmonia de paz; havia vida sem tempestade.
>
> [The herds of bulls, solemnly still on the banks, or immersed in the water between the slender reeds and the rushes, seemed to observe the movement of the river, [...] in their slow movements [...] no one would ever guess their

---

[17] Buell, *The Future of Environmental Criticism*.
[18] Michael Bennett, 'From Wide Open Spaces to Metropolitan Places: The Urban Challenge to Ecocriticism', *ISLE*, 8 (winter 2001), 31-52.

ferocious nature. In the clear sky, in the changing colours of the bare lands, in the variegated greens of the vegetation, in the whisper of the wind there was a peaceful harmony; there was a life without commotion.]¹⁹

The aestheticization of Nature is very clearly conveyed in this excerpt through the transcendent representation of common elements (the bulls, the vegetation, the river water, the sky, the wind) which are considered beautiful and sublime.

In a satirical treatment of urbanism, other authors of the period also praised the agricultural landscape. Such is the case with Júlio Dinis (1839–1871). The main character of one of his best-known novels, *A morgadinha dos canaviais* (1896), is an urban idler who travels to a village in the north of Portugal to recover from a 'city illness'. After some time in an illustrious homestead, where his idleness persists, he turns into a dreamer of the alleged countryside serenity. An ecocritical analysis of landscapes in Portuguese literature, by Isabel Alves, suggests that the ideological context of Júlio Dinis and other romantic writers' works provides the basis for this rural diegesis: '[the] natural theology, which defined the Portuguese vision of nature, [is] accentuated by the profound belief that landscape — a humanized place — is effectively a book in which man's actions may be read and his secret aspirations revealed'.[20]

The first Portuguese realist writers emerged when eminent Romantics were still producing their literary work. Among them, Eça de Queiroz went down as a portraitist of the Lisbon society of the nineteenth century, the setting in which the plots of most of his novels occur. However, he revisits the topic of countryside versus city in one of his most accomplished works, *A cidade e as serras* [*The City and the Mountains*] (published posthumously, 1901). In this novel, the author opposes Paris, where he lived in the last years of his life and where he was the Portuguese Consul, to the Douro region of Portugal, where his wife's family came from. He creates a clear image of Tormes, the family estate at Baião, in a description which appears before the reader as an exercise in observation and a detailed analysis of reality. However, the writer did not know the place he was describing very well, since he visited it only once and only for a short period of time, so we may well suppose that the setting was at least partially imagined.

In his pretension to realism, which distinguishes him from his predecessors, he lists common elements (the vineyards in terraces, the orange-tree groves, a chapel, the river stream), pointing out chromatisms, directions and proportions, without neglecting to suggest, through the character's reactions, the aesthetic dimension of the setting:

> Rolávamos na vertente de uma serra, sobre penhascos que desabavam até largos socalcos cultivados de vinhedo. Em baixo, numa esplanada,

---

[19] Alexandre Herculano, *Cenas de um ano da minha vida. Poesia e Meditação. [1831–1832]. Apontamentos de Viagem [1853–1854]* (Lisbon: Bertrand Editora, 1973), p. 189.

[20] Isabel Alves, *Landscape: Inter-relationships between Place and Soul* (Cluj–Napoca: Editura Limes, 2006).

branquejava uma casa nobre, de opulento repouso, com a capelinha muito caiada entre um laranjal maduro. Pelo rio, onde a água turva e tarda nem se quebrava contra as rochas, descia, com a vela cheia, um barco lento carregado de pipas. Para além, outros socalcos, de um verde pálido de reseda, com oliveiras apoucadas pela amplidão dos montes, subiam até outras penedias que se embebiam, todas brancas e assoalhadas, na fina abundância do azul. Jacinto acariciava os pêlos corredios do bigode:
— O Douro, hein?... É interessante.

[We were travelling along the side of a rocky mountain, above terraces planted with vines. Beyond, we could see a fine house, a place of opulent repose, with a little whitewashed chapel set in a grove of orange trees full of ripe fruit. On the river, where the dark, desultory waters did not even break against the rocks, a boat in full sail and laden with barrels was making its slow way downstream. Farther off, where olive trees were dwarfed by vast mountains, other fields — the pale green of mignonette — rose up to meet bare, sunbaked rocks drinking in the fine abundance of blue. Jacinto was still stroking his moustache.
'The Douro, eh? Very interesting.'][21]

Fialho de Almeida (1857–1911), a protagonist of Naturalism, broke with the traditional bourgeois and aristocratic novel (of which the work of Eça de Queiroz is an example) by awarding his leading roles to the poorest and most disadvantaged. In one of his short stories, set in Lisbon, the writer describes a fair, a place of popular entertainment near the Prazeres cemetery:

> Na esplanada que vai terminar à porta dos Prazeres, as pequenas barracas de lona enchiam-se de grupos; filhas de saias engomadas, olheiras fundas, com fadistas de calças esticadas sobre alpargatas de linho. As mulheres gordas, lenço vermelho, os grossos braços nus, refogavam mexilhão, vermelhas de calor; em torno os soldados passavam, de chibata, rostos vulgares e bestiais, dilatados em risos enormes; e, abanando-se, diziam brutezas às pequenas ovarinas sujas. Na confusão dos grupos os garotos sujos, vivamente alegres, corriam relanceando olhares famintos sobre os bolos secos das vendedeiras ambulantes, e de passagem pediam cinco réis. Aqui e além viam-se sobre a relva, petiscando, famílias de operários, pequenas louras e limpas, tipos de costureiras futuras, traços finos, cismadores e delicados. Os vadios esqueléticos, de calções em frangalhos, apregoavam água.[22]

[On the flat ground that runs up to the gate of the Prazeres, the small canvass stalls were filling up with groups of people; girls wearing ironed skirts, deep rings around their eyes, accompanied by Fado singers wearing their trousers stretched over linen espadrilles. Fat women with red headscarves and plump bare arms were braising mussels and flushing in the heat; around them soldiers passed with their canes, their faces common

---

[21] Eça de Queiroz, *A cidade e as serras*, ed. by Helena Cidade Moura (Lisbon: Livros do Brasil, n.d.), pp. 129–30; *The City and the Mountains*, trans. by Margaret Jull Costa (New York: New Directions Book, 2008), p. 140; also (Sawtry, Cambs: Dedalus, 2008), p. 128.
[22] Fialho de Almeida, 'A Ruiva', in *Contos*, 1st edn (Porto and Braga: Livraria Internacional de Ernesto Chardron, 1881), p. 18.

and bestial, stretched into enormous grins; and fanning themselves, they made coarse remarks to the dirty little fish-wives. In the confusion of the groups dirty urchins ran around, vivaciously cheerful, casting famished looks at the biscuits of the itinerant sellers, and asking for five-réis coins on the way. Here and there on the grass workers' families are to be seen nibbling away, fair, clean girls, looking like future seamstresses, with fine features, dreamy and delicate. Skeletal vagrants, their trousers in tatters, cry out their water for sale.]

As Julia Barella Vigal points out, referring to Naturalism in Spanish literature, here too 'un paisaje que define y determina a aquéllos que lo habitan' [landscape defines and determines those who inhabit it].[23]

In opposition to the city, Fialho de Almeida also writes about the countryside and his passion for the rural life:

> Em Agosto [...] Lisboa está deserta [...] uma nostalgia de campo acode ao espírito de quem, como eu, tem cá dentro, sob os invólucros postiços dum pensador e dum *artigoleiro*, a alma cândida, contemplativa, simplória, dum aldeão transviado à cultura dos seus campos, e dum lavrador cativo, que a todos os instantes suspira pela rabicha do arado.[24]
>
> [In August [...] Lisbon is deserted [...] a longing for the countryside rushes to the minds of those who, like me, possess within, under the artificial wrappings of a thinker and a *scribbler*, the pure, contemplative and simple-minded soul of a villager led astray from the cultivation of his fields, and of a captive farmer, who at every moment sighs for the handle of his plough.]

Moving away from the dominant theme that favoured an urban-versus-rural dichotomy, Raul Brandão (1867–1930) was the first to make a literary description of the sea, the coastline and the fishermen's lives, going against the more usual literary landscapes of the time in Portugal. His experience in Foz do Douro, where he was born the son and grandson of seamen, marks the way in which he represents the country and its people throughout his work: 'esta paisagem — mar, rio e céu — entranhou-se-me na alma, não como paisagem, mas como sentimento' [this landscape — sea, river and sky — is deeply ingrained in my soul, not as a landscape, but as a feeling].[25] His relationship with Nature had already been conveyed in previous works: 'nunca me comovi como diante da árvore mais humilde' [I have never been so moved as before the humblest of the trees].[26] In the Preface to the first volume of his *Memórias* [*Memoirs*] (1919) he also wrote: 'não posso ver uma árvore sem espanto' [I can't look at a tree without wonder], further declaring: 'sou talvez uma árvore que cresce à vontade, pernada para aqui pernada para acolá' [I am perhaps a tree growing at

---

[23] Julia Barella Vigal, 'Naturaleza y paisaje en la literatura española', in *Ecocríticas: literatura y medio ambiente*, ed. by C. Flys Junquera and others (Madrid: Iberoamericana, 2010), pp. 219–38 (p. 230).
[24] Fialho de Almeida, *O país das uvas* (Lisbon: Círculo de Leitores, 1992), p. 27.
[25] Raul Brandão, *Os Pescadores* (Lisbon: Livraria Bertrand, 1923), p. 21.
[26] Raul Brandão, *Os Pobres* (Lisbon: Empresa da História de Portugal, 1906), p. 106.

will, a branch over here, a branch over there].[27] Academics who study his works recognize in him the influence of Russian authors. He has been described as a 'Dostoevskian' researcher of the mysteries and riddles of the human soul,[28] who searched for answers in the natural environment.

While echoing romantic and symbolist tendencies, Raul Brandão also took upon himself the task of unveiling and depicting the country through his landscape descriptions. In 1926, he published *As Ilhas Desconhecidas* [*The Unknown Islands*], a book in which he described the Azores islands and the people's way of living. In 1929, together with his wife, Maria Angelina, he co-authored the work *Portugal Pequenino* [*Little Portugal*], a text we could nowadays call an 'ecological portrait'. Written for children — or more specifically 'for other people's children', as is revealed in the dedication — this novel presents a world in which nature and fantasy are entwined.[29]

In a section of the book, the protagonists are the last pack of wolves inhabiting the Serra do Marão mountain range in northern Portugal. The wolves have nothing to hunt for, they are chased by humans and their pups are starving. The concerns we now call 'environmentalist' are quite clear. In fact, the novel presents some impending threats to the natural environment that are a direct consequence of human actions:

> A florestal matou os lobos que eram uma das expressões mais extraordinárias da serra e os seus filhos dilectos. Envenenou-os por serem muitos e os julgar inúteis. Ora o lobo é uma figura indispensável à serra. À serra e à vida. O Marão, sem eles, parece mais despovoado e à vida de imaginação falta qualquer coisa que apouca o homem em lugar de o engrandecer.[30]
>
> [The Forestry [Department] killed the wolves that were one of the most extraordinary expressions of those hills and their favourite offspring. It poisoned them because they were many and it thought them useless. But the wolf is a character that is indispensable to the hills. To the hills and to life itself. Without them, the Marão [range] looks more uninhabited and something is missing from the life of the imagination that diminishes man rather than exalting him.]

These feelings of respect, acknowledging the wolf as part of a brotherhood, recognizing its intrinsic value and right to exist, might be interpreted as conservationist values, which are pioneering in the Portuguese cultural and scientific milieu of the time.[31]

---

[27] Raul Brandão, *Memórias* I (Porto: Renascença Portuguesa, 1919), pp. 9 and 24.
[28] Translated from the Portuguese. Guilherme Castilho, 'Dostoievsky e Raul Brandão', Sep. *Memórias Acad. Ciências Lisboa. Classe Letras*, 23 (1983), 133–45 (p. 145).
[29] João Pedro Andrade, *Raul Brandão: a obra e o Homem* (Lisbon: Acontecimento, 2002).
[30] Maria Angelina and Raul Brandão, *Portugal Pequenino* (Lisbon: Vega, 1985), p. 53.
[31] Margarida Lopes-Fernandes and others, 'Living with the Beast: Wolves and Humans through Portuguese Literature', *Anthrozoös*, 29.1 (2016), 5–20.

## The Twentieth Century

The rural provenance of many of the twentieth-century writers seems to be the main reason why many literary landscapes of the first half of the twentieth century were still pastoral representations. They demonstrated the mosaic of land use and local human activities like agriculture, pastoralism, forestry, hunting, fishing, etc. Although most regions of the country were depicted in the literary sceneries of narrative production of the time, in each writer's work, a local landscape, often associated with their birthplace, seemed to prevail.

In this panorama, Aquilino Ribeiro (1885–1963) stood out, due to his clear appreciation of the natural elements of landscape, flora, fauna and geology, his respect for nature and landscape, and his recognition of the destructive impact of humans on animals and plants. After a few fictional works in which landscape was a character, revealed by how its presence in the text conditioned the narrative's pulse and determined its action, the writer wrote literary itineraries of the places he knew and the experiences he lived, composing repositories of episodes and stories of village people, through which he expressed his opinions on ideas and usages that were damaging to the environment.[32] While observing the hills that he thought were once covered with oaks and chestnuts he noticed that the vegetation had been gradually disappearing: 'Oiteiros, outrora vestidos do verde movediço e espumoso dos bosques, estão hoje hediondamente nus' [Hills, once dressed in the shifting and frothy green of the woods, are today appallingly naked].[33] On the subject of deforestation, the author produced ecological, economic and aesthetic arguments:

> Todos estes montes, hoje descarnados, exerciam uma função necessária. Vestidos de floresta eram admiráveis condensadores de humidade. Ofereciam, além disso, agasalho contra a friagem, para que os valeiros se prestassem às culturas melindrosas. Eles mesmos, nas encostas orientadas a sabor do soalheiro, tornavam-se em fecundíssimos vergéis [...] Maus passos, cupidez, o arroteamento foram despovoando os montes, com prejuízo latente da prosperidade dos moradores e da beleza. A terra suculenta escorreu para os rios que a rolaram para o mar. Ficou pedra. Mais de metade de Portugal é ossatura.

> [All these hills, now naked, played a necessary role. Dressed in forest, they were wonderful humidity condensers. Besides that, they offered a shelter against coldness, so that the ditcher-diggers would manage to work on the delicate cultures. And these same hills, on the sun-facing slopes, became extremely fertile orchards. [...] Bad decisions, greed and the clearing of land have gradually depopulated the hills, with latent damage to the prosperity of local residents and their beauty. The succulent earth was swept into rivers

---

[32] See his four books of chronicles: *Aldeia: terra, gente e bichos* [*Village: Land, People and Animals*] (1946), *Geografia sentimental* [*Sentimental Geography*] (1951), *Arcas encoiradas* [*Leathered Chests*] (1953) and *O homem da Nave* [*The Man of the Table Land*] (1954).
[33] Aquilino Ribeiro, *Aldeia: terra, gente e bichos* (Lisbon: Livraria Bertrand, 1964), p. 118.

that carried it to the sea. Only stone was left. More than half of Portugal has been worn down to the bare bones.][34]

On his estate at Soutosa (Moimenta da Beira), living things were valued for their utility to humans (as food, means of transportation or workforce), their intrinsic value and the role they played in Natural History: 'Terra, milho, géneros de cultivo são o transitório. Aves e plantas, as belas plantas da mata, tocam já ao eterno, pelo menos em relação à minha vida, e às aves voto-lhes o mesmo respeito, consideradas na sucessão zoológica' [Land, corn, types of crops are what is transitory. Birds and plants, the beautiful plants of the woods, already touch on the eternal, at least in what concerns my life, and to birds I vow the same respect, considered in their zoological succession].[35] The author himself took measures to preserve animals: 'proibi terminantemente que dentro da quinta se fizesse mal aos bichos. No rol estava compreendida toda a espécie de aves [...] e toda a ordem de roedores, desde o coelho ao texugo, exceto os ratos [...]. E não lhes fazer mal significava: não lhes tirar os ninhos, nem meter-lhes medo com espantalhos e caravelas, muito menos dar-lhes fogo. Tal como no parque Kruger' [I categorically forbade harming animals inside the farm. The list included all species of birds [...] and every type of rodent, from rabbits to badgers, except rats [...]. And not harming them meant: not taking away their nests, or scaring them with scarecrows or vanes, let alone shooting them. Just as in Kruger Park].[36]

In the same rural matrix, Miguel Torga's literary landscape emerges from a wide corpus. His relationship with the Portuguese territory is one of the most surprising aspects of his landscape writing. Like Raul Brandão, the writer devised a road map of the country, region by region, drawing its physical and human portrait, and his book *Portugal* (1950) rose from his deep personal knowledge of places and their inhabitants. It also reflects Torga's critical response to the political regime of his time, the Estado Novo, of which he was a direct victim: he was imprisoned for his political ideas (1939–40) and some of his books were banned by the state censorship, and he was also prevented from working as a doctor because of his democratic and republican views. He prefaces the text with his poem 'Pátria' [Fatherland], bringing affective resonances of the author's landscape experiences in this 'nesga de terra | debruada de mar' [scrap of land | hemmed by the sea], despite his tough and painful childhood and despite emigration, or maybe because of it, for it led him to discover other geographical places. While addressing both the 'regional' and 'national', Torga expressed the worldview of an educated man who was aware of the problems of his country and the world.[37] Additionally, the writer understood the temporal

---

[34] Aquilino Ribeiro, *Geografia sentimental* (Lisbon: Livraria Bertrand, 1985), p. 222 and p. 284.
[35] *Geografia sentimental*, p. 327.
[36] Aquilino Ribeiro, *O homem da Nave* (Lisbon: Livraria Bertrand, 1968), p. 147.
[37] See Maria Manuel Lisboa, *Paula Rego's Map of Memory: National and Sexual Politics* (Burlington, VT: Ashgate, 2003). The autobiographical work *A criação do mundo* [*The Creation of the World*] (1937–81) is, in this regard, also an enlightening element.

dynamics of landscape in its natural and cultural components and took on the role of '*fixador de memórias*' [fixer of memories]:

> Cingido á realidade humana do momento, romanceei o Douro atribulado, de classes, injustiças, suor e miséria. E esse Douro, felizmente, está em vias de mudar. [...] Desapareceram os patrões tirânicos, as cardenhas degradantes, os salários de fome. [...] Também o rio já não tem cachões, afogados em albufeiras de calmaria.
>
> [Faithful to the reality of life in those times, I wrote of a tormented Douro, of class struggles, of injustice, sweat and misery. Fortunately, the winds of change are blowing in the Douro. [...] Tyrannical landowners, degrading 'cardenhas' to house the workers, and wages barely sufficient to appease hunger, no longer exist. [...] The falls and rapids of the river, too, have been drowned in the tranquillity of man-made lagoons.]]³⁸

During this period, the harshness of the peasants' lives was portrayed depending on political and ideological positioning.[39] Rural landscapes were used as symbols of nationality by the official propaganda. Idealized as 'calm and discreet, almost childish',[40] peasants were supposedly happy in their daily work and showed elevation of spirit and deep religious feelings. At the same time, Neo-Realism was engaged in a social context that, at its onset, focused mainly on the rural environment. This movement would come to distinguish itself by 'realçar o heroísmo da luta daqueles que são os meios da sua transformação' [highlighting the heroism of the struggle of those who are the means for social transformation].[41]

With the same ideological positioning, *Levantado do chão* [*Raised from the Ground*] (1980), by the Nobel prize-winner José Saramago, devotes its first chapter to landscape. Discussing this novel, Fernanda Cunha argues that landscape is 'o suporte e o agente modelador da narrativa' [the support and modelling agent of the narrative], where the reader can 'desenhar não só a geografia física do território como também, e sobretudo, descobrir a geografia dos afectos, a esfera privada que suporta e dá espaço para a luta política' [trace not only the physical geography of the territory but also, and above all, discover a geography of affections, the private sphere supporting and opening the way to the political struggle].[42] Saramago tells us of a landscape that is ancient but

---

[38] Miguel Torga, 'Prefácio à tradução Inglesa', *Vindima* (Lisbon: Dom Quixote, 2003), p. 13; 'Preface', *Grape Harvest* [translator not named] (Coimbra: Gráfica de Coimbra, 1989), no. pagn. *Cardenhas* were rough single-storey cottages made of stone.
[39] Ana Isabel Queiroz and J. Carrilho, 'Stone Metaphors about a Village: A "Stone Vessel" or "The Most Portuguese"', Ecozon@, 2.1 (2011), 13–33.
[40] Carlos Queiroz, *Landscapes of Portugal* (Lisbon: Secretariado Nacional de Informação, 1940), p. 13.
[41] A. Pinheiro Torres, 'Neo-Realismo (1935–1950)', in *História da Literatura Portuguesa*, vol VII, *As Correntes Contemporâneas*, ed. by Óscar Lopes and Maria de Fátima Marinho (Lisbon: Publicações Alfa, 2002), pp. 183–234 (p. 209).
[42] Fernanda Cunha, *A paisagem e as palavras que lá estão: 'Levantado do chão', um romance político* (Lisbon: Apenas Livros, 2012), p. 14.

also fluid: '[...] porquanto a paisagem é sem dúvida anterior ao homem, e apesar disso, de tanto existir, não se acabou ainda. Será porque constantemente muda: tem épocas do ano em que o chão é verde, outras amarelo, e depois castanho, ou negro. E também vermelho, em lugares, que é cor de barro ou sangue sangrado' [[...] the landscape clearly pre-dates man, and despite its long, long existence, it has still not yet expired. That's probably because it's constantly changing: at certain times of the year, the land is green, at others, yellow or brown or black. And in certain places it is red, the colour of clay or spilled blood'.[43] This is a description in which the symbolic infuses the real: the expression 'spilled blood' is a clear allusion to conflict, suffering and repression, which are the main themes of the novel, set before the Carnation Revolution (25 April 1974) that freed the country from a dictatorial regime.

Words used to describe landscapes are a dynamic resource that can disappear for lack of usage, for lack of a physical and ecological reference to match it with. The Spanish writer Miguel Delibes stated, three decades ago, that he feared people would soon need to read his books with explanatory notes, as if his text had been written in an archaic or esoteric language.[44] In this respect, José Saramago reinforces the value of words, explaining that, at a time when most people live in cities, the right terms are what give the right dimension to literary representations of the rural landscape: 'Já ficaram ditos alguns e outros agora se acrescentam para ilustração geral, que as pessoas da cidade cuidam, em sua ignorância, que tudo é semear e colher, pois muito enganadas vivem se não aprenderem a dizer as palavras todas e a entender o que elas são' [we've mentioned some already, and now we add others for the purpose of general enlightenment, because townspeople think, in their ignorance, that it's all a matter of sowing and harvesting, well, they're much mistaken unless they learn all the other verbs involved and realise just what they mean].[45]

## The Twenty-first Century

Since 2000, Portuguese novels have been characterized by a vast plurality of genres, themes and styles, which can be grouped according to the concept of *cosmopolitanism*.[46] Among other definitions, the term came up in ecocritical theory as 'a way of imagining forms of belonging beyond the local and the national'.[47] These Portuguese literary landscapes incorporate the profound changes the country has undergone, during the last decades, under the influence of a globalized reality on a European and worldwide scale. The settings

---

[43] José Saramago, *Levantado do chão*, 14th edn (Lisbon: Caminho, 1999), p. 11; *Raised from the Ground*, trans. by Margaret Jull Costa (London: Harvill Secker, 2012), p. 1.
[44] Miguel Delibes, *El sentido del progreso desde mi obra* (Barcelona: Destino, 1975), p. 53.
[45] José Saramago, *Levantado do chão*, p. 89; *Raised from the Ground*, pp. 88–89.
[46] Miguel Real, *O Romance Português Contemporâneo, 1950–2010* (Lisbon: Caminho, 2012).
[47] Ursula Heise, *Sense of Place and Sense of Planet: The Environmental Imagination of the Global* (Oxford: Oxford University Press, 2008), p. 6.

are mostly urban, though some nostalgia for the rural and 'a return to nature' can be seen, in line with the current popular ideas of ecological and spiritual restoration. The depiction of landscape patterns and their modification processes play a less relevant role, although the natural and cultural contexts that arise from them and some environmental concerns are still crucial to the development of the story. To illustrate this, three novels from three contemporary writers are examined.

Lídia Jorge was born in Algarve in 1946 and spent her childhood there. During her time in that region she witnessed the emigration of the poor, the abandonment of the fields and the development of mass tourism, phenomena characteristic of the 1950s and 1960s. *Vale da Paixão* [*The Migrant Painter of Birds*] (1999) introduces a family of small agricultural landowners going through changes dictated by the transformation of the rural environment. One of the characters tries to resist, maintaining cultures and modernizing them. But the emigrant brother has a different perception of the future, arguing

> Que não valia a pena iniciar a mecanização em terras dispersas, separadas umas das outras por quilómetros de distância e altos muros de pedras. Antes que outros assaltassem essa indústria, eles deveriam investir no sector do lazer. O lazer e o ócio, era tudo o que daria dinheiro. O lazer iria ser a grande fonte de riqueza, a grande fonte de desenvolvimento, de mudança, de alteração do mundo. O lazer iria ser um modo de vida, uma finalidade, uma causa.

> [That it wasn't worth investing in mechanization on such scattered lands, separated by distance and by high stone walls. They should invest in the leisure industry before others got in on the act. Leisure was where the money would be. Leisure would be the next great source of wealth, the great engine of development and change in the world. Leisure would be a way of life, an aim, a cause.][48]

In order to represent a transforming landscape, the writer summons prodigious facts, in a magical realism frame, thus expressing damage to the harvests and the biodiversity and revealing the erosion of the bare soil:

> [a]s aves do sapal que se levantavam das terraplanagens, perto das dunas, apareciam caminhando no restolho sequeiro, vesgas, tresmontadas, pondo ovos fora do tempo e do lugar. Umas ervas desapareciam, outras que nunca tinha visto alastravam. Os figos amadureciam abertos em nove partes, as azeitonas verdes ficavam bicudas e pretas pela falta de chuva. Seca, a terra seca. Ele via o vento levantar a terra no ar, transportá-la consigo para outras paragens e a espessura do solo arável emagrecer e descamar-se.

> [The birds from the mudflats, fleeing the earth-moving work going on near the dunes, turned up in large, disoriented flocks in the dried stubble fields, laying their eggs out of season and in the wrong places. Certain weeds disappeared, while other unknown varieties proliferated. The ripening figs

---

[48] Lídia Jorge, *O Vale da Paixão* (Lisbon: Círculo de Leitores, 1999), p. 108; *The Migrant Painter Of Birds*, trans. by Margaret Jull Costa (London: The Harvill Press, 2001), p. 105.

split into nine segments, the green olives remained black and thin for lack of rain. The earth was so dry. He watched the wind lifting the earth into the air and carrying it off to other places, he watched the arable soil growing thin [...]]⁴⁹

Mário de Carvalho was born in Lisbon, in 1944, in a family from the Alentejo region. He regarded changes in urban and rural landscapes from a highly politicized, critical position. *Fantasia para dois coronéis e uma piscina* [*Fantasy for Two Colonels and a Swimming Pool*] (2003) raises the question of the 'new rurality': how the countryside is once again brought to life, but this time as a place of recreation rather than a place for work or production. The reader is led to question the exercise of power (e.g. authority and wealth), the decision-making process and the people's participation in the construction of society. Two retired army colonels move to Alentejo and refurbish *montes* (the typical architectural ensemble of agricultural estates in this Southern region of Portugal), to try to fulfil their desire of creating an idealized countryside and to demonstrate their prosperity, symbolically represented by the swimming pool, where no one bathes. Then, the landscape changes:

> Lá em baixo, na paisagem, incrustada na duríssima permanência das coisas, onde só mandam altos castelos, menires e cromeleques, destoa azulínea, e sobressalta com a transparência, a piscina, modernaça e tratada a poder de fluidos caros e especiosos [...] espécie de olho de boi, desnaturado na paisagem, que é de prados e chaparrais, embalados por badalos espaçados de rebanhos.
>
> [Down there, in the landscape, inlaid in the extremely rough permanence of things, where only high castles, menhirs and cromlechs rule, the bluish transparent and very modern swimming-pool clashes and startles. It is treated with fine, expensive fluids [...] a kind of skylight, clashing with the landscape, made of meadows and thickets of dwarf oaks lulled by the occasional sound of cattle bells.] ⁵⁰

The countryside becomes a new *globalized* reality. Their basic needs, as well as their needs for comfort, can be easily fulfilled with a drive to the ATM or the supermarket in the nearest village. The idleness of the everyday life moves the characters' concerns away from their place of residence. This neo-rural environment, where the traditional labours that characterized it are completely absent, becomes a place where garbage collection and the moral basis for the killing of wild species become everyday topics.

*Deixem passar um Homem Invisível* [*Let an Invisible Man Pass*] (2009), by Rui Cardoso Martins tells us about a flood (coincidence or not, the writer was born in 1967, the year in which Lisbon suffered the worst flood of most recent times). The novel criticizes the way in which the capital's urban expansion led to the occupation of flood-risk areas, with consequences for people's safety and

---

49  Lídia Jorge, *O Vale da Paixão*, p. 163; *The Migrant Painter Of Birds*, pp. 161–62.
50  Mário de Carvalho, *Fantasia para dois coronéis e uma piscina* (Lisbon: Caminho, 2003), p. 19.

environmental quality:

> Os picos de precipitação — os reais ou os imaginados — originam cheias, sobretudo porque Lisboa se expandiu ao longo de uma orografia acidentada e sem as requeridas medidas de ordenamento e respeito ambiental.
>
> [The peaks of rainfall — real or imaginary — provoke floods, above all because Lisbon has expanded along an uneven hilly terrain, without the required measures in town planning and respect for the environment.][51]

Besides the lack of planning, the writer lists other territorial management issues which do not seem to have been properly addressed:

> Muitas saídas estavam entupidas com prédios novos, betão, barracas e muros, outras cobertas de lixo, garagens subterrâneas escavadas à noite no leito dos riachos [...]. Nos vales de Chelas, ao lado das hortas de couve e nabiça, dos talos submersos espetados no solo como bandeiras, afundavam-se viadutos e pilastras erguidos no sítio errado por ordem de alguém.
>
> [Lots of outlets were clogged with new buildings, concrete, shacks and walls. Others were covered with garbage, underground garages dug by night in the stream beds [...]. In the Chelas valleys, alongside the vegetable patches of cabbage and turnip, and the submerged stems stuck in the soil like flags, viaducts and pilasters were sinking, put in the wrong place on someone's order.][52]

It is in this daily landscape, and because of it, that a big hole forms on the street pavement. The waterproofing of a great part of the urban soil leads to the flow of unbearable quantities of rain into the subterranean ducts at moments of very intense rainfall, causing these structures to burst and the earth above them to drop down. The Fire Chief, who is in charge of the rescue team, resorts to history to explain the accident suffered by the missing characters:

> [n]ão se esqueçam que isso sucede quando chove desta maneira louca, é uma cidade toda mal feita no solo e subsolo, cheia de ribeiras domesticadas com canos gigantes, que não está nem nunca esteve pronta para precipitações.
>
> [[d]on't forget this happens when it pours as wildly as that, this is an extremely poorly made city at surface and subsurface level, full of streams tamed through giant water pipes, which is not and has never been ready for rainfalls.][53]

Rui Cardoso Martins, like many other contemporary writers who contributed to the literary imagery of Lisbon in the twenty-first century, portraying the city as it was lived and experienced, does not turn away from the discussion on the vulnerabilities inherent to the concentration of population and the inevitable reflection on the environmental sustainability issues. Upon the urban landscape falls a critical eye that both aestheticizes the social and the

---

[51] Rui Cardoso Martins, *Deixem passar o homem invisível* (Lisbon: Dom Quixote, 2009), p. 11.
[52] *Deixem passar o homem invisível*, pp. 17-19.
[53] *Deixem passar o homem invisível*, p. 21.

constructed monumentality, and marks the denaturalization, lack of planning and degradation. In the framework of the current literary representation, the urban area is a global place.[54]

## Conclusion

In their construction of the literary text, Portuguese writers ascribed to landscape different ways of expression and different roles in the narrative composition, in line with a chronological alignment and the artistic and ideological movements from each temporal context. However, the extended study of literary landscapes does not reveal its transformation only on an aesthetic or political level.

From the twentieth century onwards, the scales, themes and issues summoned during the construction of the narrative's sceneries, or related to them, started to reflect the changes in the landscapes that served as their referential. The local (or regional) landscape is, then, the object of the writer's attention. The first half of the twentieth century already witnessed concerns over the dynamics induced by the overexploitation of natural resources, which harm soils, vegetation, some animal species and the human populations from the affected areas. The record of urban experiences from different social classes plays witness, throughout the twentieth century, to the expansion of the city and the attraction of people, namely writers, from rural to urban spaces (especially Lisbon) and coastline areas.

The national and global-scale phenomena that impacted the landscape and triggered the environmental concerns which emerged in the last decades of the twentieth century have only recently found a place in Portuguese literature. In line with a growing social awareness and a set of new public policies, these texts, in particular, cast a critical eye over the processes of construction and deconstruction of the landscape values, highlighting the need to correct some practices that are not respectful to the environment or the quality of life. Literary works from the twenty-first century align themselves with a general trend that Lawrence Buell calls 'eco-globalist', derived from 'ecoglobalism, a whole-earth way of thinking and feeling about environmentality'.[55]

This work was supported by the FCT – Portuguese Foundation for Science and Technology [UID/HIS/04209/2013 and IF/00222/2013/CP1166/CT0001].

---

[54] Ana Isabel Queiroz, 'Planeta Lisboa', in *Falas da Terra no século XXI: What do we see green?*, ed. by Ana Isabel Queiroz and Inês de Ornellas e Castro (Lisbon: Esfera do Caos, 2011), pp. 145–61.
[55] Lawrence Buell, 'Ecoglobalist Affects: The Emergence of U.S. Environmental Imagination on a Planetary Scale', in *Shades of the Planet: American Literature as World Literature*, ed. by Wai-Chee Dimock and Lawrence Buell (Princeton, NJ: Princeton University Press, 2007), pp. 227–48 (p. 227).

# How to Construct a Master: Pessoa and Caeiro

JERÓNIMO PIZARRO

*Universidad de los Andes, Colombia*

In 1935, the year of his death, Fernando Pessoa announced, in a famous letter, that in 1914, after a 'triumphal day' on which he wrote a great number of poems, he had found his 'Master', Alberto Caeiro.[1] Did the events of this day actually happen? Is the invention of a Master possible? Let us look through the documents Pessoa left behind,[2] and examine how Pessoa constructed Caeiro, his first heteronym.[3]

According to the most widely accepted account of the facts, on 8 March 1914 Pessoa went over to 'a high chest of drawers' and wrote, standing up, thirty or so poems all at once, 'numa especie de extase cuja natureza não conseguirei definir' [in a kind of ecstasy I'm unable to define].[4] That day was, he said, the 'triumphal day' of his life; the day on which, after he began writing under the title *O Guardador de Rebanhos* [The Keeper of Sheep], someone 'appeared' within him, whom he immediately named Alberto Caeiro: 'apparecera em mim o meu mestre. Foi essa a sensação immediata que tive' [my master had appeared in me. That was what I immediately felt].[5] The complexity of this statement can be understood when the following facts are taken into consideration: (a) the only poems dated 8 March are Poem I and Poem II, which were only given that symbolic date retrospectively (see Fig. 1);[6] (b) there is a series of 'early poems'[7] dated 4 March 1914; and (c) there is a text from *circa* 1929, which points to the 'triumphal day' as being 13 March 1914.[8]

At this point we might conclude that the discussion is about the veracity of certain facts: when did he actually write these poems? Did he write them

---

[1] Fernando Pessoa, *Eu sou uma antologia: 136 autores fictícios*, ed. by Jerónimo Pizarro and Patricio Ferrari (Lisbon: Tinta-da-china. 2013), pp. 641–53. The letter, to his friend Adolfo Casais Monteiro, is translated by Richard Zenith in *The Selected Prose of Fernando Pessoa* (New York: Grove Press, 2001), pp. 251–60.
[2] Pessoa's archive (Espólio 3) is housed at the National Library of Portugal (BNP).
[3] Pessoa only used the term 'heteronym' for three of his 136 fictitious authors. See Jerónimo Pizarro, *Pessoa Existe?* (Lisbon: Ática, 2012), pp. 73–97.
[4] Pessoa, *Eu sou uma antologia*, p. 646; *The Selected Prose*, p. 256.
[5] Pessoa, *Eu sou uma antologia*, p. 647; *The Selected Prose*, p. 256.
[6] (BNP/E3, 145-3, 145-4).
[7] (BNP/E3, 67-38a). Pessoa himself used this expression when he referred to these poems.
[8] Fernando Pessoa, *Páginas íntimas e de auto-interpretação*, ed. by Georg Rudolf Lind and Jacinto do Prado Coelho (Lisbon: Ática, 1966), p. 103.

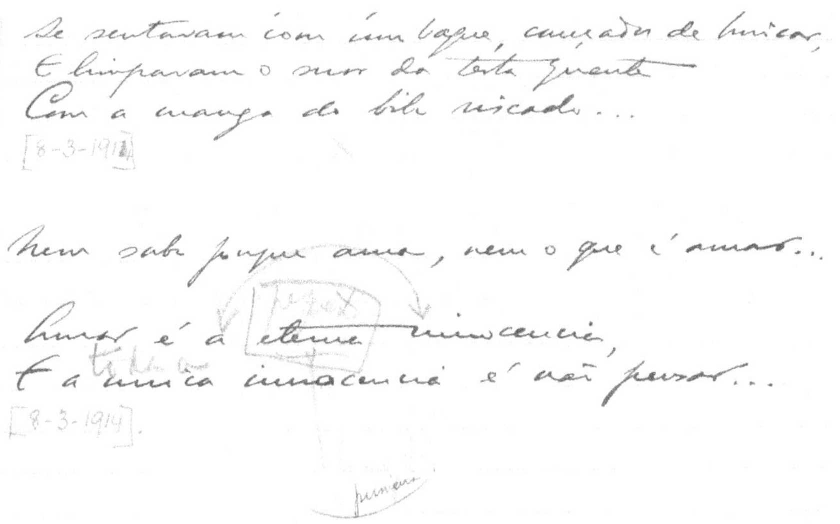

FIG. 1. Pessoa's notebook, with annotations, showing the final verses of Poems I and II of *O Guardador de Rebanhos*.

standing up? How many poems did he write on that famous day? Were there more triumphal days in Pessoa's life? Had he already come up with the title (*O Guardador de Rebanhos*)? Had Caeiro been contemplated as an author from the beginning? However, the factual information is not so easy to verify. The archive usually contradicts Pessoa's statements, and it is just as interesting to note when this happens as to explain why Pessoa does not narrate Caeiro's construction in factual terms. Ivo Castro is emphatic on this point: 'Não há evidência para dizer que o título do ciclo, ou o nome de Caeiro, ou a ideia de ciclo, e menos ainda a sua arquitectura, tenham sido concebidos antes da escrita dos poemas, apesar dessa alegação fornecer em boa medida a substância do "dia triunfal"' [There is no proof that the title of the cycle, the name Caeiro, or the idea of a cycle, and even less its construction, were already conceived before the poems were written, although it is that claim which, to a large extent, provides the substance for the 'triumphal day'].[9] As we can see, the archive contradicts Pessoa, giving us a good reason to return to the original sources, but, in order to create the foundational myth of the heteronyms, and to construct a Master with a group of disciples (among which he included himself), Pessoa had to both simplify and amplify what had occurred in March 1914. It is not very Platonic to cross out, copy, double-check, and rewrite, and we should not forget that Caeiro is something of an oral teacher and a spontaneous poet, as he explains when he says: 'Escrevo versos num papel que está no meu pensamento' [I write poems on

[9] Introduction to Fernando Pessoa, *Poemas de Alberto Caeiro*, ed. by Ivo Castro (Lisbon: Imprensa Nacional–Casa da Moeda, 2015), pp. 11–12.

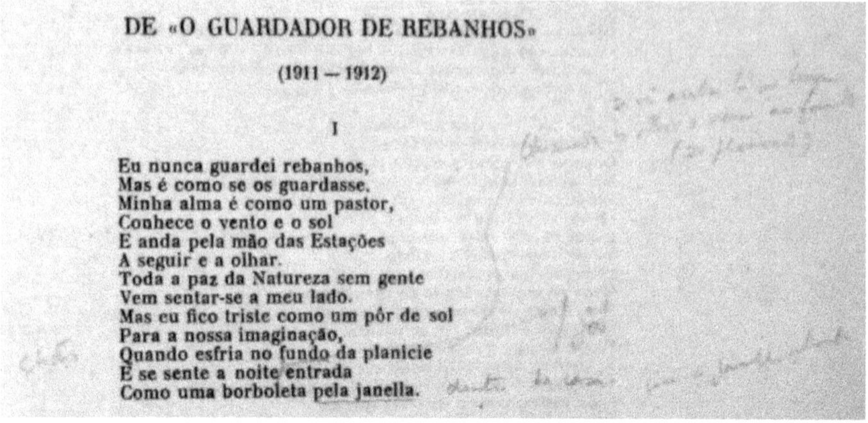

## DE «O GUARDADOR DE REBANHOS»

(1911 – 1912)

I

Eu nunca guardei rebanhos,
Mas é como se os guardasse.
Minha alma é como um pastor,
Conhece o vento e o sol
E anda pela mão das Estações
A seguir e a olhar.
Toda a paz da Natureza sem gente
Vem sentar-se a meu lado.
Mas eu fico triste como um pôr de sol
Para a nossa imaginação,
Quando esfria no fundo da planicie
E se sente a noite entrada
Como uma borboleta pela janella.

FIG. 2. Annotations by Fernando Pessoa on his copy of *Athena* (CFP, 0-28 MN). This copy of *Athena* was digitalized and catalogued before it was auctioned.

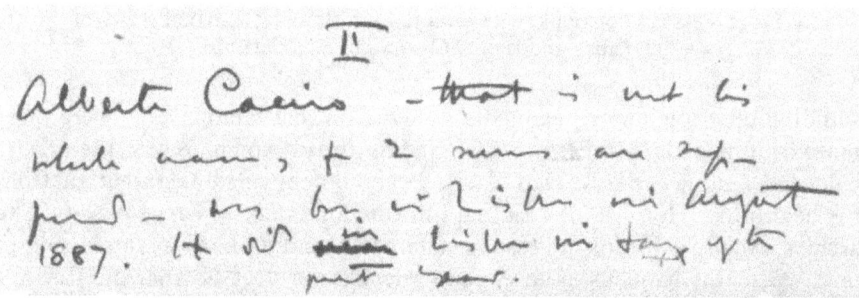

FIG. 3. 'Alberto Caeiro — that is not his whole name, for 2 surnames are suppressed — was born in Lisbon in August 1887. He died near in Lisbon in /January/ of the present year. (BNP/E3, 14B-12; the slashes indicate passages about which the author is unsure).

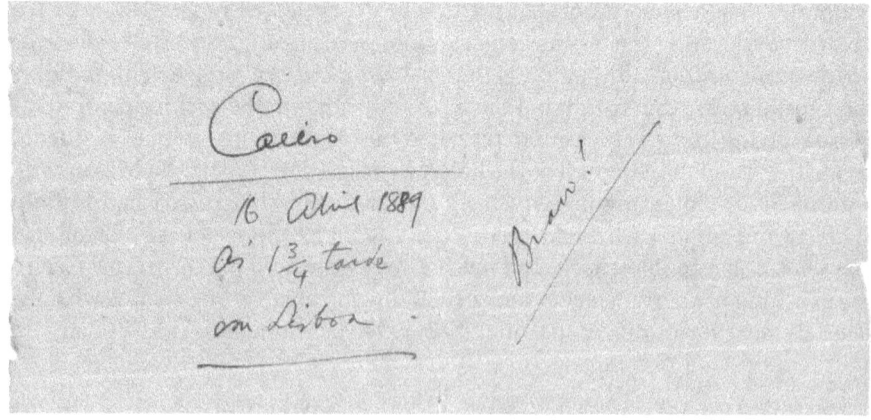

FIG. 4. 'Bravo!' for Alberto Caeiro

the paper in my thinking].[10] Caeiro mocks the poet's artistry: 'E ha poetas que são artistas | E trabalham nos seus versos | Como um carpinteiro nas taboas!...' [And there are poets who are artists | And they work on their verses | Like a carpenter with boards!...].[11]

\* \* \* \* \*

Alberto Caeiro's main work is actually a notebook in which Pessoa collected together the 49 poems that make up the cycle, 23 of which he published in 1925 in *Athena*, a magazine he co-edited with Rui Vaz between 1924 and 1925.[12] Some time later, in 1931, Poem VIII appeared in *Presença* magazine. It is difficult to call *O Guardador de Rebanhos* a complete book, because if Pessoa had published it during his lifetime it could have taken the form of a booklet, and because those who did publish this potential book did not always have to hand all the elements that would make up its genetic dossier. A notebook which contains a complete copy of the cycle was found and published by Ivo Castro in 1986.[13] This discovery followed the 1946 version edited, in Portugal, by Luiz de Montalvor and João Gaspar Simões, entitled *Poemas de Alberto Caeiro*, and the Brazilian version edited by Maria Aliete Galhoz, entitled *Obra Poética* in 1960.

The text that appeared in *Athena* with annotations by Pessoa (see Fig. 2) came to light in 2008, during the digitalization of his personal library, during which photographs were taken of many books and magazines owned by the poet's heirs. These books and magazines were never donated to the Casa Fernando Pessoa; in fact, in 2008, the annotated copy of *Athena* was sold at auction.[14] Photographs were also taken of all the books and magazines that had effectively been given to the Casa Fernando Pessoa fifteen years earlier, on the occasion of its inauguration. The subsequent editions of Caeiro's works, first the *Poemas completos de Alberto Caeiro* by Teresa Sobral Cunha (1994) and then the *Poesia de Alberto Caeiro* by Fernando Cabral Martins and Richard Zenith (2001), were prepared without taking into account this copy of *Athena* and without a thorough knowledge of Fernando Pessoa's personal library.[15] To summarize: the Caeiro's genetic dossier was incomplete until 2008, and only in 2015 was the first critical edition, by Ivo Castro, published, thereby making a more reliable Caeiro available. Editions of *O Guardador de Rebanhos* must include the complete cycle (the notebook and the poems published in *Athena*

[10] Fernando Pessoa, 'O Guardador de Rebanhos, in *Obra completa de Alberto Caeiro*, ed. by Jerónimo Pizarro and Patricio Ferrari (Lisbon: Tinta-da-china, 2016), p. 36; *The Collected Poems of Alberto Caeiro*, trans. by Chris Daniels (Exeter: Shearsman Books, 2007), p. 16.
[11] Pessoa, *Obra completa de Alberto Caeiro*, p. 64; *Collected Poems of Alberto Caeiro*, p. 58.
[12] *Athena: revista de arte* (Lisbon: Imprensa Libanio da Silva, 1924–25).
[13] See Pessoa, 2016; <http://purl.pt/1000/1/alberto-caeiro/index.html>.
[14] Pessoa, *Obra completa de Alberto Caeiro*, p. 379. For information about the Casa Fernando Pessoa (CFP), a museum, cultural centre and library devoted to the poet's life and work, see <http://casafernandopessoa.cm-lisboa.pt>. Pessoa's library is housed at the CFP.
[15] Jerónimo Pizarro, Patricio Ferrari and Antonio Cardiello, *A biblioteca particular de Fernando Pessoa*, bilingual edition (Lisbon: Dom Quixote, 2010).

and *Presença*), because Caeiro is a fabulous, hybrid being, half manuscript and half print. Until 1986, Caeiro was known as being half old manuscripts and half print. After 1986, he was half notebook and half print. Since 2008, he has become half notebook and half print (with marginalia). Caeiro himself says he never alters what he writes,[16] but, as mentioned above, the archive contradicts him.

Or it contradicts him in part, since Pessoa gives the year of Caeiro's death as 1915; he may have done this in 1916, after his friend Mário de Sá-Carneiro committed suicide, on 26 April. And yet Pessoa continued writing Caeiro poems after 1915. In other words, if we admit the fictitious dates of Caeiro's birth (1889) and death (1915), then it had to be Pessoa, or Pessoa *qua* Caeiro, who corrected some of the Caeiro poems. It is not only the above-mentioned dates that are fictitious, but also some of the dates of his two main cycles: *O Guardador de Rebanhos* and *Poemas Inconjuntos*.[17] Both were partially published in *Athena* in 1925, the first as if it had been written between 1911 and 1912, and the second as if it had been written between 1913 and 1915. These dates contradict the idea of there being one triumphal day in 1914, which we know was the year in which *O Guardador* was actually composed, as Pessoa made official during his correspondence with the directors of the *Presença* magazine between 1928 and 1935. When Adolfo Casais Monteiro read, in 1935, that Caeiro had appeared on 8 March 1914,[18] he could well have asked Pessoa why *O Guardador* was dated 1911–12 in *Athena* magazine (1925). It seems, then, as if the date of Caeiro's (fictitious) death led Pessoa, at first, to 'bring forward' the dates of *O Guardador* and *Poemas Inconjuntos*. Later, that date, 1915, would not have been problematic and Pessoa must have accepted the idea of Caeiro writing his whole *oeuvre* in less than a year: between March 1914 and early 1915 (January, according to a manuscript in which Caeiro's year of birth is recorded as 1887 and not 1889; see Fig. 3).[19]

As one can see, the dates vary and it takes some time for them to become more stable or fixed. In a letter dated 13 January 1935, the one Jorge de Sena christened the letter about the genesis of the heteronyms, it is given as 8 March. That same letter provides other details about Caeiro, some of them validated and complemented by an earlier horoscope and astrological calculations. Thus, for example, there is a piece of paper on which Pessoa wrote: 'Caeiro 16 Abril 1889 ás 1¾ tarde em Lisboa. Bravo!' [Caeiro 16 April 1889 at 1¾ afternoon in Lisbon. Bravo!] (Fig. 4).[20] This source of information is much more precise than others, for the 1935 letter does not give us either the day or the time of Caeiro's birth, nor does the foreword written by Ricardo Reis (Fig. 5).

[16] Pessoa, *Obra completa de Alberto Caeiro*, p. 352; *Collected Poems of Alberto Caeiro*, p. 182.
[17] There are several translations of this title: Disjunctive Poems, Discontinuous Poems, Detached Poems, Miscellaneous Poems, Uncollected Poems, Ungrouped Poems. I use Edwin Honig's translation: Disjunctive Poems.
[18] Pessoa, *Eu sou uma antologia*, p. 646.
[19] Pessoa, *Obra completa de Alberto Caeiro*, p. 297.
[20] Fernando Pessoa, *Cartas astrológicas*, ed. by Paulo Cardoso, with the collaboration of Jerónimo Pizarro (Lisbon: Bertrand, 2011), p. 71.

HOW TO CONSTRUCT A MASTER: PESSOA AND CAEIRO    61

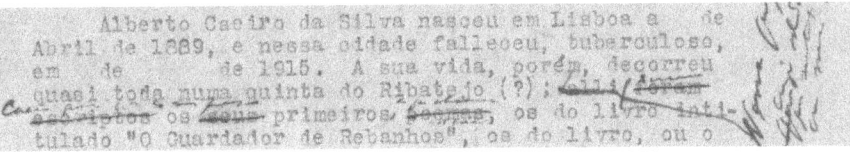

FIG. 5. First lines of the prologue written by Ricardo Reis (BNP/E3, 21-73). 'Alberto Caeiro da Silva nasceu em Lisboa a — de Abril em 1889, e nessa cidade falleceu, tuberculoso, em — de — 1915. A sua vida, porém, decorreu quasi toda numa quinta do Ribatejo; só os primeiros dois anos d'elle, e os ultimos mezes, foram passados na sua cidade natal. Nessa quinta isolada cuja aldeia considerava por sentimento como sua terra, escreveu Caeiro quasi todos os seus poemas – os primeiros, a que chamou "de creança", os do livro intitulado "O Guardador de Rebanhos"' [Alberto Caeiro da Silva was born in Lisbon on the — of April 1889, and died of tuberculosis in that same city on the — of — 1915. He spent, however, most of his life in a country estate in Ribatejo; he only spent his first two years and the last months of his life in the city of his birth. In that isolated estate, in a village he considered his heartland, Caeiro wrote almost all his poems – the first ones, which he called 'a child's work', are collected in the book called *The Keeper of Flocks*].

Whether or not Caeiro died in 1915 (he certainly did not die then in Pessoa's soul, nor that of Álvaro de Campos who was yet to write his 'Notas para a Recordação do meu Mestre Caeiro' [Notes for the Memory of my Master Caeiro]), the truth is that his construction took a lifetime, that is, at least 21 years (1914–35). If Pessoa had lived longer than 47 years (1888–1935), he surely would have continued to develop Caeiro and would have given him an even greater fictional density.

Now that we have reached, what is, to some extent, an overall view of Caeiro, it may be interesting to turn back to the moment of his gestation, in March 1914, in order to consider carefully who exactly that Shepherd, the keeper of sheep, was, particularly during the days when he started writing *O Guardador de Rebanhos*.

\* \* \* \* \*

The two poems Pessoa dated, belatedly, as being written on 8 March 1914, are the first two poems of the cycle. Nevertheless, these poems may have been written on 4 and 8 March 1914, respectively, and belong, especially the first, to a series of 'early poems'. In the notebook which contains a complete copy of the cycle there are at least three 'early poems', dated, which Pessoa hesitated to include in the cycle: Poem XVI (*c.* 4 March 1914), Poem XVII and Poem XVIII (both *c.* 7 March 1914). These poems were written over a period of four days; Poem XVI has the same date as Poem I, Poem XIX, Poem XXXV and Poem XXXIX (all *c.* 4 March 1914); Poems XVII and XVIII bear the same date as Poem XX, Poem XXI and Poem XXII (all *c.* 7 March 1914). If nothing else, this means that ten poems were written in two days, that on maybe the 5 and 6 of March another ten were

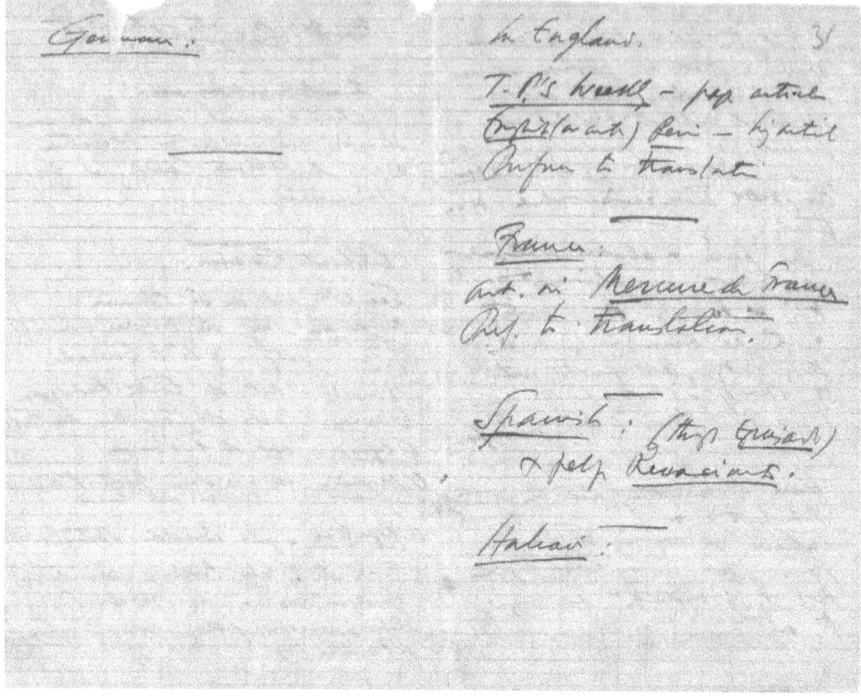

FIG. 6. Spreading the news about Caeiro's poetry (BNP/E3, 14B-16)

written, and that it is possible that the thirty or so poems Pessoa claimed, in 1935, to have written in a single day may in fact have been written over a full week, between 4 and 11 March 1914 (the date of Poem XXVI). Pessoa appears, then, to have condensed into one day a series of events that may actually have happened over the course of a week or more. Indeed, it is becoming more and more common to hear scholars speak of a 'triumphal *month*'!

What is interesting about the three poems Pessoa hesitated to include (and which did not appear in 1925 in *Athena*), is that they are texts in which Caeiro is 'sick', since his objectivism is tinged with subjectivism. Poem XV begins: 'As quatro [↑ duas] canções que seguem' [The four (↑ two) songs following this one],[21] thus introducing the next three compositions (XVI, XVII and XVIII). These 'songs', Caeiro says:

> Separam-se de tudo o que eu penso,
> Mentem a tudo o que eu sinto,
> São do contrario do que eu sou...
>
> Escrevi-as estando doente
> E porisso ellas são naturaes [...]

---

[21] Pessoa, *Obra completa de Alberto Caeiro*, pp. 49 and 399; *Collected Poems of Alberto Caeiro*, p. 37.

[Separate themselves from anything I think,
Make lies of everything I feel,
Are the opposite of what I am...

I wrote them when I was getting sick
And so they're natural]²²

Right from the start Pessoa planned a Shepherd who would fall sick, but he did not name him immediately. He also imagined a fictitious author who would manifest as a healthy poet (when in good health) and a sick poet (when his health deteriorated). Poem XVII is especially significant, because it is a text about which Pessoa wrote: 'Aqui, na poesia 17, é que colhemos em acção as influencias fundadoras de C[aeiro] — Cesário Verde e os neo-panteistas portugueses. E o 7º verso é Cesário Verde puro. O tom geral podia quase ser de Pascoaes' [In the seventeenth poem, we are able readily to discern Caeiro's foundationary influences: Cesário Verde and the Portuguese neopantheists. And the seventh line is pure Cesário Verde. The tone in general is almost Pascoaes].²³ The sick Caeiro was able to evoke the Realism of Cesário Verde, whom Pessoa so much admired and quoted in the *Livro do Desassossego* [*The Book of Disquiet*] (first Portuguese publication 1982); but first and foremost he was an antagonist of the Portuguese Neo-Pantheists, whose main figure was Teixeira de Pascoaes, of whom Caeiro says in an interview: 'Quando leio Pascoaes farto-me de rir. Nunca fui capaz de ler uma cousa d'elle até ao fim...' [When I read Pascoaes I laugh so hard, I've never been able to finish anything of his...].²⁴

In actual fact, Pessoa preferred to mock Pascoaes without making Caeiro fall sick, associating the Shepherd with a poetics of unlearning. In a poem which was published in *Athena*, written on 13 March 1914, he wrote: '[...] os poetas dizem que as estrellas são as freiras eternas | E as flores as penitentes convictas de um só dia' [poets say that stars are the eternal nuns | And the flowers are penitent and certain for a single day], but, in the end, 'as estrellas não são senão estrellas | Nem as flores senão flores, | Sendo por isso que as vemos estrellas e

---

²² Pessoa, *Obra completa de Alberto Caeiro*, p. 49; *Collected Poems of Alberto Caeiro*, p. 37.
²³ Pessoa, *Obra completa de Alberto Caeiro*, p. 51; *Collected Poems of Alberto Caeiro*, p. 39.
²⁴ Pessoa, *Obra completa de Alberto Caeiro*, p. 234; *Collected Poems of Alberto Caeiro*, p. 159. Nevertheless, in 1916, in a letter to an English editor, Pessoa wrote: 'If you can conceive a William Blake put into the soul of Shelley and writing through that, you will perhaps have a nearer idea of what I mean. This movement [Portuguese Saudosism] has produced two poems which I am bound to hold among the greatest of all time. Neither is a long one. One is the "Ode to Light" of Guerra Junqueiro, the greatest of all Portuguese Poets [...]. The other poem, which certainly transcends Browning's "Last Ride Together" as a love-poem, and which belongs to the same metaphysical level of love-emotion, though more religiously pantheistic, is the "Elegy" of Teixeira de Pascoaes, who wrote it in 1905. — To this school of poets we, the "sensationists", owe the fact that in our poetry spirit and matter are interpenetrated and inter-transcended. And we have carried the process further than the originators, though I regret to say that we cannot as yet claim to have produced anything on the level of the two poems I have referred to', in Fernando Pessoa, *Sensacionismo e outros ismos*, ed. by Jerónimo Pizarro (Lisbon: Imprensa Nacional–Casa da Moeda, 2009), pp. 402–03. Pessoa and Caeiro do not necessarily share the same opinion; in fact, it is known that Pessoa mentioned having felt 'disgusted' as he wrote Poem VIII of *O Guardador*; see Pessoa, *Obra completa de Alberto Caeiro*, p. 374.

flores' [stars are only stars | And flowers only flowers, | And therefore we see them as stars and flowers].²⁵

My point is that Pessoa did not reveal the Sick Shepherd, or the Amorous Shepherd, who he started to outline in July 1914, during his lifetime. The Pantheistic Caeiro and the Caeiro in love are aspects of this heteronym that were discovered posthumously. We know texts by Caeiro that Pessoa's contemporaries did not know. For example, Pessoa published 41 poems between 1925 and 1931, but there are 115 in the 2016 edition of the complete works of Caeiro (published by Tinta-da-china).

Pessoa wrote at least four poems on 4 March 1914 (I, XIX, XXXV, and XXXIX) and it is likely that he wrote more. If we examine these poems, it is easy to show that they already heralded the beginning of a poetic cycle: in Poem I, the Shepherd is already present, the process of thinking is already somewhat 'uncomfortable', and a typical case of manifestation takes place: Caeiro sees himself as an other: 'Olhando para o meu rebanho e vendo as minhas ideias, | Ou olhando para as minhas ideias e vendo o meu rebanho' [Looking after my flock and seeing my ideas, | Or looking after my ideas and seeing my flock].²⁶ Besides, Caeiro desires to be understood as a spontaneous poet, 'qualquer cousa natural' [something natural].²⁷ Poem XIX is one of the songs written when Caeiro was sick and it gives an account of a subjective evocation produced in the poet by the moonlight falling on the grass. Poem XXXV is almost a reaction to the former. The moonlight reappears, not to awaken memories (of an old servant) but to allow Caeiro's objective poetics to surface:

> O luar atravez dos altos ramos,
> Dizem os poetas todos que elle é mais
> Que o luar atravez dos altos ramos.
>
> Mas para mim, que não sei o que penso,
> O que o luar atravez dos altos ramos
> É, além de ser
> O luar atravez dos altos ramos,
> É não ser mais
> Que o luar atravez dos altos ramos.
>
> [The moonlight through high branches,
> All the poets say it's more
> Than moonlight through high branches.
>
> But for me, who don't know what I think,
> What moonlight through high branches
> Is, besides being
> Moonlight through high branches,
> Is being nothing else
> But moonlight through high branches.] ²⁸

---

[25] Pessoa, *Obra completa de Alberto Caeiro*, p. 56.
[26] Pessoa, *Obra completa de Alberto Caeiro*, p. 32; *Collected Poems of Alberto Caeiro*, p. 16.
[27] Pessoa, *Obra completa de Alberto Caeiro*, p. 33; *Collected Poems of Alberto Caeiro* p. 16.
[28] Pessoa, *Obra completa de Alberto Caeiro*, pp. 63–64; *Collected Poems of Alberto Caeiro*, p. 57.

All of Caeiro is condensed in these verses and in his reaction against mystic and pantheistic poetry of romantic lineage and local pretentions (such as Saudosismo). Poem XXXIX confirms that on 4 March 1914 a Shepherd already existed and that Pessoa had already found his poetics. The poem closes with two lines: 'As cousas não teem significação: teem existencia. | As cousas são o unico sentido occulto das cousas' [things have no meaning: they only have existence. | Things are the only hidden meaning of things.].[29] In some texts written in English to help Caeiro's work circulate in Europe, Pessoa translated these verses: 'Things have no meaning: things have existence | Things therefore are the only occult meaning of things',[30] presenting them as a synthesis of Caeiro's philosophy.

Regardless of the exact day and the air of triumphalism that day may have exerted on Pessoa, the truth is that Caeiro was simultaneously a surprise and an achievement. The first poems revealed something new to Pessoa: an objectivism that he would come to describe as pagan and lead him to exclaim that Pan was reborn. It also allowed him to elaborate the figure of the Shepherd surrounded by 'Toda a paz da Natureza sem gente' [All the peace of Nature without people].[31]

\* \* \* \* \*

Pessoa must have experienced something very close to a triumphal day or a series of triumphal days in early March 1914. The exact day was not really important, and he was aware of that. His main task was to construct Caeiro, and after Caeiro the two other heteronyms, Ricardo Reis and Álvaro de Campos. Pessoa describes the creation of the 'coterie' of heteronyms as a process that meant placing 'aquillo tudo em moldes de realidade' [it all in a framework of reality].[32] In the next sentence, he explains: 'Graduei as influencias, conheci as amisades, ouvi, dentro de mim, as discussões e as divergencias de criterios' [I ascertained the influences at work and the friendships between them, I listened in myself to their discussions and divergent points of view].[33] In the specific case of Caeiro, who appeared before Campos and Reis (which explains why it is so difficult when it comes to attributing a poem to Caeiro or to Campos, for instance), Pessoa tried to reproduce Walt Whitman's strategies to make his creation 'real'. When he came up with an ambitious plan to present and publicize the work of Caeiro in many European countries, Pessoa probably thought about the anonymous notices or self-reviews that Bliss Perry refers to in *Walt Whitman: His Life and Work* (1906), one of the most underlined and annotated books in his library:

---

[29] Pessoa, *Obra completa de Alberto Caeiro*, p. 66; *Collected Poems of Alberto Caeiro*, p. 61.
[30] Pessoa, *Obra completa de Alberto Caeiro*, p. 258.
[31] Pessoa, *Obra completa de Alberto Caeiro*, p. 31; *Collected Poems of Alberto Caeiro*, p. 15.
[32] Pessoa, *Eu sou uma antologia*, p. 647; Pessoa, *The Selected Prose*, p. 257.
[33] Pessoa, *Eu sou uma antologia*, p. 647; Pessoa, *The Selected Prose*, p. 257.

> Throughout his career as a poet, [Whitman] had no scruples about composing laudatory anonymous notices of himself, and sending them to the newspapers. [...] It has sometimes been urged that his anonymous defense of *Leaves of Grass* was called forth by the abusive attacks upon it, but the fact that at least three of his elaborate articles appeared almost immediately after the publication of the book shows that they were part of a deliberate campaign. Believing absolutely in himself and his book, he took a large and unconventional view of the publicity involved.[34]

Perry mentions the reviews that Whitman published in three newspapers: *United States Review, Brooklyn Daily Times* and *American Phrenology Journal*. Pessoa, when he intended to launch Caeiro, was no less assertive:

> *Um grande poeta materialista*
> *(Alberto Caeiro)*
> Entre o grande número de casos curiosos que existem na literatura, o caso de Alberto Caeiro é dos mais curiosos.
>
> ———
>
> Alberto Caeiro:
> *Seculo* — art[igo] do Sá Carneiro.
> *Montanha* — art[igo] do Ribeiro Lopes (?)
> *El Tea* — artigo do A[lfredo] P[edro] Guisado.
> (S. Miguel) — art[igo] do Côrtes-Rodrigues.
> *Economia* — art[igo] do Carvalho Mourão (?)
> *A Aguia* — art[igo] de F. Pessoa.
> *O Mundo* — ver se se obtem Santos-Vieira.
> (pelo lado anti-clerical ◊)
> *A Republica* — pelo Boavida Portugal.

(Torres de Abreu talvez consiga qualquér cousa. Se Albertino da Silva pudesse fallar, mesmo que atacasse!)

> *[A great materialist poet*
> *(Alberto Caeiro)*
> Of all the curious cases that exist in literature, Alberto Caeiro's is one of the most curious.
>
> ———
>
> Alberto Caeiro:
> *Seculo* — article by Sá Carneiro.
> *Montanha* — article by Ribeiro Lopes (?)
> *El Tea* — article by Alfredo Pedro Guisado.
> (S. Miguel) — article by Côrtes-Rodrigues.
> *Economia* — article by Carvalho Mourão (?)
> *A Aguia* — article by F. Pessoa.
> *O Mundo* — see if we can get Santos-Vieira.
> (on the anti-clerical side ◊)
> *A Republica* — by Boavida Portugal.

---

[34] Bliss Perry, *Walt Whitman: His Life and Work*, with illustrations (London: Archibald Constable and Co., Ltd; Boston and New York: Houghton Mifflin & Co., 1906), pp. 105–06. (CFP 8–434).

(Torres de Abreu might get something. If only Albertino da Silva could say something, even if it is an attack!)][35]

The plan moves from Portuguese to English, from clearly defined (and real) authors to future authors (Thomas Crosse, a fictitious author, was to receive a request to write a preface to the English translation of Caeiro's poems, just as Ricardo Reis was to receive one to preface the Portuguese edition):

> In England:
> *T. P.'s Weekly* — page article
> *English* (or another) *Review* — big article
> Preface to translation
>
> ———
>
> *France*: Art[icle] in *Mercure de France*
> Pref[ace] to translation.
>
> ———
>
> *Spanish*: (through Guisado)
> & perhaps *Renascimento*.
>
> ———
>
> *Italian*: ◊
>
> ———
>
> *German*: ◊[36]

Just like other plans, Pessoa did not manage to carry this one to completion (Fig. 6), either on paper, or in practice. But at least many of the fragments of the article Pessoa was writing for *Águia* magazine, drafts of the article to be sent to England and fragments of the preface to the English translation still exist today. Pessoa was to end his relationship with *Águia* on the 12 November 1914 (in a letter to Álvaro Pinto).[37] Caeiro's launch into Europe was to remain an unfulfilled promise, but a strategy had been outlined, and, some time later, his celebrity would be assured with the arrival of Ricardo Reis, Álvaro de Campos, António Mora and Thomas Crosse. Pessoa did not introduce Caeiro to the public until 1925, in *Athena*, but he and all his others had been talking about the Master since 1914. Bernardo Soares even quotes him in the *Livro do Desassossego*.[38] Before unveiling a few of Caeiro's poems, Pessoa was already well acquainted with the *Guardador*, and had known him for several years, even before his premature death.

---

[35] Pessoa, *Obra completa de Alberto Caeiro*, p. 223.
[36] Pessoa, *Obra completa de Alberto Caeiro*, pp. 223–24.
[37] For Pessoa, there was a 'radical e inevitavel' [radical and inevitable] conflict of interests between the spirit that produced Saudosist works and the spirit that produced works such as his own and those of Mário de Sá-Carneiro. See Pessoa, *Sensacionismo e outros ismos*, p. 23.
[38] See specially the fragment that begins: 'Releio passivamente, recebendo o que sinto como uma inspiração e um livramento, aquellas phrases simples de Caeiro' [I re-read, passively, those simple lines by Caeiro [...] receiving from them what I feel to be both inspiration and liberation]. Fernando Pessoa, *Livro do Desassossego*, ed. by Jerónimo Pizarro (Lisbon: Tinta-da-china, 2013), p. 295. Fernando Pessoa, *The Book of Disquiet*, trans. by Margaret Jull Costa (London: Profile, 2010), p. 102.

* * * * *

It would be impossible to comment here on all the texts Pessoa wrote about Caeiro, whether under his own name, or anonymously, or under other names. The truth is that Caeiro was not only intended to be the author of a single central book (*O Guardador*, just like the Penny Poets edition of *Leaves of Grass*),[39] but also the inspiration for Portuguese Neo-Paganism, as the catalyst to awaken other sleeping creatures (Reis and Campos), and as a great and unexpected literary revelation. As such, Caeiro is created just as much by the poems of two or three poetic cycles as he is a figure forged by others, in an endless hall of mirrors.

More than a 'miracle' that happened in 1914, though he may have been that too, Caeiro is a figure Pessoa worked on throughout his life and which he was still developing in 1935, up until his death. In this sense, there is one Caeiro who poses a synchronic challenge to us, whose poems we read without thinking of dates; and there is another one who challenges us diachronically as we try to track the process of his construction and his many voices against a timeline. One text states that Caeiro was born in 1887, but there are other texts which aver that he was born in 1889. In a similar way the Caeiro of Ricardo Reis exists just as much as the Caeiro of Álvaro de Campos, and they are very different. Reading Caeiro synchronically and diachronically, contrasting one view of a character to the view of many, can enrich our interpretation. This multiplicity is one of Fernando Pessoa's greatest achievements. We can read Caeiro as a canonized author; but we can also read him as a work in progress, constructed from what Pessoa wrote *qua* Caeiro and what Pessoa *qua* others said of their Master. As Hans Walter Gabler wrote once:

> No creation of the human mind springs to instant life and perfection without revision. Whether preserved or not, there must always have been discrete textual states, in temporal succession, of a literary composition. Thus the work may be said to comprise all its authorial textual states. By such definition, the work attains an axis and extension in time from earliest draft to final revision. Its total text presents itself as a diachronous structure correlating the discrete synchronous structures discernible, of which that conferred by publication is only one, and not necessarily a privileged one. It is thus a kinetic system of signification [...].[40]

We are so used to reading authors as closed entities, and yet I understand Caeiro as an invitation to discover the concept of the open author, that is to

---

[39] Cf. Patricio Ferrari, 'On the Margins of Fernando Pessoa's Private Library: A Reassessment of the Role of Marginalia in the Creation and Development of the Pre-heteronyms and in Caeiro's Literary Production,' in *Luso-Brazilian Review*, 48.2 (2011), 23–71 (pp. 45–46). See also Walt Whitman, *Poems by Walt Whitman*, ed. by William Thomas Stead (London: 'Review of Reviews' Office, [1895]), 'The Penny Poets, No. XXVII'. Catalogue number, 8–664 MN.

[40] Hans Walter Gabler, 'The Synchrony and Diachrony of Texts: Practice and Theory of the Critical Edition of James Joyce's *Ulysses*', in *Text. Transactions of the Society for Textual Scholarship*, ed. by D. C. Greetham and W. Speed Hill (New York: AMS Press, 1984), pp. 305–26 (p. 309).

say, of an author constructed over time and by others (among whom we, his readers, are all included). The Caeiro of *Athena* is not the same as our Caeiro, and he will always be multiple if his readers are many. In the radiant centre of the Pessoan constellation there is a plural Master, who changed every day. Pessoa tried to place him 'in a framework of reality' and he failed, to some extent, because he did not finish his task; but this failure is also a victory, because we are now able to approach Caeiro as the author of a closed and static work of fiction (described in titles such as *Complete Poems* or *Complete Works*), but also as an open and fluid entity (described in titles as *Poemas Inconjuntos* [*Disjunctive Poems*] or *Andaime* [*Scaffolding*]). Caeiro is Caeiro, but he is also what Caeiro became at every different moment in time and in every dialogue he had with other imaginary creations, like a character on the stage. With Pessoa we take our leave of the 'sujeito idêntico, permanente, substancial' [identical, permanent, substantial subject][41] of Cartesian philosophy, even when the Shepherd says stars are only stars.

---

[41] João Constâncio, 'Pessoa & Nietzsche: sobre "não ser nada"', in *Nietzsche e Pessoa: ensaios*, ed. by Bartholomew Ryan, Marta Faustino and Antonio Cardiello (Lisbon: Tinta-da-china, 2016), 161–84 (p. 163).

# A Life Framed: Serafim Alves de Carvalho's *Emigrar... Emigrar: as contas do meu rosário* (1986)

CARMEN RAMOS VILLAR[1]

*University of Sheffield*

Taking Paul Longley Arthur's concept of framing as an 'act of enclosing by organising material into some kind of order',[2] this article will approach Carvalho's text *Emigrar... Emigrar: as contas do meu rosário* (1986) [*Emigrating... Emigrating: A Life Parceled Out in Pieces*] from four different perspectives and examine the different ways in which Carvalho's textual self is constructed in his account. To do so, the article will first frame its close reading of this text around how Carvalho's self is textually constructed; second, around how Carvalho's ghost-writer and editor, Rui de Castro, crafted Carvalho's self; third, around the effect of the interplay of the text and the photographs; and finally on how the aims of the publishing house have affected the production of Carvalho's textual self. As the article will conclude, Carvalho's text was shaped in a very specific way to illustrate the ideological qualities desired by the Portuguese government in the mid-1980s. In choosing to focus on the fourth analytical frame in particular, this article expands on current readings of how Carvalho's text contributed to the ethnic debate present in Portuguese-American autobiographical texts.[3]

Before beginning a close reading of Carvalho's text along these four frames, it will be useful to summarize the contents and composition of *Emigrar... Emigrar:*

---

[1] I wish to thank Dr Eleanor Jones for her thorough reading of the script and Debbie Madden for her keen eye for a good turn of phrase. I also wish to thank the anonymous peer reviewers for their very insightful comments, and Margarida Rendeiro for helping me find alternative sources to those suggested by them. Should there be any mistakes, they are entirely my fault. Unless otherwise indicated, all translations provided are my own.

[2] Paul Longley Arthur, 'Out of Frame', *Auto/Biography Studies*, 29.1 (2014), 1–9 (p. 2).

[3] See, for instance, José I. Suárez, 'Four Luso-American Autobiographies: A Comparative View', *MELUS*, 17.3 (1992), 17–32; Francisco Cota Fagundes, 'Portuguese Immigrant Experience in America in Autobiography', *Hispania*, 88.4 (2005), 701–12, and 'La experiencia inmigrante de los portugueses en los Estados Unidos a través de sus autobiografías', *Migraciones y exilios*, 11 (2010), 11–28; and Reinaldo Silva, 'Her Story vs His Story: Narrating the Portuguese Diaspora in the United States of America', in *Narrating the Portuguese Diaspora: Piecing Things Together*, ed. by Francisco Cota Fagundes, Irene Maria Blayer, Teresa F. A. Alves and Teresa Cid (New York: Peter Lang, 2011), pp. 49–62 and 'After Great Pain, a Formal Reappraisal of America Comes: Estrangement upon Returning to the Ancestral Land in Four Portuguese-American Autobiographies', *Gávea-Brown*, 34–35 (2013), 29–48.

*as contas do meu rosário*. The second-eldest of nine children in an impoverished family, Carvalho was born in the Portuguese village of Arouca, near Porto, in 1898. At a very early age, he went to work as a shepherd in a nearby village, and then continued to move from job to job. At age seventeen or eighteen, in order to escape military conscription, he covertly crossed the border to Spain, finding work in the Asturian mines. It was here that he attended school for the first time and learned to read, write and speak Spanish, as well as obtaining a false Spanish passport. In 1918, at the end of the First World War, he crossed over to France, and briefly to Belgium. In France, he worked in a variety of jobs and obtained, via dubious means, first a French passport and then a Portuguese passport. Having saved up the money he needed to enter the United States, he secured a place working on board a ship. On the way, he went to work in a coal mine near Cardiff, to see if life and conditions in Britain were better, but only stayed for a day. He arrived in the United States in August 1920 and, after falling prey to a couple who stole all his possessions, he took a train to his cousin's place of residence in Connecticut, where he worked in a coin factory until the effects of the economic recession forced him to leave the job, a year later. He then found work in various coalmines: first, until 1926, in Kentucky, then in Pennsylvania, and finally in West Virginia. However, the declining economy of the late 1920s, and the concomitant collapse of the coal industry, forced him to move to Newark to work as a road labourer. In 1926, he spent a brief period in Portugal in order to get married, but returned to the United States a few months later. On his return, he worked first at a Ford factory in New Jersey, then moved to New York and became a salesman for a wine merchant; finally, in 1945, he opened up a shipping and wooden pallet manufacturing company, operating from the famous Wall Street in New York. From the 1950s onwards, he travelled to Portugal regularly, particularly following his establishment of a fruit farming business. He returned to live in Portugal definitively in 1981, having sold the shipping business. In 1985, a few months before his death and the posthumous publication of his account, Carvalho received the *Medalha de Valor e Mérito* [Medal of Value and Merit] from the Portuguese government.

As the Introduction by Maria Manuela Aguiar implies, *Emigrar... Emigrar: as contas do meu rosário* was commissioned by the Secretaria de Estado das Comunidades Portuguesas/Centro de estudos as part of a series called 'Portugueses de longe escrevem' [Portuguese Write from Afar].[4] The Preface by Rui de Castro states that he heard Carvalho's account from his own lips.[5]

---

[4] Serafim Alves de Carvalho, *Emigrar... Emigrar: as contas do meu rosário* (Lisbon: Rocha/ Artes Gráficas, 1986), p. 1. Hereafter, page numbers will be given in the text. It was unusual for autobiographies of this kind to be published in this way. Usually, either authors financed publication themselves, or they were published by an independent publishing house. The Introduction suggests that the book was a commission following Carvalho's receipt of the *Medalha de Valor e Mérito*. The series in which Carvalho's text was published, 'Portugueses de longe escrevem', was a short-lived initiative by the Secretaria de Estado das Comunidades Portuguesas, launched in 1986.

[5] Although there has been every effort to ascertain who Rui de Castro was, I have not been able to trace any information about his life, or why he was chosen as a ghostwriter and editor for Carvalho's

In fact, Carvalho dictated his account to Castro who, as a ghostwriter, then edited the text prior to its publication in December 1986. The book is 203 pages long, divided into twenty-nine very short chapters of at most three pages of text, interspersed by photographs that either relate to a particular episode in that chapter or that act as general illustrations for the material covered in that chapter. Toward the end of the text, the number of photographs increases significantly, from one or two per chapter to a maximum of eight in Chapter 26.

**Carvalho, the Self in the Frame**

Carvalho's account is narrated in a simple, matter-of-fact tone, which reflects both his period of childhood and the hardships suffered due to his family's financial circumstances. This understated mood serves to emphasize a humble, self-sacrificing, and resourceful personality. These character traits are made clear from the outset of the story, when he describes his first job as a shepherd:

> Se na minha casa havia miséria, para onde fui ela não era menor e se alguma coisa ganhava e se tinha sido menos uma boca a sobrecarregar a pobre vida dos meus Pais, o que é um facto é que ali não via futuro e, por isso, só estive lá um ano. (p. 29)

> [If we were poor in my house, we were no worse off than anyone else and at least I was earning and it was one less mouth to feed at home, but there was no future for me there and, because of that, I only stayed there for a year.]

This quote also offers a very restrained summary of the reasons behind leaving his first job, further emphasizing his humble character — within a few paragraphs, the reader concludes that Carvalho's father had come to rescue him from malnourishment and neglect at the hands of his boss. In what becomes a running theme in Carvalho's account, he moves from job to job, conscious of the need to ease the extreme privation of his family as well as to ensure his own survival. For Carvalho, the concept of providing help to his family stretches beyond immediate family to include not only his wife's family, but also ultimately Portugal as a whole, within the wider concept of the nation as family. For instance, he regularly sends money to his parents and helps them buy land (pp. 21 and 79), he supports his in-laws financially (p. 157),[6] and his idea for a fruit growing business aims to reduce the price of that commodity in Portugal (p. 197). The aim, as Carvalho presents it in his account, is to provide practical

life. Similarly, I have also been unable to trace Orlando Miranda, the person credited with obtaining the photographs that illustrate Carvalho's account. Any information relating to these, and to why the 'Portugueses de longe escrevem' series emerged, and was discontinued after only three publications, would be very gratefully received.

[6] For further reading on the importance of the remittances sent by Portuguese emigrants to their families at key moments of Portuguese history see Maria Ioannis Baganha, 'Social Marginalization, Government Policies and Emigrant's Remittances: Portugal, 1870–1930', in *Estudos e Ensaios em Honra de Vitorino Magalhães Godinho* (Lisbon: Sá da Costa, 1988), pp. 431–48.

solutions to ease the financial burden experienced by this broadly defined 'family', emphasizing once again his self-sacrificing and generous nature, as well as his adaptability.

Carvalho experiences his emigrant status in a positive manner, an outlook reflected by the tone in which he revises the traditional concept of what constitutes an emigrant. Carvalho describes himself as an emigrant from the moment he leaves his place of birth, even while within the same country's boundaries (p. 35). Emigrating allows him the means by which to improve, help, and learn. Carvalho sees every hardship he suffers as character building, as can be seen in his nostalgic description of his first job:

> um ano de trabalho feito por uma criança mal alimentada, à chuva e ao frio, sem comodidades as mínimas. Mas eu tenho saudades desses recuados tempos e não deploro o tempo por lá e por outros lados passado mais ou menos nas mesmas condições. Nessa miséria de vida afirmei o meu carácter. Ganhei forças e avivei a minha inteligência para que pudesse vir a realizar trabalhos mais compensadores. (p. 29)

> [a year of work, outside in the rain and cold, carried out by a malnourished child without the most basic of comforts. But I miss those far-away times and I don't regret the time I spent in more or less the same conditions there or elsewhere. This miserable life shaped my character. I gained strength and sharpened my intellect so that I could later have more rewarding jobs.]

Here, Carvalho evokes the idea of learning lessons from the 'school of life', described as a series of ongoing journeys, trials and obstacles to overcome (pp. 85 and 201).[7] Carvalho presents his story as an example to an imagined youth of the world, commenting that hard work and determination can bring success (p. 15). This sentiment is reiterated in the last chapter, where Carvalho dispels the idea of being a hero. Instead, he is careful to point out that his success is born out of not having failed at certain crucial points (p. 201). By not presenting himself as a hero, but rather as someone who ultimately was able to succeed, Carvalho's words reflect a disarming honesty while once again underscoring his humble personality.

Carvalho's account is punctuated by an ongoing preoccupation with modernization and the resulting changes from it through comments such as this: '[q]ue saudades do sossêgo desses tempos, mas progresso é progresso e parar é morrer!' [how I miss those tranquil times, but progress is what it is, and to stop is to die!] (p. 163). These comments are perhaps coloured by Carvalho's experience of having to return to live permanently in Portugal in 1981 due to

---

[7] Cota Fagundes' translation of the second part of Carvalho's title, *Emigrating... Emigrating: A Life Parceled Out in Pieces* echoes the idea of emigration as a never-ending journey in Carvalho's text (see 'Portuguese Immigrant Experience', p. 701). Considering the reference to rosary beads in the Portuguese title, especially as the rosary is prayed keeping in mind certain important religious events or mysteries, Carvalho could be seen as praying his personal rosary by revisiting episodes that are important to the shaping of his character as he tells the story of his life.

the modernization of the shipping industry.[8] When a comment regarding the pace of social change appears, he takes care to explain certain social customs that were affected by this change. To offer two examples, Carvalho explains the manufacture of bricks before the process was industrialized (p. 47), and the practise of transporting liquid manure in barrels from pig farms, the so-called *água-choca*, to use as compost on cultivated land (p. 59). Describing social customs that modernity may have superseded, or be about to supersede, enables Carvalho to carefully construct an image of authority, of being a cultural mediator to the past, and of highlighting how far things have come.

This image as a cultural mediator, carefully cultivated by Carvalho, promotes empathy and trust in the narrative he relates. This sense of trust causes the reader to defer their scrutiny of Carvalho's actions and the dubious anecdotes in his account. For example, in the anecdote of the *guerra da água-choca*, Carvalho comments that he organized the other young *água-choca* carriers to beat up the older men in order to avenge the mistreatment they had been subjected to as they competed for the business of carrying that 'commodity'. Milkmaids in the village also become involved in the beating when they run to the aid of the older men. In addition to the lack of milk supply on the day it occurred, this episode results in Carvalho's rapid departure from the village when the authorities begin searching for him. This episode becomes an important event in Carvalho's life; as he comments when he returns to the village to ask for his future wife's hand in marriage, the *guerra da água-choca* is an 'ocorrência trágica que, no entanto, considero fundamental na minha existência' [tragic event that, nonetheless, I consider fundamental to my existence] (p. 135).[9] The episode of the *guerra da água-choca* also becomes a point of reference whenever Carvalho wishes to highlight how he overcame unfair treatment. For instance, while working in a French mine, the narrator rallies the group of Portuguese miners to beat up a Moroccan who has hit him (p. 105). Carvalho's reference to the *guerra da água-choca* episode here seemingly persuades the reader of the validity of his behaviour, perpetuating his image as an honourable man. Carvalho implicitly reinforces this moral and prudent self-image in certain statements, such as the explanation of his decision not to work in the Welsh mines:

> Mas à noite, bem se vê que era costume, fui obrigado a pagar uma rodada de cerveja aos mineiros [de Cardiff] que se encontravam no bar. Não gostei do uso porque o que eu queria era ganhar dinheiro. Também não sou nem nunca fui homem de bares e de copos. Vender vinho, isso sim, desde que se ganhasse dinheiro; bebê-lo só às refeições e com cautela. (p. 119)

---

[8] The explanation given by Carvalho is that the introduction of metal containers in the shipping business replaced wooden pallets, forcing him to sell up (pp. 179 and 197). Taking into account Silva's analysis of Carvalho's text, the preoccupation with modernization voiced by Carvalho perhaps arises from his disappointment at seeing his business ventures in Portugal fail due to the economic landscape of Portugal in the 1970s. See Reinaldo Silva, 'Her Story vs His Story', p. 57 and 'After a Great Pain', pp. 31–35.

[9] Here, Carvalho refers to the fact that his wife was the daughter of his boss at the time of the *guerra da água-choca* episode.

[At night, as was the custom, I had to get a round of beer for the Cardiff mineworkers at the pub. I didn't like the custom because all I wanted to do was earn money. Also, I have never been someone that drinks or goes to pubs. Selling wine was fine as long as I earnt money, but I only drink it in moderation at mealtimes.]

The moral undertone of this comment is undermined by his desire to earn money, which is at odds with the idea that he is an honourable and generous man. Carvalho's ring-leading actions in the episode of the *guerra da água-choca* could be dismissed as a folly of youth, considering that he must have been barely a teenager. The attack on the Moroccan miner in France could also be explained by his immaturity and inexperience, reflecting an inability to think through his actions in what was a very tense atmosphere of different cultures coexisting in the same space. This tense atmosphere might be the reason that Silva remarks, when analysing the many situations involving Carvalho's violent behaviour in his account, that extreme violence was necessary 'to stay on top to survive, no matter what'.[10] On close inspection, however, Carvalho is revealed as a troublemaker, unaware that his actions were sometimes inappropriate. Carvalho's morality is also placed in question when the reader considers the highly dubious and underhanded way in which he illegally obtains his passports.[11] This mixing of questionable moral statements with episodes of problematic behaviour causes the reader to repeatedly evaluate the appropriateness of Carvalho's actions. The result is a contradiction between Carvalho's self-image as an honourable and moral man, and the reader's perception of Carvalho's self in the final text.

## Rui de Castro in the Frame

As José Suárez comments, Castro 'not only transcribed, edited, and polished the [text], but may have determined [its] form'.[12] Suárez goes on to leave this fact to one side in his analysis, concentrating instead on the ethnic contribution made by Portuguese-American autobiographers. This article will expand upon Suárez's analysis by examining the inconsistencies in Carvalho's self; namely, the division and formatting of chapters, and a narrative intrusion by Rui de Castro that frequently affects the style of the account. These inconsistencies could be the result of the means by which the final text was created. It is important to note at this point that Carvalho dictated his account to Rui de Castro in September 1985, and that Carvalho died prior to its publication in December 1986. From the layout of the final text, it is clear that Carvalho's account was significantly edited to fit within the short chapter format that was chosen for the final text.

---

[10] Silva, 'Her Story vs His Story', p. 57.
[11] Carvalho recognizes obtaining the Portuguese passport as a point at which to turn a new leaf when he comments that 'não precisava de andar com mentiras que, mais tarde ou mais cedo, poderiam dar mau resultado' [I didn't need to tell lies which, sooner or later, might catch up with me] (p. 113).
[12] Suárez, 'Four Luso-American Autobiographies', p. 17.

The format of the chapters is furthermore at odds with the text's original form as a taped conversation, in which the octogenarian Carvalho would be expected to talk freely, fluidly and uncritically. The division of chapters sometimes seems awkward; it appears that the account given in Chapter 25, for example, which outlines how Carvalho met Henry Ford in person whilst working at his factory in the early 1930s, describing how he was rewarded for having suggested a way to increase productivity in the factory's assembly line, would sit more comfortably as part of the previous chapter. Chapter 25 begins instead with the following rather contrived sentence: 'Para terminar esta pequena história relacionada com a minha passagem pela Ford, direi que, numa certa altura em que eu estava debruçado sobre o meu trabalho...' [to finish this short tale about my time working at Ford, I'll just say that, at one point when I was concentrating on my job...] (p. 135). This sentence seems more likely to be an editorial addition on Castro's part intended to divide and link the two chapters, as opposed to a verbatim utterance by Carvalho. Perhaps Carvalho's raw account as given to Castro might have been too fragmented, or certain episodes were revisited or clarified in different sessions, thereby presenting editing problems for Castro that resulted in inconsistencies in the final text.

Carvalho's account also seems stylistically awkward at certain points. For example, in the last sentence of Chapter 8, where Carvalho described how he met and worked for his future father-in-law, he seemingly addresses the reader directly: 'No capítulo seguinte, vai o caro leitor saber como o mafarrico as tece' [in the next chapter, my esteemed reader will see how the devil was at work] (p. 59). This last sentence provides a cliffhanger to the next chapter, which describes the *guerra da água-choca* episode, and which is one of the longest, perhaps unsurprisingly given the importance Carvalho attaches to it. There are also certain instances where editing inconsistencies are apparent, such as '[n]ão sei se o leitor sabe' [I'm not sure if the reader knows] (p. 109), or '[o]s estimados leitores estão a ver' [as my dear readers can see] (p. 157). While these may represent a simple editing choice, designed to replace a polite form of address between Castro and Carvalho, they appear inconsistent when the reader considers that this is a transcribed oral account. There are other, more natural instances of orality that have not been edited out, such as '[c]omo disse' [as I said] (p. 119). While the decision behind these chapter divisions and word substitutions might be based on practical editing decisions taken by Castro, in order to group certain themes and events coherently in the final text, such inconsistencies highlight the need to take care over how Carvalho's self is interpreted by the reader; it is clear that Castro has added to Carvalho's account.

## Text and Photographs in the Frame

The inconsistencies in Carvalho's account, outlined above, appear also in the relationship between photographs and the text in the published version. There are photographs that accompany the text, but which the text does not reference. For instance, on page 185 there is a photograph of the house in New Jersey in which Carvalho's brother lived, but there is no mention anywhere in Carvalho's account that his brother emigrated to the United States. Furthermore, in the introduction, there is a photograph of Carvalho in a wheelchair receiving the *Medalha de Valor e Mérito* from the Portuguese government in 1985. Here, it is unclear whether he still has both of his legs, but two later photographs, on pages 41 and 202 respectively, show that one of his legs has been amputated.[13] Once again, there is no mention of this discrepancy anywhere in the text. The omissions might again be practical editing decisions made by Castro, grouping together certain themes and events coherently and leaving out sections that could threaten this coherency; it is difficult to determine whether this is the case. However, the effect of omitting from the text incidents or events that are tantalizingly present in the photographs recalls Barthes' punctums, or details that hold the reader's attention.[14] In this case, the omissions hint at something important being withheld, either by Castro or Carvalho, raising questions as to why.

There are many instances where the photograph and the narration of Carvalho's life are very closely linked, recalling Kuhn's observation that a 'photograph is a prop, a pre-text: it sets the scene for recollection',[15] enabling the construction of a narrative that makes sense of the past. This can be seen, for example, when Carvalho remembers joining the festivities in S. Bento da Porta Aberta, to avoid being spotted by the police before his clandestine crossing to Spain (p. 91). In the caption that accompanies a photograph of the S. Bento da Porta Aberta church, Carvalho notes the changes to the location as his memory recalls what happened:

> A bela fachada da igreja onde se venera S. Bento da Porta Aberta, no Gerez. No tempo em que por ali passei, não existia. Só a imagem do Santo e algumas pedras a dar-Lhe guarida bem como às cabras montezas que ali passavam a noite. (p. 90)

---

[13] Reinaldo Silva comments that the amputated leg revealed in the last photograph in Carvalho's account 'may have been the most violent blow he experienced in his entire life' (see 'Her Story vs His Story', p. 57), but he does not note the lack of its mention in the text. Silva also suggests that Carvalho requested a ghostwriter because he was conscious of his lack of a formal education (see 'Her Story vs His Story', p. 50). However, perhaps Carvalho requested a ghostwriter for more practical reasons: in recognition of his deteriorating health when he was approached with the project of publishing an account of his life.
[14] Roland Barthes, *Camera Lucida: Reflections on Photography*, trans. by Richard Howard (London: Vintage, 2000).
[15] Annette Kuhn, *Family Secrets: Acts of Memory and Imagination* (London: Verso, 2002), p. 13.

[The beautiful church façade where St Benedict is worshipped is in Gerez. It was not there when I passed through. There was just an image of the Saint in some stone sheltering which also provided shelter for mountain goats who spent the night there.]

This suggests that Carvalho uses photographs as props to aid the construction of his life narrative. There are also photographs included in the text because they have triggered Carvalho to juxtapose the past with the present, much like the caption reproduced above. Carvalho's positioning as a cultural mediator is also aided by the use of photographs whose captions highlight particular social customs, such as in the chapter where Carvalho explains his job as an *água-choca* carrier. Here, the reader finds photographs of a typical *água-choca* carrier (p. 66), and of a milkmaid (p. 69) from Vilar do Andorinho, where Carvalho worked, which serve as illustrations for Carvalho's account. Thus, the photographs and captions used in Carvalho's account provide a further layer to support Carvalho's construction of himself as an authoritative cultural and historical mediator, while at the same time bringing the action closer to the reader's experience, and aiding the reader's sense of the narrative's authenticity.

A photograph depicting Carvalho's reunion with the family of one of his mining co-workers (p. 85) provides another punctum in the narrative. A closer look at the photograph reveals that Carvalho is using crutches. It seems a missed opportunity on the part of Castro to mention Carvalho's ailing health, or how the leg came to be amputated. This raises a further set of questions regarding the decisions behind the construction of the final text, beyond Castro's editing. Did Carvalho return to places in his past as a way to prepare for his dictation of the account to Castro, or was it Castro's suggestion to do so? Did Castro suggest looking over photographs as preparation before, or even during, Carvalho's dictation? Whose choice was it to include which photographs when putting the final touches to the book prior to publication? It is impossible to determine how much Carvalho prepared before dictating his account to Castro, and whether this preparation was suggested by Carvalho or by Castro. It is also unclear whether it is Carvalho or Castro that is providing the photographs. However, as has been shown, what is clear is that some photographs are used to trigger the memory of certain episodes in Carvalho's life, even if some memories are not present in the final text.

The captions that accompany the photographs undermine the construction of Carvalho's self. The captions under the photographs imply that they were written (dictated even?) by Carvalho. Most of them read as if Carvalho were taking us through his photographic album and telling us snippets of information about them, which seems rather contrived. At the end of the book, the photographs are attributed to Orlando Miranda. There are certain photographs that one would not expect either Carvalho or Castro to possess. Could Castro have asked Orlando Miranda to obtain photographs of places mentioned by Carvalho in his account, after the initial editing of the text? The photographs of Afonso Costa (p. 100)¹⁶ and Henry Ford (p. 161) could provide evidence of this idea. In effect, the photographs included in Carvalho's text recall Watt's description of the use of photographs in biographies to provide a script through which the reader interprets and corroborates a particular version of reality presented by the biographer.¹⁷

There are inconsistencies between what the text states, and what the photograph supposedly depicts. Looking at the photograph of a letter written by Eisenhower (US President 1953–61), for example, the caption tells us that the letter accompanied Carvalho's renewed US passport (pp. 191 and 192). In the text, Carvalho vainly posits that the letter is in honour of the services he provided for the US government with his shipping business during the Second World War, and that the letter was written by Eisenhower personally to show the high esteem in which Carvalho was held. However, this interpretation is contradicted by Carvalho's previous assertion that he had worked for a wine merchant in New York during the Second World War, and that he had only started his shipping business after 1945 (p. 179). Moreover, on closer inspection, Eisenhower's letter appears to be a generic letter sent to all emigrants who acquired a US passport, in order to ensure that the recipient was fully cognisant of the privilege of having a US passport and to urge them to behave in an appropriate manner when travelling abroad. Could it be that the contradiction between text and photograph arises because Castro has added to Carvalho's account when editing? It seems strange that Carvalho's account, a transcription, states that the letter is included in the final text — an odd comment to make if he was dictating his account to Castro (p. 191). Considering Carvalho's presentation as a humble man, reflected in both the content and tone of the text, it would also be inconsistent for Carvalho to have misinterpreted the content of the letter. In any case, it seems unlikely that Carvalho could have misinterpreted the intention of the letter given that he lived in the United States from 1920 to 1981 (over 60 years in total). Although the photograph upholds the image of Carvalho as a self constructed through achievement, this perception relies on the reader not knowing English, or not understanding the contents and context of the letter. Thus, as this article will argue in due course, Castro might be deliberately misinterpreting the content of the photograph for a specific purpose.

Considering all of these factors, the credibility of what is read and observed about Carvalho is unwittingly undermined by editing decisions that were supposed to be supported by photographic evidence. The use of photographs as documentary evidence, presumably by Castro, has ironically resulted in weakening the legitimacy of Carvalho's constructed self. The omissions in the

---

¹⁶ Afonso Costa was a Portuguese lawyer, minister and prime minister during the First Portuguese Republic. He led the Portuguese delegation that signed the Treaty of Versailles, although it is unclear from the text whether that is when Carvalho's path crossed with his.
¹⁷ Stephen Watt, 'Photographs in Biographies: Joyce, Voyeurism, and the "Real" Nora Barnack', in *Photo-Textualities: Reading Photographs and Literature*, ed. by Marsha Bryant (London: Associated University Presses, 1996), pp. 57–72 (p. 58).

text may be the result of Castro's choosing to disregard events for which there is no photographic evidence. This is unlikely, however, as the presence (or, to be more exact, the absence) of Carvalho's amputated leg would have warranted at least some explanation in the text. It might be that Castro was being steered towards presenting a particular version of Carvalho's life.

**The Aims of the Publishing House in the Frame**

As the cover of *Emigrar... Emigrar: as contas do meu rosário* shows, the book was published under the 'Portugueses de Longe Escrevem' series of the Secretaria de Estado das Comunidades Portuguesas/Centro de Estudos, suggesting it was a commissioned piece.[18] The Introduction, written by Maria Manuela Aguiar, the Secretária of the Comunidades Portuguesas [Minister for the Overseas Portuguese Communities] at that time, reproduces the speech she gave when Carvalho received the *Medalha de Valor e Mérito* in 1985. The prologue echoes the idea of Carvalho's life providing an example to an imagined collective youth, and closely echoes two of Carvalho's preoccupations: the presentation of his life as an example of determination and adaptability, and the effects of modernization on society (p. 1). Castro's introduction is also careful to outline the main traits of Carvalho's account. Castro heaps praise on Carvalho, noting that he fought to improve the life of his family, and learnt a resourcefulness in Portugal that enabled him to survive and to adapt to many difficult situations. Castro furthermore comments that although Carvalho was able to find personal and financial success in the United States, he never forgot Portugal. He is also at pains to emphasize Carvalho's humble character and his rags-to-riches story, stating that the book is dedicated:

> à emigração portuguesa, seja ela da América, da África ou da Europa, mas destina-se especialmente — pelo menos é esse o objectivo da sua principal e única figura — à juventude dum Portugal que necessita que o façam reviver. [...] Na juventude, está o futuro deste Portugal de oito séculos. (p. 9)
>
> [To Portuguese emigration, be it from America, Africa or Europe. It is particularly aimed at — at least this is the main objective and envisaged readership — the youth of a Portugal that needs to come back to life. [...] The future of the eight-century-old Portugal lies in its youth.]

Castro goes so far as to refer to Carvalho as 'um verdadeiro português' [Portuguese through and through] (p. 7) at the same time that he is 'um homem como qualquer outro, como qualquer de nós' [a man like any other, like any one of us] (p. 9); someone who, to paraphrase Castro, never lost his tenacity or love

---

[18] A statement made by Aguiar in the Introduction strongly suggests that Carvalho was approached by the Secretaria de Estado das Comunidades Portuguesas to publish his life story, which is unusual for this kind of text. There is, however, some disagreement as to whether Carvalho chose to write in Portuguese and publish his text in Portugal because it was cheaper, suggesting Carvalho chose to publish it on his own (see Suárez, 'Four Luso-American Autobiographies', p. 25, and Fagundes, 'Portuguese Immigrant Experience', p. 711).

for his family (which can here be read also as family-as-nation, in what seems a deliberate extension of the word, as explored earlier). Both Aguiar's and Castro's introductions guide the reader toward a particular reading of Carvalho's self, and a particular aim behind the publication of the text; if Carvalho could, and did, succeed against all odds, then so too can everyone and anyone else.

This aim acquires a particularly powerful meaning when we consider the socio-political situation in Portugal in December 1986, when the book was published. Coinciding with Portugal's entry into the European Economic Community (known today as the EU) in that year, the text could be seen as part of the celebrations surrounding the success of the democratic process started by the April Revolution of 1974.[19] For Portugal, the 1970s marked the beginning of a reorientation of its national discourse, a need to look beyond an inward orientation of Portugal as the head of a vast overseas empire.[20] The April Revolution also accelerated the period of social change which had begun in the late 1960s, and Europe presented an alternative to the empire, enabling an outward orientation of the national discourse towards seeing itself as being in Europe, and part of a global system.[21] For Portugal, entry into the EU was thus an important reorientation in terms of its national identity, and the emigrant became a central part of this reorientation. Feldman-Bianco, writing in 1992, comments that 'in preparation for the unification of Europe, the term "immigrant" was recently abolished and replaced by the expressions "Portuguese Abroad" and "Portuguese spread around the world"'.[22] These communities of emigrants were assimilated into 'the new and expanded construction of a "global" Portuguese nation' in Portugal's reconfiguration of its national identity parameters.[23] Portugal increasingly saw itself as a nation with a global community brought about by the historical movement of its people, and the former colonies and emigrant communities across the world were absorbed into this new discourse.

Carvalho's account was commissioned and published at a very specific time, and could be seen as serving a very specific purpose for the Portuguese state. Its function is akin to how biographies and life stories are currently examined in what Lechner terms as the 'validated subjectivities' of biographical narratives, whereby

---

[19] For a more detailed examination see Eduardo Lourenço, 'Psicanálise mítica do destino português', in *O Labirinto da Saudade* [1st edn 1978] (Lisbon: Gradiva, 2004), pp. 23–66.

[20] See Boaventura de Sousa Santos, 'State and Society in Portugal', in *After the Revolution: Twenty Years of Portuguese Literature, 1974-1994*, ed. by Helena Kaufman and Anna Klobucka (London: Associated University Presses, 1997), pp. 31–74, and António Barreto, 'Portugal na periferia do centro: mudança social, 1960 a 1995', *Análise Social*, vol. 30.5, no. 132 (1995), 841–55.

[21] See António Barreto, *op. cit.*, Russell Hamilton, 'Lusofonia, Africa, and Matters of Languages and Letters', *Hispania*, 74.3 (1991), 610–17 and Boaventura Sousa Santos, 'Between Prospero and Caliban: Colonialism, Postcolonialism, and Inter-Identity', *Luso-Brazilian Review*, 39.2 (2002), 9–43.

[22] Bela Feldman-Bianco, 'Multiple Layers of Time and Space: The Construction of Class, Ethnicity, and Nationalism among Portuguese Immigrants', *Towards a Transnational Perspective on Migration: Race, Class, Ethnicity, and Nationalism Reconsidered*, 645 (1992), 145–74 (p. 150).

[23] Ibid. p. 149.

[o]n the one hand it allows for an understanding of the forms of experience and concrete interpretations of a narrator, on the other, it sheds light on the social and political meaning of private experiences (biographical narratives) allowing for an attempt at collective understanding of experience (research based on and into these narratives).[24]

Lechner also asserts that the emigrant narratives 'represent a silent heritage that actually could bring a valuable contribution to Portuguese history, culture, and society'.[25] What Lechner calls attention to here is not only what the life narratives say, as this article has examined, but also how the narratives are then used to fit within a collective experience and a particular political narrative. Carvalho's comments about being an emigrant from the moment he left his childhood home; of being an everyman, yet a person worthy of being honoured with the *Medalha de Valor e Mérito*; and of being an example for a collective youth, yet a hero by force of circumstances, fits within the reconfiguration of Portuguese national identity described above. Carvalho embodies the characteristics of an outward looking, global Portuguese citizen, or rather he is made to embody these characteristics. This would explain the text's editing inconsistencies, the inclusion of curious commentaries on social history that punctuate the account, its emphasis on changes in society due to modernization, and its emphasis on Carvalho's humility, simplicity and sense of honour.

The use of photographs in Carvalho's account brings to mind Linda Haverty Rugg's warning that 'uninterrogated presentations of photography and autobiography [...] can work towards the most powerful support of unconscious ideological assumptions'.[26] With this in mind, and returning to the photograph of the letter sent to Carvalho by Eisenhower, Castro might be deliberately misinterpreting the content and intent of the letter in Carvalho's account in order to fulfil the editing steer. To suggest that Eisenhower sent the letter personally, as recognition of Carvalho's role in the Second World War, fits within the wider aim of inspiring Portuguese youth to emulate Carvalho's example. Moreover, as stated above, the matter-of-fact narrative tone found in Carvalho's account should be seen not only as a feature of Carvalho's narration, but also as a deliberately cultivated style to steer the reader away from questioning Carvalho's actions too closely, thus undermining the image of Carvalho as a role model. In effect, there is a particular sense of Carvalho's self being constructed, perhaps crafted and honed, not only by Carvalho — who is carefully considering his audience (Castro/Secretaria de Estado das Comunidades Portuguesas/wider Portuguese public) — but also by Castro, who is under guidance to fulfil the aims expected from the final text.

It is perhaps for this last reason that Carvalho's book seems neutral in its

---

[24] Elsa Lechner, 'Autobiographical Writings by Portuguese Emigrants in Newark: Glocal Emancipation and Resisting Stereotypes', *Journal of Lusophone Studies*, 1.2 (2016), 51–71 (p. 59).
[25] Ibid., pp. 55–56.
[26] Linda Haverty Rugg, *Picturing Ourselves: Photography and Autobiography* (Chicago, IL, and London: University of Chicago Press, 1997), p. 2.

political statements at first glance. In many ways, Carvalho's account could be seen as an exercise in editing that offers a subtle examination of Portugal's situation in the twentieth century, without any overt or personal undermining or criticism. As Aguiar indicates in her introduction, Carvalho's book is more than just

> uma simples colectânea de recordações, de episódios pitorescos ou mesmo dramáticos, que são apresentados com notável sobriedade quanto à sua escolha e à expressão literária, o que não obsta a que evoquem muito concretamente, juntamente com o material fotográfico de grande interesse também aqui reunido, muito [sic] dos problemas sociais, dos usos e costumes, da evolução do estilo de vida neste século XX, sobretudo até a década de 60, com suas constantes, e muitas vezes profundas, mudanças. (p. 1)

> [a simple collection of memories, of interesting or dramatic episodes, presented with remarkable self-restraint both with regards to their choice of what to include and their literary expression. Alongside all this, the very interesting photographic material included palpably evokes many of the social problems, the customs and behaviours, of the evolution in the way of life in the twentieth century, especially until the 1960s, with its constant and, often, deep changes.]

In other words, the account's emphasis on the changes resulting from modernization provides a subtle commentary on the evolution of Portuguese society, and how Portugal has responded to socio-historic changes throughout the twentieth century. Specifically, Carvalho's life stands as an example of how changes in land ownership laws introduced at the turn of the twentieth century affected rural communities. Carvalho's account also serves to illustrate the interaction between different social layers in Portuguese society, the treatment of the workers by richer families, and the lack of empathy between classes at the beginning of the twentieth century. Carvalho's life furthermore provides an example of how widespread emigration helped the Portuguese economy throughout the twentieth century. Overall, what Carvalho's account subtly alludes to is a society that is no longer present in the Portugal of 1986, when the text was published. The editing steer thus seems to present a Portuguese society that is ostensibly in the process of being phased out, in the process of changing for the better, thanks in large part to people like Carvalho and to the modernization of Portuguese society.

That said, Carvalho does make reference to historical events, both within Portugal and beyond. For instance, Carvalho crosses over to France and works in the French mines to replace the labour lost when German prisoners of war are freed (p. 99). When he returns to the United States in 1927, having travelled to Portugal to get married, he briefly remarks on the unstable atmosphere in Portugal: '[s]e algo foi conseguido, nem o soube, porque, entretanto, parti e nas vezes que cá vinha, talvez por estar numa grande nação, na maior e mais desenvolvida nação do mundo, nunca senti que as coisas mudassem para melhor quanto era necessário' [I really don't know if anything was achieved in the meantime because I moved to and from Portugal and, because I lived in a great nation, the greatest and most developed in the world, I never felt that things changed for the better as much as was needed] (p. 155).[27] In other words, rather than simply perceiving the apolitical nature of Carvalho's account as an editing strategy on the part of Castro to fulfil the aims of its publication, it is also pertinent to consider that Carvalho comments on political situations only when they directly affect him. Such a reading is supported by Eduardo Mayone Dias, who notes that the poor education of the Portuguese emigrant, coupled with the tendency to seek isolation when s/he emigrated, resulted not only in a lack of political sophistication, but also in a deliberate political reticence.[28] This observation is echoed by Suárez, who notes that this reticence was 'not because [it] lacked a defined ideology, but perhaps out of a sense that politics can bias a reader and detract from the story'.[29] It must also be remembered that Carvalho spent a total of sixty years in the US at a time that being an emigrant (read: different) was not appreciated by either Portugal or the US, as Feldman-Bianco describes, and thus would naturally steer him away from making political statements about either society. The comments made, therefore, represent not only an editing steer followed by Carvalho and/or Castro, but also a historical reference made to situate the reader within significant world events that brought about global change. The result, as stated above, remains; this is a text that highlights how far Portugal has come.

## Concluding Remarks

Rereading Rui de Castro's comments that the book was dedicated 'à emigração portuguesa, seja ela da América, da África ou da Europa' (p. 9) confirms this article's close reading of Carvalho's text as a deliberate cog within the wider machine of Portuguese national identity building in the 1980s. A book commissioned by a department of the Portuguese government, Carvalho's account has been used to aid, and even to illustrate, a particular set of political aims within Portugal. The contradictions and inconsistencies found in the text suit a particular political and social function in Portugal's global configuration of its national identity. Carvalho's account, therefore, is an example that exposes the mechanisms though which the Portuguese state constructed itself as a global nation made up of different emigrant communities in the mid 1980s — a discourse of national identity that is still present today.

[27] According to José Suárez, this is the closest that Carvalho comes to praising the US (p. 20). The understated praise might be due to Carvalho being aware of the audience for his text.
[28] Eduardo Mayone Dias, 'A Literatura emigrante portuguesa na California', Arquipélago (1983), 467–568 (p. 480, p. 564).
[29] Suárez, 'Four Luso-American Autobiographies', p. 28.

# Writing on Behalf of Those Women 'Que Não [?] Têm Escrita': Gendered Boundaries inside and outside the Fiction of Mia Couto

TOM STENNETT

St Anne's College, Oxford

> Eu vou trabalhando, lutando, tentando dar voz aos que não a têm [...]. Tento desenterrar alguns pontos obscuros, aquelas realidades obscurecidas pela sociedade.
>
> [I go on working, fighting, trying to give voice to those who are voiceless [...]. I try to unearth some obscure points, those realities hidden by society.]
> (Paulina Chiziane)[1]

In an interview given in August 2015, Mozambican author Mia Couto describes himself as a hybrid individual whose identity is made up of 'contradictory worlds': 'I'm a white guy and an African; the son of Europeans and Mozambicans; a scientist living in a very religious world; a writer in an oral society'.[2] Couto describes the plurality of his identity with an image that recurs frequently in his work, the crossing of a boundary — in this case, the road that separated his family's colonial-style residence in Beira from the black children with whom Couto was encouraged to mix as a child. Boundaries have always been important in Mia Couto's literary work. In his texts, the crossing of frontiers highlights the arbitrary nature of the boundary traversed and implies the (potential) collapse of a wall that had previously separated two categories. For example, in 'Identidade', the first poem of the 1983 collection of poetry *Raiz de Orvalho*, the 'need' to become someone else, 'um outro', is evoked in a text where the frontier between the present and the future is blurred, as the poet finds himself simultaneously dying in one world, and being born in a present-future reality:

> No mundo que combato
> morro
> no mundo por que luto
> nasço (*RO*, 13)

---

[1] Paulina Chiziane in an interview with Rosália Estelita Gregório Diogo, 'Paulina Chiziane: As Diversas Possibilidades de Falar Sobre o Feminino', *Scripta*, 14.27 (2010), 173–82 (p. 182).
[2] Maya Jaggi, 'Mia Couto: "I am white and African: I like to unite contradictory worlds"', *Guardian*, 15 August 2014, <https://www.theguardian.com/books/2015/aug/15/mia-couto-interview-i-am-white-and-african-i-like-to-unite-contradictory-worlds> [accessed 2 September 2016].

*Portuguese Studies* vol. 33 no. 1 (2017), 85–104
© Modern Humanities Research Association 2017

[In the world in which I fight
I die
in the world for which I fight
I am born][3]

These lines foreshadow Couto's interest in the liminal spaces along boundaries as areas of artistic creation; zones typically created by either rendering the frontiers between two ordinarily separate categories porous, or by removing the boundary between them entirely. For example, in another poem from *Raiz de Orvalho*, 'Palavra que desnudo', Couto employs the Portuguese word 'fronteira', only to undermine its usual meanings as either a line dividing two or more categories, or one that marks the extremity of a territory:[4]

percorro a imperceptível
fronteira do meu corpo
e sangro
nos teus flancos doloridos (*RO*, 17)

[I cross over the imperceptible
frontier of my body
and bleed
on your aching flanks][5]

As the boundary becomes indistinct, so the body of the poet and that of the beloved coalesce into one being — a complete fusion of two entities, male and female, that takes place in the 'versos [...] tão íntimos' (*RO*, 7) [very intimate verses] of Couto's first collection of poetry.

Following *Raiz do Orvalho*, the implications of Couto's rupturing of boundaries have moved beyond the merely personal as the author's concern has become markedly social and political. The image of the boundary, as well as its symbolic dismantling or blurring, appears in many contexts in Couto's works.[6] In this article, I examine how boundaries relate specifically to gender

---

[3] English translations of quotations in Portuguese are my own renderings unless otherwise stated. Lines 11–14 of 'Identidade' (dated September 1977) in *Raiz de Orvalho e Outros Poemas* (Lisbon: Caminho, 1999), p. 13.

[4] The Porto Editora Online dictionary gives the following five definitions for the entry '*fronteira, nome feminino*': 1. linha que delimita territorialmente um Estado, fixando a sua extensão [a line that delimits the territory of a State, marking its extension]; 2. linha que separa dois países, regiões, territórios, etc.; estrema [a line that separates two countries, regions, territories, etc.; boundary line]; 3. zona adjacente a essa linha [a zone adjacent to this line]; 4. o que separa duas coisas distintas ou contrárias [that which separates two distinct or contrary things]; 5. *figurado* limite; termo [*figurative* limit; boundary]. <http://www.infopedia.pt/dicionarios/lingua-portuguesa/fronteira> [accessed 10 August 2016].

[5] Lines 9–12 of 'Palavra que desnudo' (dated April 1981) in *Raiz de Orvalho e Outros Poemas* (Lisbon: Caminho, 1999), p. 17.

[6] For critical studies of boundaries in Mia Couto's work see, for example, Phillip Rothwell, *A Postmodern Nationalist: Truth, Orality and Gender in the Work of Mia Couto* (Lewisburg, PA: Bucknell University Press, 2004); Bill Ashcroft, 'The Multiple Worlds of Mia Couto', *A Companion to Mia Couto*, ed. by Grant Hamilton and David Huddart (Woodbridge: James Currey, 2016), pp. 106–24; and Patrick Chabal's reading of 'As Baleias de Quissico' [The Whales of Quissico] in 'Mia Couto or the Art of Storytelling', in *A Companion to Mia Couto*, ed. by Hamilton and Huddart, pp. 86–105 (pp. 96–97).

in three novels: *Jesusalém* [The Tuner of Silences] (2009), *A Confissão da Leoa* [The Confession of the Lioness] (2012) and *Mulheres de Cinza* [Women of Ash] (2015).[7] The relationship between boundaries and gender has been studied by Phillip Rothwell in his seminal work *A Postmodern Nationalist: Truth, Orality and Gender in the Work of Mia Couto*, with regard to some of Couto's earlier collections of short fiction. In the chapter 'Playing Gam(et)es with Gender: Subverting Orthodoxy through Sexual Confusion', Rothwell argues that inside Couto's fiction there is frequently a blurring of the boundary between masculinity and femininity, which is dramatized through characters such as the cross-dressing man Zé Paulão from 'Sapatos de Tacão Alto' [High-Heeled Shoes] and the *machista* Joãotónio, who becomes Joãotónio/Joanatónia after his wife becomes more sexually dominant in 'Joãotónio, No Enquanto' [Joãotónio, For the Time Being]. According to Rothwell, the undermining of a rigid gender binary in these stories 'runs in parallel with his [Couto's] dissolution of other frontiers, most noticeably those of race and class', as the dismantling of the binary masculinity/femininity leads to a disavowal of 'the innate legitimacy of all boundaries'. Ultimately, the result of the dissolution of the boundaries between races and social classes, catalysed by the dismantling of a rigid gender binary, is an 'identity [...] that eschews racial apartheid, rigorous taxonomy, or defined hierarchies'.[8]

Couto's exploratory dismantling of the masculinity/femininity binary takes place within the experimental space of the *conto*. The novels *Jesusalém*, *A Confissão da Leoa* and *Mulheres de Cinza*, on the other hand, represent lengthy examinations, more appropriate to the novel, of the plight of women who live under absurd and violent patriarchal orders. Gender inside these communities is not rooted in fluidity, as no crossover between masculinity and femininity is permitted.[9] However, Couto does enact a blurring between masculinity and femininity *outside* these communities, by aligning writing, or at least the sort

---

[7] Throughout the article, I use the following abbreviations in brackets, accompanied by a page reference, after quotations in Portuguese from *Jesusalém* (*J*), *A Confissão da Leoa* (*CL*), and *Mulheres de Cinza* (*MC*), all published in Lisbon by Caminho, in 2009, 2012 and 2015 respectively. Quotations in Portuguese from *Jesusalém* and *A Confissão da Leoa* are followed by David Brookshaw's renderings in English, from *The Tuner of Silences* (Windsor, ON: Biblioasis, 2012) and *The Confession of the Lioness* (London: Harvill Secker, 2015) respectively. For Brookshaw's translations I use the abbreviations in parentheses: *The Tuner of Silences* (*TS*) and *The Confession of the Lioness* (*CotL*). Brookshaw's translations are also followed by a page number.

[8] Phillip Rothwell, *A Postmodern Nationalist*, pp. 134, 156, 135.

[9] The one instance of gender blurring in the three novels occurs in *Mulheres de Cinza* in an analeptic episode recounting the disappearance of Imani's grandfather, Tsangatelo. Imani recalls how one day Tsangatelo decided to emigrate to the diamond minds in South Africa. A year after his departure, a messenger arrives in Nkokolani with the news that Tsangatelo has deliberately got lost in the system of underground mining tunnels. The messenger also reveals that while in South Africa Tsangatelo married a *tshipa*, 'Um desses homens que, entre os mineiros, fazem serviço de mulher' [One of those men who, amongst the miners, performs a woman's/wife's duties]. On learning that her husband has married a man, Imani's grandmother denies her husband's existence, refusing to recognize his humanity: 'Tsangatelo já não é uma pessoa! É um morto. Tsangatelo morreu' (*MC*, 127–36) [Tsangatelo is no longer a person! He's a dead man. Tsangatelo is dead!].

of writing that Couto champions, to the author's representation of the feminine (fluid, subversive and plural). The subtle, almost imperceptible dismantling of the masculinity/femininity binary on an extra-diegetic level allows Mia Couto to position himself, in the words of Phillip Rothwell, as a 'gender ambiguous writer'.[10] This manoeuvring is problematic for several reasons. First, two fictional Mozambican women writers take centre stage in *A Confissão da Leoa* and *Mulheres de Cinza*, whilst flesh-and-blood non-Mozambican poets guide the reader through *Jesusalém* via chapter epigraphs. Real, non-fictional Mozambican women writers are completely absent from the three novels. As such, female Mozambican voices are restricted to the fictional world, and not permitted into the ranks of those real figures of authority that guide the reader through the text. Secondly, Couto problematically ventriloquizes the voice of Imani, the black woman who narrates half of *Mulheres de Cinza*'s chapters, in order to cast her in the role of a spokesperson for those people who do not have access to the written word:

> *Agora entendo: aprendi a escrever para melhor relatar o que vivi. E nesse relato vou contando a história dos que não têm escrita.* (MC, 404)
>
> [Now I understand: I learnt to write in order that I might recount better what I've been through. And in this account, I will be telling the story of those that do not have writing.]

Statements like this are deeply problematic given that Mia Couto has become a literary representative for Mozambique to the outside world, 'Mozambique's de facto cultural ambassador'.[11] Couto's critical success in Portugal and internationally[12] has led to the exclusion of other voices, resulting in 'the reduction of a complex culture to the voice of a single man'.[13] Thus, in suggesting through the voice of a fictional black woman at the end of *Mulheres de Cinza* that he writes for those who cannot, Couto threatens to impinge on the space of Mozambique's real female prose writers. I argue that Couto's emphasis on women's writing, accompanied by a subtle positioning of his own writings next to those of his fictional female narrators, results in a paradoxical plurality, as Couto's inclusion of fictional spokeswomen (simultaneously for Couto *and* 'os que não têm escrita', i.e. the illiterate) does not lead the reader toward a real

---

[10] Rothwell, *A Postmodern Nationalist*, p. 138.
[11] Hilary Owen, *Mother Africa, Father Marx: Women's Writing of Mozambique, 1948–2002* (Lewisburg, PA: Bucknell University Press, 2007), p. 221.
[12] Couto's most recent accolades include the 2013 Camões Prize for Literature and the 2014 Neustadt International Prize for Literature. Couto was also one of ten finalists for the 2015 Man Booker International Prize.
[13] Rothwell, *A Postmodern Nationalist*, p. 17. In his chapter 'Mia Couto & Translation', Stefan Helgesson lists the following (twenty-one) languages into which Mia Couto's works have certainly been translated: 'Bulgarian, Catalan, Croatian, Czech, Danish, Dutch, English, Finnish, French, German, Greek, Hebrew, Italian, Norwegian, Polish, Romanian, Serbian, Slovenian, Spanish, Swedish, and Tamil'. Stefan Helgesson, 'Mia Couto in Translation', in *A Companion to Mia Couto*, ed. by Hamilton and Huddart, pp. 140–56 (p. 141 note 1).

diversity; toward the texts of Mozambican women writers such as Paulina Chiziane[14] and Lília Momplé.[15]

## Mapping Gendered Cartographies inside *Jesusalém*, *A Confissão da Leoa* and *Mulheres de Cinza*

Inside *Jesualém*, *A Confissão da Leoa* and *Mulheres de Cinza* the boundary is a dual-purpose thematic tool, the two functions of which work in tandem to evoke the rural patriarchal communities that serve as the novels' settings. Couto alternately presents gendered frontiers at their most limiting and at their most fluid. The boundaries that map the social/cultural spaces from which women are excluded are rigidly enforced, whilst Couto blurs the frontier that separates animality from humanity. The author describes on the one hand the dehumanizing process that the male inhabitants of hyper-masculine worlds undergo in the absence of femininity, and on the other the positive metamorphoses that the women of Kulumani experience in *A Confissão da Leoa*. In *Jesusalém*, femininity, linked to plurality and fluidity, ultimately infiltrates the all-male settlement that gives the novel its name via an outsider, a Portuguese woman, whilst in *A Confissão da Leoa*, a dormant, suppressed femininity violently resurges from within the women of Kulumani.

In the patriarchal communities depicted in *Jesusalém*, *A Confissão da Leoa* and *Mulheres de Cinza*, the roles that women are expected to perform are defined by highly restrictive limits, which set boundaries on where women can and cannot go. As a place where women are forbidden, the settlement of Jesusalém provides the most extreme example of enforced boundaries in the three novels. *Jesusalém*'s narrator is Mwanito, and he tells the stories of the titular community's four permanent human residents, plus Tio Aproximado, who lives at the borderline between the settlement and the outside world. Jesusalém was established by Silvestre Vitalício, Mwanito's father, following the suicide of Silvestre's wife Dordalma, who had hanged herself following a gang-rape. The settlement serves as a retreat for Silvestre while he mourns Dordalma's death, until a Portuguese woman, Marta, arrives and precipitates the return of Jesusalém's inhabitants to the city from which Silvestre had fled. Silvestre's fear of his past has led to the violent suppression of all that reminds him of his wife, Dordalma. And yet, although Silvestre tries to extinguish Dordalma and his memory of her, his wife's presence haunts the novel's first

---

[14] Paulina Chiziane was the first Mozambican woman to publish a novel in Portuguese, in 1990. Despite this, the first English translation of one of her novels, *Niketche: Uma História de Poligamia* (Lisbon: Caminho, 2002), was only published in 2016: Paulina Chiziane, *The First Wife*, trans. by David Brookshaw (New York: Archipelago, 2016).
[15] Lília Momplé is the author of *Ninguém Matou Suhura* (Maputo: Associação dos Escritores Moçambicanos, 1988) and *Neighbours* (Porto: Porto Editora, 2012). *Neighbours* has been translated into English by Richard Bartlett and Isaura de Oliveira as part of the African Writers Series as *Neighbours: The Story of a Murder* (Oxford: Heinemann, 2001).

two sections. Silvestre erects a boundary to separate the exclusively masculine sphere of Jesusalém from the outside world, represented by the city — the multiplicity, vibrancy and progressiveness of which contrast with the arid seclusion of the hunting ground that Silvestre makes into his nation. Silvestre confesses at the novel's end, in a text written by Mwanito, that this frontier was not physical, but psychological: 'A fronteira entre Jesusalém e a cidade não foi nunca traçada pela distância. O medo e a culpa foram a única fronteira' (*J*, 293) [The frontier between Jezoosalem and the city wasn't based on distance. Fear and guilt were the only frontier] (*TS*, 229).[16] Thus, the boundaries of Silvestre's pseudo-nation are mapped on a cartography of terror and self-loathing, as the shame of his past actions towards his wife is transferred onto a fear of womankind as a whole.

In contrast, Kulumani and Nkokolani, the settings of *A Confissão da Leoa* and *Mulheres de Cinza* respectively, have female as well as male inhabitants, although the roles that men and women are made to perform are strictly defined according to the mandates of tradition. *A Confissão da Leoa* is narrated alternately by Mariamar, an inhabitant of the rural village Kulumani and the last surviving daughter of her abusive father Genito Mpepe, and the hunter Arcanjo Baleiro, an outsider contracted by the authorities to hunt a group of lions that are believed responsible for a string of deaths in the local area — including the most recent fatality, Mariamar's sister Silência. Arcanjo initially believes that the lions in Kulumani all have tails and manes, but he soon discovers from various women residents that the feline creatures living in the nearby jungle are not the only lions that hunt and kill in the village. Naftalinda, an outspoken female voice in the community and the wife of Kulumani's Administrator, reveals that another group of lions is in reality the men who rape and kill a cleaning woman called Tandi for accidentally entering an exclusively male zone, the *mvera*. Naftalinda reveals to the outsider Arcanjo that some of Tandi's murderers figure among the local hunters who are competing with Baleiro to track down and kill the lions (*CL*, 160). Tandi's murder represents the fate that awaits women who transgress the exclusionary, gendered boundaries set by local traditions to keep women away from the sacrosanct zone of masculine initiation. Furthermore, that Tandi dies of her injuries because the local nurse, fearing reprisals from the same group of men, refuses to treat her (*CL*, 161), reveals the murderous efficiency of Kulumani's communal patriarchal system: a mechanism validated by traditional beliefs and in which both men and women are complicit.

The consequences of a woman entering an exclusive, masculine space are also alluded to in *Mulheres de Cinza*. Chikazi, the mother of the novel's narrator, Imani, explains that 'desgraça eterna' [eternal disgrace] would fall on any woman who dared enter the jungle where young boys, like Imani's brother

---

[16] The name of Silvestre Vitalício's settlement is rendered as 'Jezoosalem' in David Brookshaw's English translation.

Dubula, were circumcised and initiated 'em assuntos de sexo e mulheres' [in the subjects of sex and women] (MC, 59).

## Separating the Men from the Beasts

In *Jesusalém*, *A Confissão da Leoa* and *Mulheres de Cinza*, the violent policing of socially imposed boundaries leads to the blurring of the frontiers between species. In *Jesusalém*, the blurring of the human and animal worlds is implicit in the location of the settlement that gives the novel its name: Jesusalém is an old hunting ground. Hiding out in the arid world of a toxic and wounded masculinity, Silvestre becomes a tyrannical patriarch whose desertion from humanity is consummated through his sexual relationship with a jenny, Jezibela — the animal being a means by which Silvestre may satisfy his sexual urges (*J*, 106). Silvestre is not the only male character to cross this frontier in the novel. The boundary between the animal and human worlds is also blurred by Couto during Marta's account of the gang-rape of Dordalma in a letter to Mwanito. When Dordalma leaves home to meet her lover Zacaria Kalash, wearing an outfit so stunning that it would 'cegar um mortal' [leave mere mortals groping], the men who stare at her in the streets do so with eyes full of a predatory lust: 'Raiavam nas pupilas dos machos as mesmas dilatadas veias que enchem os olhos dos predadores' [The males gazed at her, their pupils dilated, their eyes predatory]. This animalistic language returns later in the passage to describe the men who subsequently rape Dordalma: 'Dordalma foi arremessada ao solo, entre babas e grunhidos, apetites de feras e raivas de bicho' (*J*, 256–57) [Dordalma was thrown onto the ground amid grunts and salivations, feral appetites and animal frenzy] (*TS*, 202).

The local hunters contracted by Kulumani's administrator in *A Confissão da Leoa* undergo a similar metamorphosis in the ceremony that signals the beginning of the hunt for the lions surrounding the village. Arcanjo writes that these men's acts of sexual and physical violence turn them into the very beasts that they hunt:

> Durante um tempo os homens dançam e, à medida que rodam e saltam, vão perdendo o tino e, em pouco tempo, desatam a urrar, rosnar e sujar os queixos de babas e espumas. Então percebo: aqueles caçadores já não são gente. São leões. Aqueles homens são os próprios animais que pretendem caçar. (*CL*, 160)
>
> [The men dance for a little longer, and while they are gyrating and jumping they begin to lose their inhibitions, and soon they are screaming, growling, and soiling their chins with froth and spittle. It's then that I understand: Those hunters are no longer humans. They are lions. Those men are the very animals they seek to hunt.] (*CotL*, 113)

The external threat of the lions, which are believed to be solely responsible for the killings in Kulumani, has created an atmosphere of war in the village. A blind man warns that these lions are by-products of the civil war between the Frente de Libertação de Moçambique (FRELIMO, 'Front for the Liberation of Mozambique') and the Resistência Nacional Moçambicana (RENAMO, 'Mozambique Resistance Movement') that ended in Mozambique in 1992.[17] The blind man asserts that the fighting during the civil war has now been replaced by these lions, who terrorize Kulumani's population (CL, 119). However, his words will be shown to be true only because the people of Kulumani have transferred their fears onto an external tormentor, the power of which is more imaginary than real.

In *Mulheres de Cinza*, soldiers rather than hunters undergo a process of dehumanization through the activities of their violent profession. *Mulheres de Cinza* is the first novel of a trilogy called *As Areias do Imperador*, which is set in southern Mozambique at the end of the reign of Ngungunyane, the last ruler of the Gaza Empire, the second largest empire ruled by an African.[18] Ngungunyane came to power after the death of Gaza's previous emperor, Muzila, in October 1884, and he immediately began to assert his supremacy over geographical regions that Muzila had begun to lose towards the end of his reign, whilst at the same time negotiating with the Portuguese governor of Lourenço Marques (now Maputo), the seat of the Portuguese colony. These negotiations resulted in an agreement whereby Portugal would recognize Ngungunyane's jurisdiction, in return for various concessions. However, several factors led to a breakdown in the relationship between the Portuguese in Lourenço Marques and Ngungunyane, resulting in a war between the two parties.[19] Ngungunyane was captured by Mouzinho de Albuquerque in December 1895, sent to Portugal to be paraded before the crowds in Lisbon, and thereafter exiled to the Azores, where he remained for eleven years before his death. The defeat of Ngungunyane came at an opportune time for the Portuguese, who had been

---

[17] Initially a military unit funded by the Rhodesian security forces, and later by apartheid South Africa, RENAMO developed into a major opposition force to the ruling party, FRELIMO, during the 1980s. RENAMO was infamous for carrying out massacres and mutilations against rural populations, which included the recruitment of child soldiers through an initiation process that involved forcing these children to kill villagers or even members of their own family. The conflict ended with a UN-brokered peace deal in 1992. See Malyn Newitt, *A History of Mozambique* (London: C. Hurst, 1995), pp. 563–77; Malyn Newitt, 'Mozambique', in *A History of Postcolonial Lusophone Africa*, ed. by Patrick Chabal (London: C. Hurst, 2002), pp. 209–35.
[18] Ngungunyane's name is normally rendered in English as Gungunhana.
[19] These factors include: the internal problems that beset Gazan society in the 1890s, which were exacerbated by the wars with the Chopi people, a result of the movement of Gaza's capital south; Gaza's increasing isolation following the signing of partition treaties between Portugal and Britain, and the conquest of the Ndebele in 1893, which isolated Gaza as the only surviving independent monarchy in Southern Africa; the outbreak of conflict involving Tsonga chiefs, which brought Tsonga forces (who represented a significant part of the Gaza military) outside Lourenço Marques between October 1894 and January 1895; and the appointment of a hawkish Portuguese commissioner in January 1895, who presented an ultimatum to Gaza in August of the same year. For an account of the fall of the Gaza State, see Malyn Newitt's chapter 'Mozambique: The Making of the Colonial State', in Malyn Newitt, *A History of Mozambique* (London: C. Hurst, 1995), pp. 356–85.

humiliated by the other colonial powers with the Ultimatum of 1890.[20] For Malyn Newitt, Portuguese 'pacification' of the Gaza State was fundamental in shaping modern Mozambique: 'The end of the Gaza monarchy opened the way for the Portuguese colonial state in the south to achieve some level of organization and to begin the immediate task of economic exploitation and the longer term process of development'.[21]

Like *A Confissão da Leoa, Mulheres de Cinza* has two narrators: Imani, a Portuguese-speaking fifteen-year-old girl from the coastal Chopi tribe, and Germano de Melo, a Portuguese sergeant exiled to Mozambique for taking part in a Republican uprising in Porto, to whom Imani is assigned as an interpreter. War rages between the Portuguese colonial forces that Germano de Melo serves (although with dwindling conviction as the novel progresses) and Ngungunyane's Nguni forces — with Nkoklani, the village where Imani lives, sitting somewhere in between the two sides of the conflict, as a Mozambican community supporting the Portuguese forces against Ngungunyane, and which sees Ngungunyane's Nguni as invaders in their territory (*MC*, 20–21).

The war between Gaza's forces and the Portuguese is devastating for the land, transforming the novel's setting into an inferno where the inner demons of the Portuguese and Mozambican soldiers teem, as Couto employs hellish and demonic imagery to evoke the dehumanization of combatants on both sides of the conflict. In an episode from Germano de Melo's final chapter, a group of characters including the sergeant and Imani discover a fire that has destroyed a Portuguese camp, setting off explosives and scaring away the Portuguese soldiers' horses (*MC*, 395). Soon after, the runaway horses appear before the party like a nightmarish apparition: 'como uma assombração vinda das entranhas da noite' [like an apparition come from the depths of night]. The animals gallop, 'as crinas acesas pelas fagulhas' [manes coruscating with sparks], and rush past 'como se fossem aladas criaturas do apocalipse' (*MC*, 393–94) [like winged creatures of the Apocalypse]. The Portuguese bring with them explosives and guns and, contrary to the putative Christian aims of the colonial

---

[20] In 1885 the Portuguese Foreign Ministry had produced the famous Mapa Cor-de-Rosa ('Rose-Coloured Map'), which set out Portugal's claims in Central Africa, showing a band of Portuguese territory stretching from the western coast of the continent (Angola) all the way across to the east (Mozambique). The Berlin Congress of 1884–85 had seemed to establish effective occupation as the sole admissible criterion for international recognition of European claims in Africa. The British had dismissed the notion that the Portuguese would be able to ensure effective occupation of the disputed regions on the Rose-Coloured Map, and were therefore surprised by the successes that the Portuguese military had achieved in those geographical areas by the end of 1889. The British Foreign Office, fearing public humiliation, drew up a memorandum 'on the misconduct and deviousness of the Portuguese', and on 8 January 1890 Lord Salisbury issued an ultimatum to the Portuguese to withdraw all forces active in the disputed areas. Portugal's acquiescence to Britain's demands was perceived as a national humiliation in Portugal, with the first Republican uprising in Portugal following soon after in 1891, in Porto. Newitt, *A History of Mozambique*, pp. 341–55; James Anderson, *The History of Portugal* (Westport, CT; London: Greenwood, 2000), pp. 138–39; A. H. de Oliveira Marques, *History of Portugal*, vol. II: *From Empire to Corporate State*, 2nd edn (New York: Columbia University Press, 1976), pp. 72–75; 110–18.

[21] Newitt, *A History of Mozambique*, p. 378.

project, have participated in the creation of scenes of a Christian hell-on-earth. As for the Nguni soldiers, Imani's description of the invaders' commanders, who decorate themselves with *simba* pelts 'até perderem a forma humana' [until they lose all human resemblance], joins together the dehumanizing language of animality with the vocabulary of warfare. For Imani, this is the purpose of a soldier's uniform, to 'afastar o soldado da sua humanidade' (*MC*, 24) [distance the soldier from his humanity]. In climates of fear, as the boundaries between (hu)mankind, on the one hand, and the demonic and animal realms on the other, become blurred, so the warriors, hunters, fathers and husbands of Jesusalém, Kulumani and Nkokolani distance themselves from their humanity and transform into the very monsters, physical and oneiric, they claim to fight.

## Rewriting Patriarchal Symbols through Multiplication and Feminization in *A Confissão da Leoa*

In Couto's work, it is not just men that are transformed in extreme environments. Women also undergo metamorphoses in *A Confissão da Leoa*, as Couto provides feminine counter-examples to the male hunters who transmogrify into brutal animals. Thus, the transformations that take place in the dire, rural landscape of Kulumani are gendered, since male characters often, but not always, experience negative mutations into violent monsters, whilst the female protagonists experience, or manage to catalyse in other characters, more positive transformations. As we have seen, the lions in *A Confissão da Leoa* are not all feline animals. Indeed, in the novel the word 'leão' comes to designate any person who acts with animalistic violence. In the case of the beasts that circle Kulumani, this violence is simply a part of their nature as lions. However, the men who turn into lions do so at the expense of their humanity. One such transmutation takes place in the novel's opening pages, when Genito Mpepe rapes Hanifa Assulua:

> A minha mãe ocorreu, então, que por cima dela não estava o seu homem, mas um bicho dos matos, sequioso de seu sangue. Durante o ato amoroso, Genito Mpepe se convertera numa fera que literalmente a devorava. Dissolvida na avidez do outro, ela permanecia paralisada, à mercê dos seus felinos apetites. (*CL*, 24)

> [Then it occurred to my mother that it wasn't her man who was on top of her, but a creature from the bush, thirsty for her blood. During the act of love, Genito Mpepe had turned into a wild beast that was devouring her. Weakened by his fervour, she was helpless, at the mercy of his feline appetite.] (*CotL*, 10–11)

This transformation of a male character into a 'bicho dos matos' [creature from the bush] during a violent act contrasts with Mariamar's meeting with a lioness in her second chapter, where the animal is described as 'delicada e feminina como uma dançarina, majestosa e sublime como uma deusa' (*CL*, 62) [delicate and feminine as a dancer, majestic and sublime as a goddess] (*CotL*, 40). Whereas Genito's metamorphosis comes at the expense of his humanity, Mariamar experiences a feeling of (human) kinship with the lioness she encounters. The lioness's 'inquisitive' gaze leads the narrator to believe that the animal recognizes her, and the creature even greets Mariamar 'com respeito de irmã' (*CL*, 62) [with a sisterly respect] (*CotL*, 40). The sororal link that connects Mariamar and the lioness, as well as the verbs for which the lioness is the grammatical subject, emphasize the creature's humanness. Thus, the lion is a gendered image: when men undergo the metamorphosis from human into beast it is a process of de(hu)manization and debasement, whilst the lioness is a symbol of a sublime, awesome and, paradoxically, humanized power.

The meeting between Mariamar and the lioness reveals that the lions are the receptacle of many of the fears harboured by the people of Kulumani, especially the men. For the male inhabitants of Kulumani really fear the women they subjugate and exploit. Couto explains race relations in Mozambique at the end of the colonial period in a similar way in his 1999 novella *Vinte e Zinco*. One of that text's epigraphs, an extract from *Voodoo in Haiti* by Alfred Metraux, points to the way in which the relationship between colonizer and colonized is based on fear:

> Quanto maior era a subjugação dos negros, mais eles lhe [ao senhor] inspiravam medo. [...] Talvez alguns escravos se tenham realmente vingado sobre os seus tiranos — mas o medo que reinava nas plantações tinha origem em mais profundas camadas da alma — era a feitiçaria e o mistério de África que perturbavam o sono dos senhores da 'casa grande'. (*Voodoo in Haiti*, Alfred Metraux (1959), quoted in *VZ*, 11)
>
> [The greater the subjugation of the blacks, the more they provoked fear in him [the colonial master]. [...] Perhaps some slaves really had got their revenge on their tyrants — but the fear that reigned in the plantations had its origins in deeper layers of soul — it was the witchcraft and the mystery of Africa that disturbed the sleep of the owners of the 'casa grande'.]

In *A Confissão da Leoa*, the lioness Mariamar encounters becomes symbolic of the terror that the women of Kulumani inspire in their male subjugators:

> Todos acreditam que são leões machos que ameaçam a aldeia. Não são. É esta leoa [...] que tanto terror tem espalhado em todas as vizinhanças. Homens poderosos, guerreiros munidos de sofisticadas armas: todos se prostraram, escravos de medo, vencidos pela sua própria impotência. (*CL*, 62)
>
> [They are all convinced that it is male lions who are threatening the village. It's not. It's this lioness [...] that has spread such terror through the neighborhood. Powerful men, warriors equipped with sophisticated weapons: All of them have prostrated themselves, enslaved by fear, vanquished by their own impotence.] (*CotL*, 40)

As the symbol of the fear of the men of Kulumani, the figure of the *leoa* is linked several times to a legend from the novel's opening, in which Mariamar powerfully declares: 'Deus já foi mulher' [God was once a woman]. In this opening myth Mariamar suggests that Nungu, identified as a masculine deity ('o actual *Senhor*', my emphasis), is no more than a name that has been foisted upon a divinity which is *essentially* female: 'Antes de se exilar para longe da sua criação e quando não se chamava Nungu, o actual Senhor do Universo parecia-se com todas as mães deste mundo' (*CL*, 13) [Before he exiled himself far from his creation, and while he had still not assumed the name of Nungu, the current Lord of the Universe looked like all the mothers in this world] (*CotL*, 3). Later in the novel, Mariamar makes a connection between the fear that the men of Kulumani have of their wives and daughters, epitomized by the lioness, with her own story of female divinity, declaring that the source of the men's fear are the dormant goddesses that rest inside all women (*CL*, 197). Mariamar's and Hanifa's metamorphoses into the lionesses who are pushed into committing violent acts — such as the murders of Igualita and Uminha, killed by their sister Mariamar so that the twins be spared a life of abuse — reveal mother and daughter's numinous essence, or what passes for divinity in these terrestrial infernos.

By the end of *A Confissão da Leoa*, Arcanjo's fear of woman's divine nature turns to awe. When Mariamar drops her journal in front of Arcanjo at the end of the novel, she reveals the opening line of *A Confissão da Leoa*. The hunter realizes that he is surrounded by goddesses, and that 'naquele rasgar de mundos, são mulheres que costuram a minha rasgada história' (*CL*, 269) [in that rupturing of worlds, it's women who stitch together my own ruptured story] (*CotL*, 192). Even in the fraught situation that Hanifa and Mariamar find themselves, mother and daughter discover ways of combating the violent, patriarchal system that oppresses them. In an environment of immobilizing fear, Hanifa transforms into the last lioness, a metamorphosis that, rather than diminish her humanity, augments it — for she acts out of love for her daughters. Thus, the lioness, which sits at the intersection of animality, humanity and divinity, is a liminal symbol; unlike the male lion, which is characterized by a dehumanized and animalistic violence. The gendered rewriting of these symbols in Mariamar's and Arcanjo's journals entails an inversion and appropriation of patriarchal emblems. By the end of the novel, the idea of 'Deus' (the patriarchal, Christian God or the African divinity Nungu) as a single, paternal figure has been undermined, feminized, and multiplied into the 'deusas' surrounding Arcanjo. Likewise, the male lion as a symbol of masculine strength, since the hunt for the presumed male lions is perceived by the hunters as a way of outwardly proving their masculinity, is transformed into the majestic and, importantly, humanized image of the lioness.

## Contaminating Masculine Unity with Feminine Plurality

In *Jesusalém*, *A Confissão da Leoa* and *Mulheres de Cinza*, access to the female characters Marta, Mariamar and Imani is more direct than in Couto's previous texts. The author dispenses with masculine mediators, in a new and concerted effort to expose his readers to fictional women writers. We do *hear* women's voices in Couto's earlier texts, but those who speak are denied the agency of authorship. Their discourse is relayed to us via masculine intermediaries. For example, the source for the tale of 'Lenda de Namarói' (a *conto* from *Estórias Abensonhadas*), an unnamed woman, is relegated to anonymity and refused ownership of her legend, as it is implied that our access to the text has only been made possible because a priest recovered it.[22] A chain of potential owners of the tale is established and foregrounded at the beginning of the text by the master-author, Couto. He uses a subversive 'legend' — in which women, in their capacity as writers and mothers, reclaim their position as originators and creators — to undermine the creation story in Genesis. In Couto's version, women precede men *and* they are a necessary condition for man's existence as, according to the legend, men were originally created in an anthropophagous process. Barren women were swallowed by their fertile counterparts. After three days, these infertile women were reborn as the first men (*EA*, 141). Women are required to end man's sterility in the same way that the exclusively male world of Jesusalém will be barren until Marta, a Portuguese woman, arrives and catalyses the male characters' departure and their return to the city. In 'Lenda de Namarói', women-as-mothers break the deadlock of infertility through their ability to give birth, entailing a dismantling and reconstruction of the patriarchal chain of the account in Genesis. Whereas in Genesis, God makes man in His own image before *subsequently* fashioning woman from one of Adam's ribs, God is altogether removed in Couto's secular and subversive rewriting.

Although women are (re)cast in their role as creators in 'Lenda de Namarói', this is only achieved in a text that dismantles the account from the Book of Genesis. This brings us back to the crucial paradox that women are placed in the primary role of origination in a text where the source, the unnamed woman, is so far removed from what we come to read. Ultimately, the effect of this distancing is subversive, as the legend is mediated through a member of the very patriarchal structure that the text undermines. Furthermore, 'Lenda de Namarói' subverts Couto's own introductory note to *Estórias Abensonhadas*, in which the author's poetic interpretation of the post-war situation in Mozambique is evoked through imagery that links the Coutian theme of the power of dreaming to create new realities to the language of the male biological role in reproduction: 'Onde restou o *homem* sobreviveu *semente*, sonho a *engravidar* o tempo' (*EA*, 7,

[22] For two readings of 'Lenda de Namarói', see Rothwell, *A Postmodern Nationalist*, pp. 136–41 and Elena Brugioni, *Mia Couto: representação, história(s) e pós-colonialidade* (Famalicão: Húmus, 2012), pp. 157–70.

my emphasis) [Where *man* remained, his *seed* survived, a dream *to impregnate time*].²³ In the 'Lenda de Namarói', the 'semente' is the symbol of the inability of the infertile women, who become the first men, to give birth (*EA*, 141). Conversely, in Couto's introductory text the word 'semente' takes on a meaning much closer to its etymology: dreams are the 'semen(te)' that will impregnate time. As such, I agree with Elena Brugioni's assertion that 'no conto "Lenda de Namarói" o aparato crítico-conceptual da re-escrita [...] permite encarar a representação literária como uma prática de questionamento das chamadas *grandes narrativas*' [in the *conto* "Lenda de Namarói" the critical-conceptual apparatus of rewriting [...] allows [Couto] to approach literary representation as a way of questioning so-called *grand narratives*],²⁴ although I would go further and argue that in this subversive text Couto self-reflexively calls into question any attempts to inscribe a unified account of History. Couto's *estória* is, we ought to remember, only one of many that constitute the collection called *Estórias Abensonhadas*. As one tale amongst many, 'Lenda de Namarói' not only questions the status of grand narratives, it casts doubts over any text that aims toward unity or authority, parodying its own status as legend. As such, Couto's introductory note is not entirely subverted as, even if the language of male fertility will be later undermined, the underlying message is the same: we should not be content with the one reality that is foisted upon us by the cultural or religious apparatus of the society in which we live. Rather, we should be open to new realities and not be afraid to create alternatives of our own.

Couto's rewriting of the creation myth from Genesis points to two of the signature features of feminine discourse in his work: texts written by his fictional women are marked by a creative subversion and the production of new realities. However, these new realities are not created as simple counterpoints. Rather, texts like 'Lenda de Namarói' allow a creative multiplicity to seep into a repressive singleness and, once this frontier has been breached, unity becomes necessarily contaminated by plurality. In Couto's fiction, this movement towards multiple and concurrent realities is normally played out by a male protagonist who comes to listen to a variety of voices, some of which belong to women. As soon as characters such as the Italian Massimo Risi in *O Último Voo do Flamingo* [The Last Flight of the Flamingo] (2005), or the westernized Mozambican student Mariano in *Um Rio Chamado Tempo, Uma Casa Chamada Terra* [A River Called Time] are introduced to a multiplicity of voices, there is no returning to their former way of looking at the world.²⁵ This journey from

---

²³ The importance of dreaming, and the dire consequences of its denial, are a principal theme of Mia Couto's first novel *Terra Sonâmbula* (Lisbon: Caminho, 1992), translated into English by David Brookshaw as *Sleepwalking Land* (London: Serpent's Tail, 2006). For an analysis of the importance of dreams and their relationship to water imagery in Couto's writings, see Phillip Rothwell 'Seaing into the Unconscious: The Role of Water in Mia Couto', in *A Postmodern Nationalist*, pp. 91–132 and Patrick Chabal, 'Mia Couto or the Art of Storytelling', in *A Companion to Mia Couto*, ed. by Hamilton and Huddart, pp. 86–105.
²⁴ Brugioni, p. 161.
²⁵ *O Último Voo do Flamingo* (Lisbon: Caminho, 2000) and *Um Rio Chamado Tempo, Uma Casa*

unity to plurality is also played out in *A Confissão da Leoa* by the male hunter Arcanjo Baleiro, whose character arc recalls that of Izidine from *A Varanda do Frangipani* [Under the Frangipani Tree], since both characters play the role of investigators in anti-detective stories.[26] As I shall demonstrate later, that a man is the agent of this transition from a repressive unity, aligned to hyper-masculinity, to a plurality associated with femininity, is significant.

## Writing on the Cusp of Non-Existence

The texts written by the female narrators of *Jesusalém*, *A Confissão da Leoa* and *Mulheres de Cinza* perform a similar, subversive function to the tale of the 'Lenda de Namarói', with one key difference: the novels are partly narrated by women who have direct access to the (Portuguese) written word. That the Mozambican women Mariamar in *A Confissão da Leoa* and Imani in *Mulheres de Cinza* write in Portuguese is significant, as it highlights the two conditions excluding Mozambican women from the writing of national literature: literacy, and the ability to speak and write in Portuguese specifically. According to World Bank statistics, there is a stark gender imbalance in literacy rates in Mozambique, with only 45.5% of women able to read and write in 2015, compared to 73.4% of men.[27] In 1975, when Mozambique officially gained independence from Portugal, the proportion of women who were literate was far smaller, with a rate of around 10%.[28] Immediately following independence, the Mozambican revolutionary party, FRELIMO, elected Portuguese as the national language.[29] As a result, as Benedict Anderson points out, Portuguese 'is the medium through which Mozambique is imagined'. The Portuguese language was the one chosen for national unification by 'radical Mozambique'.[30] One of the consequences, as explored by Kathleen Sheldon, is that 'non-Portuguese-speaking women in Mozambique are excluded from the "imagining" of a new Mozambique'. For illiterate women, the exclusion from this imagining is even greater: 'If print language was more of a marker, illiterate women were even further dismissed'.[31] For Hilary Owen, the double barrier to the Portuguese language and the

---

*Chamada Terra* (Lisbon: Caminho, 2002) have been translated into English by David Brookshaw respectively as *The Last Flight of the Flamingo* (London: Serpent's Tail, 2004) and *A River Called Time* (London: Serpent's Tail, 2008).
[26] *A Varanda do Frangipani* (Lisbon: Caminho, 1996) has also been translated into English by Brookshaw, as *Under the Frangipani Tree* (London: Serpent's Tail, 2001).
[27] <http://data.worldbank.org/indicator/SE.ADT.LITR.ZS?end=2015&locations=MZ&start=1980&view=chart> [accessed 8 January 2016].
[28] Benedita da Silva, *Beyond Inequalities 2005: Women in Mozambique* (Maputo: Fórum Mulher; Harare: Southern African Research and Documentation Centre, Women in Development Southern Africa Awareness, 2006), p. 11.
[29] Newitt, *A History of Mozambique*, p. 547.
[30] Benedict Anderson, *Imagined Communities: Reflections on the Origin and Spread of Nationalism*, rev. edn (London and New York: Verso, 2006), p. 134.
[31] Kathleen Sheldon, *Pounders of Grain: A History of Women, Work, and Politics in Mozambique* (Portsmouth, NH: Heinemann, 2002), p. 130.

written word 'were relevant factors in delimiting women's self-identification through nationhood as a narrated process'. Citing Cynthia Ward's article 'Bound to Matter: The Father's Pen and Mother Tongues', Owen concludes that this double exclusion of Mozambican women illiterate in Portuguese from the written narration of the nation 'outlines a specific gender politics at work behind the opposition of literate and oral culture in the national imaginary', where 'men step forth as nationhood's "natural" narrators while women, bound to the primary nostalgia of the oral sphere, become, once again, the fantasized, ahistorical, and excessively embodied "other" through which male projections of the national utopia come to be narrated'.[32]

In *Jesusalém*, *A Confissão da Leoa* and *Mulheres de Cinza*, Couto displays an unwavering faith in the power of *escrita* ('writing'), which he strongly aligns to the feminine. The close association of the feminine to writing is signalled by Marta's first words in *Jesusalém*: 'Sou mulher, sou Marta e só posso escrever' (*J*, 139) ['I am a woman, I am Marta and all I can do is write'] (*TS*, 110). Silvestre, who forbids women and books from entering Jesusalém, makes the same link between femininity and writing, whilst in *A Confissão da Leoa*, Mariamar explains that the written word is a woman's only 'weapon' in a masculine world (*CL*, 97). Writing serves various functions in the texts. For Mariamar in *A Confissão da Leoa*, the confessional mode allows the simultaneous unloading of her own guilt and the guilt of patriarchy in her confessions of the crimes of Kulumani's corrupt patriarchal practices. Unlike the Catholic confessional, in which the individual confesses their personal sins to a priest, Mariamar's various confessions expose the fundamental problems of a patriarchal-society-gone-wrong. Germano de Melo's letters in *Mulheres de Cinza* perform a similar function, for his confessions are both those of his personal life and those of Portuguese colonialism as practised in Mozambique at the end of the nineteenth century.

According to Rothwell, for Marta in *Jesusalém* writing is a way of coming to terms with the loss of her lover Marcelo, whilst for Mwanito, the written word grants him access to worlds beyond his father's stifling community.[33] For both Mwanito and Marta, writing is a way of countering silence and absence, which are linked to death in *Jesusalém*. The life-giving potential of writing is placed in opposition, as Rothwell has noted, to naming, the prerogative of patriarchal authority: 'Whereas writing predominantly becomes the preserve of the feminine in *The Tuner of Silences*, naming appears, at first, to be the patriarchal preserve of men, the function of the empty father'.[34] The empty

---

[32] Owen, *Mother Africa, Father Marx*, pp. 21–22.
[33] Phillip Rothwell, '*Jesusalém*: Empty Fathers & Women's Texts', in *A Companion to Mia Couto*, ed. by Hamilton and Huddart, pp. 157–69 (pp. 163–68). For an analysis of the workings of trauma in *Jesusalém* see Grant Hamilton, 'Trauma: Repetition & Pure Repetition in *The Tuner of Silences*', in *A Companion to Mia Couto*, ed. by Hamilton and Huddart, pp. 170–87.
[34] Rothwell, 'Empty Fathers & Women's Texts', p. 164. For an analysis of the trope of the empty father in Portuguese literature see Phillip Rothwell, *A Canon of Empty Fathers: Paternity in Portuguese*

father Silvestre, formerly Mateus Ventura, renames the five inhabitants of his hamlet in an attempt to take control of language. This control is consummated through the act of inscription in the 'censo populacional' [population census], but Silvestre's servant Zacaria Kalash, who is appointed scribe, highlights the difference between the acts of writing and inscription: 'Desculpe, Vitalício. É escrever ou inscrever?' (*J*, 43) [Sorry, Vitalício. Is it write or inscribe?] (*TS*, 35; translation modified). Couto suggests that to inscribe is to attempt to crystallize the named individual and thereby control them, whilst writing is characterized by its potentially creative fluidity.

In *A Confissão da Leoa*, the liquid nature of Couto's feminine discourse contaminates the act of naming in Mariamar's sixth chapter, 'Um rio sem mar' [A River Without Sea], through the image of Mariamar's impossible daughter: 'Espuma'. Mariamar imagines naming the child that she will never have, and therefore never name, after the foamy waves of which she has always dreamed. This impossible dream is only made possible in a textual landscape where Mariamar can counter the infertility imposed upon her by her abusive father in the physical world.

The same theme of writing against absence, silence, and therefore death is prevalent in *Mulheres de Cinza*. For Imani, writing is chiefly a way of ensuring that the oral narratives of her family are not lost. Imani's writing of these untold stories is a development of her father's practice of scratching the names of the casualties of the war with Ngungyane into the ground with a sharpened stake (*MC*, 48). Imani makes the link between her father's activities and her own project at the end of *Mulheres de Cinza*:

> Agora entendo: aprendi a escrever para melhor relatar o que vivi. E nesse relato vou contando a história dos que não têm escrita. Faço como o meu pai: na poeira e na cinza escrevo os nomes dos que morreram. Para que voltem a nascer das pegadas que deixamos. (*MC*, 404)
>
> [Now I understand: I learnt to write in order that I might recount better what I've been through. And in this account, I will be telling the story of those that do not have writing. Like my father, I write the names of the dead in the dust and the ash. In order that they may be reborn out of the footsteps that we leave behind.]

As the scribe who narrates the story of those who cannot write, Imani becomes a literal embodiment of Mozambican orature: of the names written in the earth by her father Katini and the oral narratives of her grandfather Tsangatelo (*MC*, 130–31; 141–42) that risk being forgotten because they have not been written down. Hilary Owen has argued that one of the challenges for Mozambican woman writers is the construction of a narrative subject 'at the intersection of written Portuguese and oral African vernaculars': 'The figure of "woman as writer" effectively finds itself reified as oral matrix in a way that

*Narrative* (Lewisburg, PA: Bucknell University Press, 2007).

militates against conscious female agency using linguistic hybridization to women's own political ends'.³⁵ In ventriloquizing his fictional female scribe as the teller of the lost stories of Mozambique's history, Couto effectively makes Imani into the vehicle through which an oral matrix may be filtered. Thus, in Imani, Couto attempts to combine the traditionally masculine enterprise of narrating the Mozambican nation, through a critical revision of a key moment in Mozambique's history,³⁶ with the oral sphere to which Mozambican women have often been relegated.

Within the narrative of *Mulheres de Cinza*, Couto underlines the urgency of having Imani narrate the stories of her family by making her the last surviving daughter of her father and mother. In *A Confissão da Leoa*, Mariamar is also the only survivor out of her sisters, meaning that she too bears the burden of responsibility for telling both her mother's and her dead sisters' stories. The silencing and forgetting that constantly threaten to engulf the women of *A Confissão da Leoa* and *Mulheres de Cinza* serve as another, subtle, justification for the author to tell women's stories. However, even though for Couto the pen is the only way out of enforced silence, he unfortunately does not seem to recognize the pens of real Mozambican women. This failure to recognize the writings of Mozambique's female authors becomes apparent when we consider the identity of the writers who sign the epigraphs in *Jesusalém*. Except for the Herman Hesse extract that precedes the novel, and the Jean Baudrillard text that introduces the novel's second section, all the epigraphs that preface the chapters of *Jesusalém* are authored by women, including the Portuguese poet Sophia de Mello Breyner Andresen, the Brazilian poets Hilda Hilst and Adélia Prado, and the Argentinian writer Alejandra Pizarnik.³⁷ Mozambican women writers are conspicuous by their absence, and indeed Marta, the only female scribe in *Jesusalém*, is a white Portuguese woman.³⁸ The lack of Mozambican women writers will be filled by Couto himself in the two novels that follow *Jesusalém*, as we see a determined effort in *A Confissão da Leoa* and *Mulheres de Cinza* to expose writings authored by fictional Mozambican women, and

---

³⁵  Hilary Owen, 'Third World/Third Sex: Gender, Orality and a Tale of Two Marias in Mia Couto and Paulina Chiziane', *Bulletin of Hispanic Studies*, 84.4 (2007), 475–88 (p. 480).
³⁶  For an analysis of Couto's first attempt at a critical revision of history, the novel *O Outro Pé da Sereia* [The Mermaid's Other Foot], see Carmen Lucia Tindó Secco, 'The Other Feet of History: A Reading of *Choriro* by Ungulani Ba Ka Khosa and *O Outro Pé da Sereia* by Mia Couto', in *Narrating the Postcolonial Nation: Mapping Angola and Mozambique*, ed. by Ana Mafalda Leite, Hilary Owen, Rita Chaves and Livia Apa (Oxford: Peter Lang, 2013), pp. 45–65.
³⁷  For an analysis of the significance of *Jesusalém*'s epigraphs see Rothwell, 'Empty Fathers & Women's Texts', in *A Companion to Mia Couto*, ed. by Hamilton and Huddart, pp. 161–63.
³⁸  This problem persists in *A Espada e a Azagaia* [The Sword and the Assegai], the sequel to *Mulheres de Cinza*. The epigraphs in *A Espada e a Azagaia* are taken from a variety of sources, many of which are non-literary. The only epigraph written by a non-fictional woman writer is the tercet penned by Portuguese poet Sophia de Mello Breyner Andresen, which precedes Chapter 38. Otherwise, there are several epigraphs attributed to fictional(ized) female characters from the novel, such as Queen Impibekezane, Germano de Melo's Italian friend Bianca Vanzini, and Imani's mother Chikazi. *A Espada e a Azagaia* (Lisbon: Caminho, 2016).

unadulterated by editors — such as the Catholic priest Elia Ciscato in 'Lenda de Namarói — to his readership. And yet, Couto himself seems to fulfil the same role as Elia Ciscato in 'Lenda de Namarói'. In his reading of the *conto*, Phillip Rothwell argues that Elia Ciscato inhabits a 'third-gendered-space': 'the de-sexed celibate who dons a frock to celebrate the Eucharist and who is simultaneously the guardian of Christian orthodoxy'. Rothwell argues that a 'network of perspectives is established' in the text, with Mia Couto, 'the gender-ambiguous writer' sitting at the top of the authorial chain.[39] Although, in *Mulheres de Cinza*, the first — fictional — intermediary (Ciscato) has been removed, the second mediator, the master-narrator Couto, has not. Feminine discourse is still distilled through a male storyteller, a cis-man who takes a linguistically feminized name, Mia,[40] and manoeuvres himself into a position as a writer who shares many of the traits of his own fictional women writers. As such, Imani's assertion that she writes for those who do not have access to the written word is a justification for Couto's own enterprise, as a writer of novels (such as *A Confissão da Leoa*) in which a fictional woman narrator exposes the brutal reality of a rural patriarchy. Imani is not an autonomous agent: she is a fiction created by Mia Couto. Thus, Imani's justification for writing on behalf of the pen-less is by extension Couto's too. I would argue that this boundary, the one between narrator and author, is one that Couto does not and cannot successfully dismantle — if nothing else because it is a frontier that lies outside the textual worlds he creates. It is one thing to create textual spaces in which one may dream of a world where gender is not a barrier, but it is another to suggest that the reader should forget the author's background in a world where gender clearly *is* important. Couto's stated aim is to give life to the silenced voices of orature through the written word. To reach that Coutian plurality, it is important to remember that Couto's women are fictions written by a man, and not adequate replacements for the writings of Mozambique's flesh-and-blood women.

However, the boundary between masculinity and femininity is not the only frontier that threatens to dissolve outside the novels. As Rothwell argues, the blurring of the sacrosanct frontier between masculinity and femininity is often accompanied by a dismantling of other boundaries, such as those that separate racial and social categories.[41] In the case of racial boundaries, Couto has subtly invited us, normally via the voices of his characters, to rethink what the word 'race' means in several of his works. In the collection of short stories *Cada Homem É uma Raça* (1990) [Every Man is A Race], Couto appropriates the term 'raça' and redefines it in a manoeuvring that encourages the reader to ignore, at least while the book is open, that the author is white. In the book's epigraph,

---

[39] Rothwell, *A Postmodern Nationalist*, pp. 137–38.
[40] Couto explains that he owes his sobriquet to a love of cats. Rothwell, *A Postmodern Nationalist*, p. 133.
[41] Rothwell, 'Playing Games with Gender: Subverting Orthodoxy through Sexual Confusion', in *A Postmodern Nationalist*, pp. 133–57.

attributed to the seller of birds from 'O embondeiro que sonhava pássaros' [The Bird-dreaming Baobab],[42] Couto proposes an alternative definition for race, which suggests that it is often a cultural label rather than a useful biological classification: 'Minha raça sou eu mesmo. A pessoa é uma humanidade individual. Cada homem é uma raça' (*CHR*, 9) [My race is me myself. A person is an individual humanity. Every man is a race]. This new definition, which encourages us to ignore the author's white skin, is put forward by the voice of a black man problematically ventriloquized by Couto. Similarly, in *O Outro Pé da Sereira* [The Mermaid's Other Foot] (2006) the black businessman Casuarino points to the arbitrary nature of racial purity by asserting that globalization has meant that we live in an 'era da mulatização global' [era of worldwide mulattozation] and, as such, 'desde Caim somos todos mulatos' (*OPS*, 311) [since Cain, we are all mulattos]. This is not to say that Couto believes that race as a cultural/social category is unimportant in Mozambican society: his works clearly attest to the contrary. Couto creates textual spaces in which race and gender can be shown to be no more than cultural constructs. Couto's 'disavowal of the innate legitimacy of all boundaries'[43] may occur inside the textual universes that he creates. The problems arise when the blurring of the political frontiers between masculinity and femininity, and different races, threatens to occur outside the text. The third-gendered-space that appears in several experimental short stories from Couto's earlier collections, as well as the speculative achromatic space of *Cada Homem É uma Raça*, cannot be inhabited by Mia Couto himself, who writes in a world that is still governed by boundaries.

---

[42] The English translation of this *conto* appears in *Every Man is a Race*, trans. by David Brookshaw (Cambridge, UK: Proquest LLC, 2008), pp. 31–37.
[43] Rothwell, *A Postmodern Nationalist*, p. 156.

# Joaquim Maria Machado de Assis: Six *Crônicas* on Slavery and Abolition

TRANSLATED AND INTRODUCED BY
ROBERT PATRICK NEWCOMB

University of California, Davis

### Translator's Preface

One of the perennial questions surrounding the great Brazilian writer Joaquim Maria Machado de Assis (1839–1908) is the degree to which he addressed questions of race, and more specifically, slavery and abolition, in his work. A traditional view has held that despite — or perhaps because of — the fact that Machado was the great-grandson of slaves, grew up relatively poor, and was a *mulato* (of mixed European/African ancestry), he largely populated his fiction with members of Rio de Janeiro's white political and economic elites. When free or enslaved Afro-Brazilians appear in Machado's fiction, they almost always occupy supporting roles. Further, Machado's most forceful literary statements against slavery, the short stories 'O caso da vara' and 'Pai contra mãe', were published in 1891 and 1905 — that is, after legal abolition in 1888.[1] The defenders of this view chide Machado for his apparent silence on slavery, explaining this as a function of 'racial self-negation', lack of empathy, or fear that if he spoke out he would compromise his position in the imperial bureaucracy and in Brazil's overwhelmingly white literary establishment.[2]

In recent decades, this view has been challenged. Roberto Schwarz's broadly Marxist interpretation, famously presented in *Ao vencedor as batatas* (1977), situates Machado's fiction as a reflection and critique of the contradiction between the 'misplaced' classical liberalism espoused by nineteenth-century Brazil's political class and the country's economic dependence on plantation agriculture. Hence Machado's focus on the Brazilian elite is, for Schwarz, a matter of structural necessity, and the critical gaze he casts upon the elite's shortcomings and hypocrisies becomes admirable.[3] Critics have also focused

---

[1] John Gledson, 'Os contos de Machado de Assis: o machete e o violoncelo', in Machado de Assis, *Contos: uma antologia*, ed. by John Gledson, 2nd edn, 2 vols (São Paulo: Companhia das Letras, 1998), I, 15–55 (pp. 52–53).
[2] G. Reginald Daniel, *Machado de Assis: Multiracial Identity and the Brazilian Novelist* (University Park: Pennsylvania State University Press, 2012), p. 77.
[3] See John Gledson, *The Deceptive Realism of Machado de Assis: A Dissenting Interpretation of 'Dom*

on those rare but, in John Gledson's words 'unforgettable' moments in which Machado references slavery and abolition in his fiction.[4] A notable example is a scene from the novel *Memórias Póstumas de Brás Cubas* (1881) in which Prudêncio, Brás Cubas' former slave, purchases his own slave and begins to abuse him, just as he had been abused. While, for Brito Broca, the episode 'denuncia [...] a deformação moral produzida pelo regime servil' [denounces the moral deformation produced by the servile regime],[5] Schwarz opts for structural critique: '[T]he cruelty of the freed black — shocking, in that it suggests that suffering teaches one nothing — is the product of the blows that his masters had given him'.[6]

Scholars have also re-examined Machado's life and challenged the idea that he was disengaged from abolitionism. Sidney Chalhoub and Raimundo Magalhães Júnior have both investigated Machado's activities in the Ministry of Agriculture, responsible for implementing the 1871 *Lei do Ventre Livre* [Law of the Free Womb], which freed children born in Brazil to enslaved women. They found that 'Machado consistently sought to interpret the law in favor of the slave's freedom', 'defend[ing] the prerogatives of the public trust against the perennial wrath of the master class'.[7] José Américo Miranda, in arguing for Machado's abolitionism, cites a *crônica* (newspaper column) published on 14 May 1893 — and included in this selection — which recalls that Machado joined in the public festivities on 13 May 1888. Further, Miranda notes that Machado wrote a poem, '13 de Maio', to commemorate the *Lei Áurea* [Golden Law] that legally abolished slavery.[8] Finally, in 2015, the website Brasiliana Fotográfica revealed photographic evidence that Machado attended an outdoor mass on 17 May 1888, celebrated in Rio to commemorate abolition.[9]

The defence of Machado as a writer who, if not a militant, nonetheless opposed slavery and favoured abolition, has been bolstered by the increased attention paid in recent years to his voluminous production of *crônicas*, which he wrote over several decades.[10] Given that topicality is a defining characteristic of the *crônica*, it is unsurprising that these texts document Machado's 'active

*Casmurro*' (Liverpool: Francis Cairns, 1984), p. 5, n. 4.
[4] Ibid.
[5] Brito Broca, *Machado de Assis e a política: mais outros estudos* (São Paulo: Polis, 1983), p. 57.
[6] Roberto Schwarz, *A Master on the Periphery of Capitalism: Machado de Assis*, trans. by John Gledson (Durham, NC: Duke University Press, 2001), p. 74. See also Paul Dixon, *O chocalho de Brás Cubas: uma leitura das 'Memórias Póstumas'* (São Paulo: EDUSP & Nankin, 2009), p. 134, and John Gledson, *Machado de Assis: ficção e história*, trans. by Sônia Coutinho (Rio de Janeiro: Paz e Terra, 1986), p. 137.
[7] Daniel, pp. 80–81.
[8] *Maio de 1888: poesias distribuídas ao povo, no Rio de Janeiro, em comemoração à Lei de 13 de maio de 1888*, ed. by José Américo Miranda et al. (Rio de Janeiro: Academia Brasileira de Letras, 1999), pp. 12–22.
[9] 'Missa Campal de 17 de maio de 1888', *Brasiliana Fotográfica*, <http://brasilianafotografica.bn.br/?page_id=736>.
[10] See Marcus Vinicius Nogueira Soares, 'Machado de Assis: folhetim e crônica', in *À roda de Machado de Assis: ficção, crônica e crítica*, ed. by João Cezar de Castro Rocha (Chapecó, SC: Argos, 2006), pp. 365–94 (p. 365).

engagement with some of the major issues of the period', including slavery and abolition, though this engagement was obscured by Machado's practice of writing many *crônicas* — including the six translated below — anonymously or using pseudonyms.[11] It was perhaps this relative anonymity, or the imperative to comment on current events, or both, that pushed Machado to address slavery years before he would publish his two abolitionist stories.

The *crônicas* included in this selection, especially those published in the *Gazeta de Notícias* on 11 and 19 May and 26 June 1888, approach slavery and abolition in ways that are consistent with Machado's literary and philosophical worldview, in which polite society disguises a Hobbesian 'war of all against all', and egotism and vanity reign.[12] The first, which I have entitled 'The Anonymous Benefactor',[13] and which was published on 15 June 1877 in the *Ilustração Brasileira*, concerns an apparent friend of the narrator who frees a female slave when she turns sixty-five: 'She had earned him seven or eight times her purchase price. The slave woman's birthday arrived and he decided to free her... without charge!' Machado's irony exposes the selfishness that lies behind this act: the elderly slave, if the master had kept her, would have cost him more to support than she could possibly have earned.[14] What is more, this master seeks public acclamation and writes 'a simple announcement for the newspapers that reported what he had done [...] and this one bit of commentary: "Actions of this sort deserve the approval of enlightened souls".' The *crônica* is, then, doubly ironic: it exposes a case of 'false philanthropy' and an attempt to shamelessly benefit from an act of only apparent generosity.[15]

The second *crônica*, 'A Dialogue between Stars', published on 20 June 1885, in the *Gazeta de Notícias*, addresses another aspect of the problem. Anticipating the critique of political discourse contained in his novel *Esaú e Jacó* (1904), Machado ridicules the evasive, inflated rhetoric employed by Brazilian politicians and journalists. In this piece, written as a dialogue between the celestial 'Lord Sun' and his servant 'Mercury', the former is given a copy of the earthly newspaper the *Diário do Brasil*, and is confused by its language, such as the term 'servile

---

[11] See Daniel p. 83. Though as Eduardo de Assis Duarte, 'Machado de Assis's African Descent', in *Lusophone African and Afro-Brazilian Literatures*, ed. by Lúcia Helena Costigan and Russell G. Hamilton, special issue of *Research in African Literatures*, 38.1 (Spring 2007), 134–51 (p. 138) and Gledson, *Machado de Assis: ficção e história*, p. 117, both note, Machado's identity as the author of the 'Gazeta de Hollanda' and 'Balas de Estalo' series was revealed by the *Gazeta de Notícias* on 15 January 1887. See also Eduardo Luz, 'Crônica e brasilidade: a catação do mínimo e do escondido', *Machado de Assis em linha*, 5.9 (June 2012), 115–37 (p. 118).
[12] For Hobbes and Machado, see Robert Patrick Newcomb, 'Machado de Assis and English Social Contract Theory: A Reading of "Pai contra mãe"', *Espelho: Revista Machadiana*, 14/15 (2008–09), 33–63. See also Gledson, *Machado de Assis: ficção e história*, p. 117.
[13] Five of the *crônicas* were untitled. 'A Dialogue between Stars' was originally entitled 'Diálogo dos Astros'.
[14] See Daniel, p. 82.
[15] Duarte, p. 139. See also Sidney Chalhoub, *Machado de Assis, historiador* (São Paulo: Companhia das Letras, 2003), pp. 235–37, who notes that at the ministry Machado encountered many cases of masters who manipulated the law in order to free themselves of aged, unproductive slaves.

element' (*elemento servil*), euphemistically used to describe slaves. Lord Sun remarks: 'The servile... element? I don't know what that is. Servile element? I'm only familiar with the old elements.' Beyond the piece's humorous critique of flowery, imprecise language, Machado presents a serious point: language may be utilized to evade and mislead, rather than tell the truth. This idea, a major theme of Machado's novel *Dom Casmurro* (1899), is particularly troubling when applied to slavery: a failure to call slaves by their proper name may imply a willingness to gloss over abuses and betray a lack of political courage.

The third piece, 'Fugitive Slaves', was published in the *Gazeta de Notícias* on 11 May 1888, two days prior to the promulgation of the *Lei Áurea*. It describes how Brazilian landowners frequently hired escaped slaves as paid labourers. Machado's narrator breezily explains: 'From the moment self-interested men first violated the principle of solidarity under the common law, this became a simple struggle for life, and I, in all struggles, always take the side of the winner.' This statement, with its invocation of Spencer's formulation, the 'struggle for life', recalls Quincas Borba, the mad philosopher who first appears in the *Memórias póstumas de Brás Cubas*, and whose system of *Humanitismo* satirizes biological determinism. Further, the *crônica* suggests, in its description of property owners, that in an unjust system principles and interpersonal solidarity count for little. Machado would return to this theme in his two abolitionist stories, in which slavery creates the context for his protagonists to condone the suffering of an enslaved person to advance personal objectives. Finally, as Gledson notes, Machado's choice of words (*alugados*, or 'rented' to describe hired fugitive slaves, for example) suggests a continuity between coerced labour under slavery and the exploitative working conditions that would prevail following abolition.[16]

Of the six *crônicas* featured here, the fourth, 'Freeing Pancrácio', has received the most critical attention. Published in the *Gazeta de Notícias* on 19 May 1888, the piece is narrated by a slave owner who, just prior to abolition, decides to free his slave Pancrácio, and celebrates his apparent magnanimity with a banquet, which he publicizes to the press. Thus the *crônica* returns to the theme of false philanthropy, though here the narrator, beyond simply seeking public acclamation to satisfy his ego, utilizes his unearned reputation for generosity to launch a political career. As he announces at the end of the *crônica*: 'My plan is set. I'm going to run for the office of deputy, and in the campaign circular I'll send to the voters, I'll describe how long before slavery was legally abolished, I, in the modest setting of my home, freed one slave, an act that moved everyone who learned of it.' Additionally, the piece describes how the master convinces Pancrácio to stay on as a hired labourer. The nominally free Pancrácio earns a pittance, and suffers the same physical abuses that had been routine when he was enslaved. Machado thus intuited that the *Lei Áurea* was not a panacea,

---

[16] See Gledson, *Machado de Assis: ficção e história*, pp. 123–24, and *Por um novo Machado de Assis: ensaios* (São Paulo: Companhia das Letras, 2006), p. 155.

that abolition would not undo deeper social inequalities, and that former slaves would continue to suffer.[17]

The fifth *crônica*, 'Buying Freed Slaves', was published on 26 June 1888 in the *Gazeta de Notícias*. Its narrator is a diabolical scam artist, who proposes a version *à brasileira* of the character Chichikov's scheme from Nikolai Gogol's novel *Dead Souls* (1842). He plots to visit former slave owners and backdate bills of sale for their emancipated slaves to a date prior to abolition. These fraudulent titles would then allow the narrator to receive indemnification for his 'losses'. The scheme rests on the ultimately unfounded assumption that the Brazilian government would compensate land owners for their freed slaves.[18] While not as sophisticated as his previous slavery-themed *crônicas*, 'Buying Freed Slaves' adds to Machado's picture of the dark side of abolition, in which slave owners and scoundrels are ready and willing to profit from emancipation. Further, as Gledson notes, the *crônica* addresses the hot-button issue of indemnification, which had yet to be resolved when it was published.[19]

The sixth and final piece, 'Celebrating Abolition', was published on 14 May 1893 in the *Gazeta de Notícias*. It looks back fondly on the *Lei Áurea* promulgated five years previously. Machado writes:

> There was sun, and a good deal of it, on that Sunday in 1888 when the Senate passed the law, which the Regent approved, and after which all of us spilled out onto the streets. Yes, even I, a person as timid as a snail, went out into the streets, and joined the procession in an open carriage, the guest of, if you'll beg my pardon, a heavyset friend who has now left us. Everyone was happy. The scene was one of general delirium. Truly, this was the only day of public delirium that I've witnessed.

This piece differs in tone and narration from the previous five, with acid critique replaced by wistful nostalgia, and the 'voluble' Machado's practice of narrating his *crônicas* from a variety of perspectives abandoned in favour of a straightforward, autobiographical approach.[20] Indeed, Machado's account of his celebratory carriage ride with Ferreira de Araújo, founder and editor-in-chief of the *Gazeta de Notícias*, was confirmed in the 21–22 May 1888 edition of that newspaper.[21] Though, this being Machado, his memory is tinged with melancholy. He confesses: 'I fear that our rejoicing is fleeting, that our memory of the past will die with it.' Here Machado, at fifty-three, confronts the ultimate adversaries of the delirious happiness he describes as having broken out in

---

[17] See Gabriela Kvacek Betella, *Bons dias: o funcionamento da inteligência em terras de relógios desacertados: as crônicas de Machado de Assis* (Rio de Janeiro: Revan, 2006), p. 108; Daniel, p. 82; and Gledson, *Machado de Assis: ficção e história*, p. 126.
[18] See Gledson, *Machado de Assis: ficção e história*, p. 141.
[19] See Gledson, *Por um novo Machado de Assis*, pp. 170–71.
[20] See Ivanete Bernardino Soares, 'O *ethos* narrativo em *Bons dias!*, de Machado de Assis', *Machado de Assis em linha*, 5.10 (December 2012), 102–21 (p. 105); Gledson, *Por um novo Machado de Assis*, p. 150.
[21] *Gazeta de Notícias*, Rio de Janeiro, 21–22 May 1888. Page 1, <http://memoria.bn.br/DocReader/docreader.aspx?bib=103730_02&PagFis=13811>.

the wake of the *Lei Áurea:* the passage of time and the inevitability of death. Nonetheless, in the midst of '[a]ll of these melancholy ideas', Machado notes that 'the sun finally broke through the clouds', allowing him to celebrate, if momentarily, a law that, though no panacea, nonetheless marked a step forward for Brazil.

### The Anonymous Benefactor[22]

I have found a man, and so I will snuff out the light. Diogenes, go hang yourself in the Elysian Fields of your paganism, you penniless philosopher, you unfortunate vagrant, you seeker after impossible things! Yes, I have found a man. And do you know why, you accursed philosopher? Because I wasn't looking for him, but was calmly drinking my coffee, shifting my gaze between the day's newspapers and the sun rising in the sky. When I least expected him, there he was before me.

And when I say that I found him I am saying too little, for all of us found him. It wasn't just me, but the entire city, that is, if the city's attention wasn't occupied by something more serious (the bullfights, for example, or Ombre,[23] or the cosmorama[24]), which is not entirely implausible.

And when I say that I found him, I am speaking in error, because I didn't find him. I didn't see him. I don't know him. I found him without finding him. This is surely an enigmatic statement, of the sort I'd like you, reader, to make if you are interested in this sort of thing.

While I assume that the reader has a penetrating mind, I should clarify that the man of whom I speak is the anonymous benefactor of the orphans of the Santa Casa,[25] a man who donated 20:000$000 without giving his name.[26]

Without giving his name! This simple fact earns for him our admiration. It's not that his action was superhuman, for this is the nature of Christian charity, in whose name the children of the Evangelist fashion their charitable acts for the newspaper gazettes.[27]

But in truth, this is a unique case. Twenty *contos*, given without any announcement in the newspapers, without a tip of the hat, without a celebratory ode, without anything; twenty *contos*, which fell from the benefactor's money pouch into the recipients' hands, without first passing through the printing presses, those blessed printing presses, those adorable printing presses, which

---

[22] Originally published on 15 June 1877 in *Ilustração Brasileira* as the first numbered section of a four-part *crônica*.
[23] A card game known in Portuguese as *voltarete*.
[24] A visual representation of parts of the world, generally landmarks, which makes use of mirrors and lenses.
[25] Machado refers to the Santa Casa da Misericórdia do Rio de Janeiro, an institution founded in the sixteenth century.
[26] 20:000$000 equals twenty million *réis* (twenty *contos* of *réis*), or twenty thousand *mil-réis*.
[27] Here Machado uses the term 'inventaram' [invented], which suggests the idea of false philanthropy, the topic of this piece.

report everything, even secret actions! This is a Christian act, but one as rare as pearls.

For this reason I declare: I found a man. The anonymous donor to the Santa Casa is the man of the Gospels. I imagine that he is defined by two principal characteristics: a spirit of charity, which should be and truly is anonymous, and a certain disdain for Fame's clarion call, for the beat of the drum, and for the sound of publicity's fife. Now then, these two characteristics represent two forms of strength. Those who possess them are, in a sense, already rich. And the reader should know that the action of the Santa Casa's anonymous benefactor inspired a friend of mine to undertake his own admirable act.

He owned a female slave who was sixty-five years old. She had earned him seven or eight times her purchase price. The slave woman's birthday arrived and he decided to free her... without charge![28] Without charge! That alone was generous. Now then, it was only his right hand that was aware of this act (his left hand ignored it),[29] and so his right hand took up a pen, wet it in the inkpot, and wrote a simple announcement for the newspapers that reported what he had done, along with the black woman's name, his name, the motivation behind the action, and this one bit of commentary: 'Actions of this sort deserve the approval of enlightened souls.'

Typical of what the right hand would do!

The *Jornal do Comércio* later reported on the anonymous donation to the Santa Casa, which was known only to its illustrious protagonist. My friend recoiled: he hadn't shared his act with the newspapers, though he found the occasion to tell everyone he knew that Clarimunda no longer worked for him.

— Did she die?

— Oh, why no!

— Did you free her?

— Let's talk about something else. Are you going to the theatre today?

To expect more of him would have been cruel.[30]

---

[28] The slave master's action anticipates the *Lei dos Sexagenários* [Sexagenarians' Law] (1885), which mandated that all slaves in Brazil be freed once they reached sixty.

[29] Here Machado refers to Matthew 6. 3: 'But who thou doest alms, let not thy left hand know what thy right hand doeth.'

[30] The slave master's evasion suggests that he may not have actually freed Clarimunda, or that he did free her, but was conflicted, with his 'right hand' in favour and his 'left hand' opposed or unaware.

## A Dialogue between Stars[31]

LORD SUN — Mercury, hand me today's newspapers.

MERCURY — Yes, my lord. (*Searching for the newspapers*). I've always admired how Your Brilliance can read so many newspapers. Are they all interesting? Oh look, here's the *Escorpião*.[32]

LORD SUN — Some are more interesting than others. But even though not all of them are interesting, it's important to read them to know what's going on in the Universe. Has the *Via-Láctea* arrived?

MERCURY — Here it is.

LORD SUN — This is one of the smaller newspapers. It has a circulation of about three hundred billion.

MERCURY — That's not bad! Here are the *Eclipse* and the *Fase*...

LORD SUN — These aren't as good.

MERCURY — Here are the *Crescente*, the *Bela Estrela Canopo* and the *Revista das Constelações*. I think that's all of them. The only one missing is the *Cometa*, but as you know, it only appears at great intervals. They say that it's going to close down.

LORD SUN — (*distracted*) *Il faut qu'une porte soit ouverte ou fermée.*[33]

MERCURY — Amusing! Very amusing!

LORD SUN — (*aside*) What I said wasn't amusing at all. It was a statement like any other, but he has to laugh all the same. (*Aloud*) All right then, leave me now.

MERCURY — I beg your pardon, sir... here's a newspaper I've never seen before... the *Diário do Brasil*. Is Your Brilliance familiar with it?

LORD SUN — The *Diário do Brasil*? No.

MERCURY — It was left here with the others. There are three issues. I think it's from Earth...

LORD SUN — Mercury, you know that as far as Earth is concerned I only read what they say about the heavens, to see what they think of us down there. *Diário do Brasil*? The very name is barbaric! Give it here...

MERCURY — (*looking through an issue*) Still, there are some interesting items... Why here is Your Brilliance's name! It's a letter addressed to you. There must be more in the other issues. Here's one more, and another.

LORD SUN — Letters to me? Those who write them must have something novel or interesting to say. If this weren't the case, then they wouldn't write to me.

MERCURY — Right! Quite right!

LORD SUN — (*aside*) What I've just said is wholly false, but he finds everything

---

[31] Originally published on 20 June 1885 in the *Gazeta de Notícias*.
[32] The newspapers and magazines invented for this *crônica* have celestial names, and refer to constellations, suns, solar and lunar phenomena, and the like.
[33] This is the title of a dramatic piece by the French Romantic writer Alfred de Musset (1810–1857).

I say either 'amusing' or 'right'. (*Aloud*) Mercury, I need to be alone. Go pay a visit to Ursa Major.

MERCURY — Yes sir! (*Aside*) I picked up those issues of the *Diário do Brasil* at the gates to the Firmament, so that they would reach His Brilliance's hands. Now let's wait for him to read them and for them to make an impression. (*Leaves*).

LORD SUN — Let's take a look at these letters. There are three of them... They treat me quite harshly, even worse than that.[34] The servile... element? I don't know what that is. Servile element? I'm only familiar with the old elements. There used to be four of them, and now there are around a dozen. It says here that if I bathe in a barrel of oil I won't come out clean — but I don't take baths. Why, by the devil, would I take a bath in a barrel of oil? I confess that I don't understand. (*After some time*) Here it seems that they call on me not to forget an unforgettable duty. I like this, because a duty is such a weighty responsibility that even if it is unforgettable, it may still be forgotten. Probably the word is in fashion. It's elegant, so they use it. Unforgettable! They say that in that country words are like suits. Someone appears with a new suit, and everyone copies it, until it becomes commonplace. Then another appears. First there was the fashion for *immaculate*, then came *incomparable*, then *brilliant*, and now *unforgettable*. (*Pauses*) It's beginning to bore me. Mercury!

MERCURY — Here, sir!

LORD SUN — Haven't you left already?

MERCURY — Yes, I had left. I was five thousand kilometres away when Your Brilliance deigned to call for me.

LORD SUN — Mercury, I don't understand these letters. They are saying things to me that I don't understand in the slightest. I never directed any wind to course through the National Representation.[35] I don't even know where that is. Is it a new constellation?

MERCURY — Metaphorically yes, it is referred to as a constellation, but in a natural sense, no, it is not.

LORD SUN — So then what is it?

MERCURY — With Your Brilliance's permission, it is the assembly of men the people choose to take care of their business, to make laws, and approve taxes. It's made up of a majority and a minority.

LORD SUN — So then this part of the letter refers to the Moon, which is likewise divided into waxing and waning phases...

MERCURY — Amusing! Very amusing!

LORD SUN — (*aside*) He is unbearable! You readers can testify that I only said that to kill time, but that devil thinks that everything I say that is not

---

[34] Lord Sun mistakenly assumes that these open letters, written to the Brazilian Emperor Dom Pedro II (1825–1891; r. 1831–89) and concerning slavery, are addressed to him.

[35] Here Machado uses the euphemism 'Representação Nacional' to refer to Brazil's legislature.

'right' must then be 'amusing'. (*Aloud*) Mercury, these letters are probably for the Emperor of that country. They call him the sun, like Louis XIV.[36] It's just a metaphor, and has nothing to do with me.

MERCURY — This could well be true. I confess to Your Brilliance that it was I who was at the door to receive them, and was asked to give them to you personally. That's what happened: the name fooled me.

LORD SUN — Send them to the Emperor, who naturally has received many others.[37] Do you know if he keeps all of them?

MERCURY — No my lord, I don't know.

LORD SUN — If I were him, I would only keep those that are elegantly written. Now then, Mercury, petty spats come and go, but style remains. (*Aside*) Just look at this fool: now that I say something a bit more intelligent, he keeps quiet.

## Fugitive Slaves[38]

Good day!

Let us consider the difference between a clear-eyed, wise man of profound thoughts, one who can cause a conscience to examine itself most deeply (that is, a man like me), and the rest of the population.

Everyone stopped to watch the men as they marched down the street. They saw the bands, the banners, the noise, the tumult. They approved or disapproved of the procession, whether it called for abolition or for something else. But no one had an explanation for it, or for anything; no one extracted a meaning, and then an opinion, from what he saw. I believe that I just wrote a line of poetry.

For my part, I did not have an opinion. This wasn't a case of indifference. It was just that it was difficult for me to come to an opinion. Someone once told me that this is because some people have two or three opinions, and this unfair accumulation naturally leaves others with no opinion at all. To correct this, what is necessary is a great economic revolution, etcetera. It became clear to me that this man was a socialist, and I told him to shove off.[39] This was one more line of poetry, but it managed to rid me of a tedious man. And so often the opposite occurs with me!

These were not acts of manumission *en masse*, which have occurred over the past few days, these acts of *unconditional* manumission that have exploded like bombs[40] amid the discussion concerning the law of emancipation.[41] These were purely voluntary gestures, acts without any obvious explanation. Now it is

---

[36] Louis XIV (1638–1715; r. 1643–1715): King of France, often referred to as 'the Sun King'.
[37] Machado appears to refer to the custom in imperial Brazil of publishing 'letters to the Emperor' in newspapers and as pamphlets as a means to critique imperial policy or bring pressing issues to the attention of the Emperor and reading public.
[38] Originally published on 11 May 1888 in the *Gazeta de Notícias*.
[39] Machado's original phrase is 'mandei-o à fava'.
[40] Machado's original phrase is 'que vêm cair como estrelas no meio da discussão'.
[41] This is the *Lei Áurea* [Golden Law], adopted on 13 May 1888.

true that I like freedom, but the right to property is no less legitimate.[42] Which would I choose? I remained this way, like a shuttlecock (and I here suggest nothing untoward), bouncing back and forth between the two alternatives, until the wisdom and depth of spirit that God have blessed me with as a reward for my humility showed me the rational course and the bases for my decision.

Everyone knows that in Campos fugitive slaves hired themselves out as labourers.[43] The same occurred in Ouro Preto, but for a more specific reason: many fugitive slaves lived there.[44] These were slaves, that is, individuals who, due to the laws then in place, were obliged to serve another. They had fled, that is, had escaped from their masters, contrary to the law. These slaves had no occupation, but one day they found they could earn a salary, and it seems a good one at that.

Who hired them? Who travelled to Ouro Preto to hire these slaves who had escaped from landowners A, B, and C? Why, landowners D, E, and F! It was these men who hired these slaves out from under their fellow landowners, and who took them back to their properties.

I did not care to know anything more about this. From the moment self-interested men first violated the principle of solidarity under the common law, this became a simple struggle for life, and I, in all struggles, always take the side of the winner. I do not claim that this strategy is original, though it is lucrative. Not everyone understood me (because there are many stupid people in this world).[45] Someone even told me that these landowners did this not because they failed to understand that they were working against their own interests, but to annoy Clapp.[46] I imagine that I rolled my eyes.

— Yes sir, it so happens that Clapp made up his mind to go to Ouro Preto, to get those slaves and return them to their masters, even going so far as to give their masters some small compensation and pay the slaves' train fare home. It was for this reason that...

— So which one of us is mad?

— Why you, sir! It is you who have lost what little sense you had. I wager you've failed to notice that there's something in the air...

— I have noticed. I think it's a parakeet.

— No sir, it's the Republic.[47] Do you not think that this represents a necessary change?

[42] Here Machado refers to one of the core tenets of political and economic liberalism, the right to property, which slave owners cited in defending their ownership of other human beings.
[43] Machado presumably refers to the city of Campos dos Goytacazes, in the northern region of what was in 1888 the province of Rio de Janeiro.
[44] Ouro Preto: city in what was then the province of Minas Gerais.
[45] Here Machado uses the term 'burro' [donkey, ass]. Machado occasionally used the donkey in his writing to explore and critique human nature.
[46] João F. Clapp: Brazilian abolitionist and president of the Confederação Abolicionista [Abolitionist Confederation].
[47] The Brazilian monarchy fell on 15 November 1889, when a coalition of army officers and republican activists declared a Republic. Historians commonly cite abolition as key in bringing about this change, as it led landed elites to abandon the monarchy.

— Sir, with respect to the government, I am with Aristotle, from his chapter on hats. The best hat is the one that fits one's head. And for now, this one does not fit too badly.

— It fits terribly. The wheels are coming off the axles. Brazil must either be a Monarchy or a Republic, which the *Rio-Post* called for on 21 June of last year.[48] Do you speak German?

— No.

— You don't speak German?

After I told him again that I didn't speak it, imitating Moliere's doctor, he spat this bit of devilish nonsense at me:

— *Es dürfte leicht zu erweisen sein, dass Brasilien weniger eine konstitutionelle Monarchie als eine absolute Oligarchie ist.*[49]

— And what does this mean?

— That the flower must bloom from this final tree.

— What flower?

— The...[50]

Good night.

## Freeing Pancrácio[51]

Good day!

I belong to a family of prophets *après coup, post factum*, after the fact,[52] or whatever the Dutch call it. I will tell you, and swear if necessary, that I knew about the Law of 13 May in advance. And so on Monday, before the debate on the law took place, I tried to free a young fellow of mine of about sixteen years of age. Freeing him was nothing to me. Losing him for a thousand would be the same as losing him for fifteen hundred, so I organized a dinner.

I invited five people to the dinner, which my friends called a banquet for lack of a better name, though the newspapers said there were thirty-three in attendance, to give it a symbolic importance (Christ died at thirty-three).

At the moment of the midway toast (or *coup du milieu*, though I prefer to speak my own language), I rose with a glass of champagne in hand, and declared that in accordance with the principles taught by Christ eighteen centuries ago, I would restore my slave Pancrácio to freedom, that the entire nation should act on these principles and follow my example, and that freedom is a gift from God,

---

[48] The *Rio-Post* was a German-language newspaper published between 1886 and 1888.
[49] Written in italics in Machado's original text. In English, the sentence reads: 'One may easily demonstrate that Brazil is an absolute oligarchy rather than a constitutional monarchy.' My thanks to Esther Gimeno Ugalde for her assistance with the German. Machado correctly transcribes this sentence from the 21 June 1887 issue of the *Rio-Post*.
[50] In the original, Machado writes 'As', which in Portuguese is the feminine plural form of 'the'.
[51] Originally published on 19 May 1888 in the *Gazeta de Notícias*.
[52] In the original Machado uses the more colourful expression 'depois do gato morto' [after the cat has died].

which no man has the right to take from another without committing a sin.

Pancrácio, who was watching us from outside the room, ran in like a hurricane and threw his arms around my feet. One of my friends (I believe it was my nephew) grabbed a glass of champagne and, toasting me as the first among *cariocas*,⁵³ asked the illustrious group to follow my example. I listened with my head lowered. I gave another speech, thanking my friends, and gave the young fellow his letter of manumission. Handkerchiefs were deployed to catch the tears of admiration spilled by the group. I fell back into my chair, and there was nothing more to it. That night I received a number of letters. I believe that my portrait is being painted, I imagine in oils.

The next day, I called for Pancrácio and with unaccustomed frankness I said to him:

— You are free. You may go where you like. Here you'll find a friendly home, one you're accustomed to, and what is more, you'll earn a salary, a salary that...

— Oh, massah!⁵⁴ I stay!

— ...a salary that will be modest at first, but will be sure to grow. Everything in this world grows. You, for instance, have grown a great deal. When you were born, you were a little squirt just this big. Now you are taller than I am. Let me see: you're four fingers taller...

— Height don't mean nothin', massah...

— I repeat, it will be a small salary, six *mil-réis*,⁵⁵ but a chicken is fed grain by grain.⁵⁶ And you're worth much more than a chicken. Yes, that's right. Six *mil-réis*. At the end of the year if you've done well, you'll earn eight. Seven or eight.

Pancrácio accepted everything, even the whack I gave him the next day for not cleaning my boots thoroughly. Such is the effect of being free. But I explained to him that the whack, being a natural impulse, did not threaten the civil rights he had acquired when I freed him. He remained free, and I remained in a foul mood. Both states were natural, and perhaps divinely sanctioned.

Pancrácio has accepted everything. Since that day, I've given him a few kicks, pulled his ears a few times, and I call him a foul beast when I don't call him spawn of the Devil. He accepts all of this humbly and (God forgive me!) even happily, I think.

My plan is set. I'm going to run for the office of deputy,⁵⁷ and in the campaign

---

⁵³ A *carioca* is a person from the city of Rio de Janeiro.
⁵⁴ Here I have transposed Machado's caricature of uneducated Afro-Brazilian speech into its US equivalent. Hence 'meu senhô' becomes 'oh, massah'.
⁵⁵ Brazil's currency during the colonial and imperial periods was the *real* (plural *réis*). *Mil-réis* refers to a unit of one thousand *réis*, while a *conto de réis* refers to one million *réis*.
⁵⁶ In Portuguese, the idiomatic expression reads: 'É de grão em grão que a galinha enche o seu papo'.
⁵⁷ The government of the Brazilian Empire (1822–89) featured a bicameral legislature, termed 'Assembleia Geral' [General Assembly] or 'Parlamento' [Parliament]. Members of the lower house were termed 'deputados' [deputies].

circular I'll send to the voters, I'll describe how long before slavery was legally abolished, I, in the modest setting of my home, freed one slave, an act that moved everyone who learned of it. That slave has (one may assume) learned to read, write, and do sums, and is now a professor of philosophy in Rio das Cobras.[58] I'll declare that the pure, great and truly prudent men are not those who obey the law, but those who anticipate it, and say to their slaves, 'you are free', before the government, which acts slowly, vacillates, and is incapable of restoring God's justice to the land, can do the same.

Good night.

## Buying Freed Slaves[59]

Good day!

If I had access to credit, I would take out a loan for twenty *contos de réis* and would buy some freed slaves. 'Buying freed slaves' is not quite the right expression. Let me explain.

Reader, are you familiar with the book *Dead Souls*, by the celebrated Russian novelist Gogol? Let us suppose that you have not read it, so that I can explain the kernel of my idea. It will take but a few words.

The serfs who work someone's land are called *souls*, and landowners are obliged to pay a tax to the State in proportion to the number of *souls* working their land. In the time between the census and the tax's collection, some serfs die, while others are born. When a *deficit* results, the landowner is taxed for the number of serfs registered with the last census, and before being corrected in the next census, the missing serfs are referred to as *dead souls*.

Chichikov, who is as much of a scoundrel as I, or is perhaps more of a scoundrel, buys the *dead souls* belonging to various landowners. This is a good bargain for the landowners, who are able to get rid of their dead, or rather the names of their dead, for next to nothing. After buying a thousand *dead souls*, Chichikov registers them as if they are still living, and receives the appropriate legal documents. This supposed property owner then takes out a loan for 200,000 roubles, and stuffs it in a suitcase and flees to where the Russian police cannot catch him.

I think that you all have understood me. Now I will share with you my plan, which is just as good, and is much more honest to boot. Honesty, as you know, is like cloth: you can purchase it cheaply or dearly, for as low as a *meia-pataca*.[60]

Reader, imagine that on 12 May you owned two hundred slaves, and that you lost them the next day, due to the Law of 13 May. I arrive at your place of business, and I inquire:

— Sir, did your freed slaves all stay on?

---

[58] Machado is perhaps referring to Rio das Cobras, a river in what was then the province of Paraná.
[59] Originally published on 26 June 1888 in the *Gazeta de Notícias*.
[60] During the colonial and imperial periods, a *meia-pataca* was worth 160 *réis*.

— Only half. One hundred stayed. The other hundred disappeared. I've heard that they've been seen in Santo Antônio de Pádua.[61]
— Would you like to sell them to me?
You react with surprise. I explain:
— Sell all of them to me, both those who have stayed and those who have left.
You are shocked:
— But sir, what interest could you have...
— That doesn't matter. Will you sell them to me?
— Freed slaves cannot be sold.
— That is true, but the bill of sale will be dated 29 April, so that it won't be you who lost the slaves, but I. The sale prices listed on the document will be those established by the law of 1885,[62] but in reality I will pay no more than ten *mil-réis* for each one.

You think it through:
— Two hundred heads at ten *mil-réis* each makes two *contos*. Two *contos* for people who aren't worth a thing, because they're free: that's a tidy profit!
Then, reflecting:
— But sir, will you take them with you?
— No sir, they will remain here and work for you. I'll only take the bill of sale.
— What salary would you like me to pay them?
— None, for me they will work for free. You can continue paying them what you are already paying.

Naturally, dear reader, you agreed to the deal, not truly understanding it. And so I visited another slave master, and another, and another, until I acquired five hundred freed slaves, which was the number I could purchase with the five *contos* I had borrowed. I then returned home, and waited.

Waited for what? For indemnification, by the devil! Five hundred freed slaves, valued at three hundred *mil-réis*, divided by half, equal one hundred fifty *mil-réis*, with a guaranteed profit of one hundred and forty-five.

Now then, about indemnification, some say that it will occur, while others say no, and for this reason I will provide collateral for the loan. If indemnification occurs, I'll pay and marry (my dear lady reader, for example).[63] If not, I'll remain a bachelor and won't lose a thing, because the money is someone else's. Tell me that's not a good bargain!

---

[61] Machado presumably refers to the town of Santo Antônio de Pádua, located in the north of what was then the province of Rio de Janeiro.
[62] Machado refers to the *Lei dos Sexagenários* [Sexagenarians' Law] (1885), which, in addition to freeing slaves of sixty years or older, mandated a new census of Brazil's slaves, and established values for slaves based on their age.
[63] Here Machado plays on the literal meanings of the terms he uses to refer to a loan (*emprestado a casamento*) and collateral (*dinheiro casamento*) — hence his narrator's flirtatious offer to marry his female reader should indemnification occur.

I am sure that at least one person has already done this, with the difference being that he will have kept the freed slaves. In the time when slavery was legal, advertisements described slaves in glowing terms: they were perfect cooks, wonderful house servants, etc. This is just what all salesmen claim about their wares — that they are selling superior cloth, beautiful chintz, and superb cretonne. If cretonne, chintz, and slaves were tasked with selling themselves, they could not be any less complimentary.

Now then, yesterday I read that a woman — I'm not sure on what street, I think it was Senhor dos Passos[64] — wished to rent out her services as a remarkable starcher and presser of clothing. If this demonstrates a lack of modesty on her part, why this is one of the bitter fruits of freedom. Though if this is someone who has already anticipated my plan...[65]

Chichikov, enough of doing things half way, or we risk losing out on half of the deal!

Good night.

### Celebrating Abolition[66]

Yesterday morning I walked out into my garden. The grass, the flowers, and the leaves were cold and covered in drops of water. It had rained all night. The ground was wet, the sky had an ugly, sad look to it, and the Corcovado was wearing a shawl.[67] It was six o'clock. The forts and the ships were beginning to fire off shots in celebration of the fifth anniversary of 13 May. A clear day did not appear likely, and I asked myself if the sun would show its face on this great anniversary. It feels so good to be able to exclaim: 'Soldiers, the sun of Austerlitz!'[68] In truth, the sun is a natural accompaniment to public celebrations, and to private ones as well. Without it something is lacking.

There was sun, and a good deal of it, on that Sunday in 1888 when the Senate passed the law, which the Regent[69] approved, and after which all of us spilled out onto the streets. Yes, even I, a person as timid as a snail, went out into the streets, and joined the procession in an open carriage, the guest of, if you'll beg my pardon, a heavyset friend who has now left us. Everyone was happy. The scene was one of general delirium. Truly, this was the only day of public delirium that I've witnessed. These memories came back to me when the birds

---

[64] Rua Senhor dos Passos is located in the historical centre of Rio de Janeiro.
[65] Machado implies that perhaps a cunning purchaser of freed slaves wrote the advertisement, and that he wished to rent out the services of this enslaved woman. Here the narrator's scheme passes over from fraud against the government and banks into one that would involve illegal enslavement.
[66] Originally published on 14 May 1893 in the *Gazeta de Notícias*.
[67] The Corcovado [Hunchback] is a mountain that is one of Rio de Janeiro's most iconic landmarks.
[68] The Battle of Austerlitz (1805), in which Napoleon defeated the Russians and Austrians, is regarded as the peak of his military success. The sun broke through the clouds at a critical moment in the battle, hence 'the sun of Austerlitz'.
[69] Princess Isabel (1846–1921): daughter of Emperor Dom Pedro II and heiress to the Brazilian throne. Isabel was serving as Regent at the time of the *Lei Áurea*.

sang out the names of those who fought and triumphed, who just yesterday were duly commemorated in this same column of the *Gazeta*. Though in the midst of all of this I perceived an indefinable sadness. Did the sun's absence portend a lack of popular enthusiasm? Had the public spirit reverted to its habitual sanity?

The newspapers arrived. I saw that a delegation representing a group named after Rio Branco planned to lay a wreath of laurels and pansies at the grave of that Statesman. I understood the motive for the act: to remember the first shot fired against slavery.[70] I remained in a melancholy state. I imagined the delegation making a modest entrance into the cemetery, turning away from a small, almost anonymous burial ceremony, and piously placing the wreath upon the grave of the victor of 1871. A delegation, a wreath. This brought other flowers to my mind. After the Senate approved the law of 28 September, flowers rained down from the galleries and the rostrums onto the heads of the victor and his allies. And these brought still other flowers to my mind...

These were flowers from other climes. *Primrose day!* Oh if we could have our own *primrose day!*[71] This Spring day is dedicated by England, that idealistic and poetic nation, to the memory of Disraeli, who died on that day thirteen years ago.[72] On this day each year, the pedestal of the statue that commemorates this Statesman and novelist is cloaked in silk and covered with an infinite number of primroses and posies. They say that the primrose was his favourite flower — hence the name given to the day. Here are newspapers that describe what occurred on the 19th of last month. *Primrose day!* Oh, would that we were given a *primrose day!* Of course we would first need pedestals.

A writer of our language from long ago — I believe it was João de Barros, though I cannot confirm this, but let's say it was João de Barros[73] — recalls a proverb that states: 'The Italians are governed by the past, the Spaniards by the present, and the French by the future.' This amounts to 'a censure of our Spain', given that Spain includes the whole of the peninsula, whereas Castile refers only to Castile.[74] Our people, who came from that very place, should be censured for the same reason. They are governed by the present, think little of the future, and not at all or very little about the past. I believe that the English combine the qualities of the three nations.

I fear that our rejoicing is fleeting, that our memory of the past will die with

---

[70] José Maria da Silva Paranhos, Viscount of Rio Branco (1819–1880): Brazilian statesman, diplomat, and leader of the cabinet that approved the *Lei do Ventre Livre* [Law of the Free Womb] in 1871.
[71] Machado wrote the name of this holiday in English, and in italics. Primrose Day, celebrated on 19 April, commemorates the anniversary of Benjamin Disraeli's death.
[72] Benjamin Disraeli (1804–1881): British conservative politician, author, and two-time Prime Minister.
[73] João de Barros (c. 1496–1570): Portuguese writer, historian, and author of the four-volume *Décadas da Ásia* (1552–1615).
[74] Here Machado refers to Spain as a geographical and cultural category equivalent to the whole of the Iberian Peninsula, a definition that prevailed in Portugal prior to the Iberian dynastic union of 1580–1640.

it, and that it will be reduced to that stereotyped formulation of the press from the days of my youth. In the end, how did we celebrate our independence? With a parade, a pageant, and a ball. These occupied the space of two lines, and there were these two lines besides: our forts and the Brazilian and foreign warships anchored at our port fired off *ceremonial shots*.[75] In this modest way we commemorated the momentous fact of our separation from the metropolis.

When I was a boy, I knew a Major Valadares by sight. He lived on Rua Sete de Setembro,[76] which was not yet known by this name, and was commonly called Rua do Cano. Every year on 7 September he would decorate his doorway with green and yellow fabric, would strew *folhas da Independência* along the sidewalk and in his hall, and would bring together friends and perhaps have music, and in this way he celebrated our great national day. It was the last word in extravagance, until the ceremonial shots were fired.[77]

All of these melancholy ideas took wing as the sun finally broke through the clouds, and by three o'clock the sun governed the whole of the sky, with the exception of some patches where the clouds dared to hold out. The Corcovado announced himself, but with such a lack of enthusiasm that it was apparent that this was an act required of a vassal, and not a gesture of courtesy, much less of friendship or admiration. When I returned to my garden, I found the flowers dry and cheerful. Long live flowers! Gladstone never speaks before the House of Commons without one pinned to his topcoat, and his great rival, now deceased, had the same habit.[78] Imagine the effect it would have had if Rio Branco or Itaboraí had worn a rose on his lapel while discussing the budget, and ask yourself if we are not a melancholy people.[79]

No, no. It is I who am melancholy, probably due to indigestion. I ate favas, and favas don't agree with me. I would dine on roses, or Spring days, and I would request of you a holiday that is celebrated for at least two years. This is already too much for a modest man.

---

[75] In Machado's original, the phrase 'salvas de estilo' is rendered in italics.
[76] These names translate as 'Seventh of September Street', a reference to the date of Brazil's independence in 1822.
[77] *Folhas da Independência*: colloquial name for the variegated croton, a plant whose leaves are often green and yellow in colour.
[78] William Gladstone (1809–1898): British liberal politician, statesman, four-time Prime Minister, and rival of Disraeli.
[79] Joaquim José Rodrigues Torres, Viscount of Itaboraí (1802–1872): Brazilian politician who opposed the *Lei do Ventre Livre*.

# Reviews

Cacilda Rêgo and Marcus Brasileiro (editors), *Migration in Lusophone Cinema* (New York: Palgrave Macmillan, 2014). 232 pages. Print and e-book.

Reviewed by Paulo de Medeiros (University of Warwick)

Migration has been a constant of human history throughout the ages. In recent times it has continued to increase — the United Nations reports 244 million international migrants in 2015 — and now constitutes one of the more acute problems facing the world. In a sense, issues of migration have become a defining element of the way in which politics are conducted, as we witness a renewal of xenophobic and nationalistic rhetoric across the globe, and markedly so in Europe and the Americas. Film has become a privileged medium in which to debate the complex issues surrounding migration and the myriad ways in which it intersects with questions of identity and representation in its various meanings. None of this is new, of course: at least since the beginning of the 1980s there has been increased scholarship on migratory flows and in 2007, for instance, the European Film Academy devoted its conference to 'Migration in Movies'. Yet, in spite of the continuous growth of such studies, the present volume can rightly be seen as pioneering and as a first attempt at collectively thinking through some of the most pressing questions of our time through the lens of the cinemas of a number of Portuguese-speaking countries, especially Brazil and Portugal. It is an important and timely contribution to film studies, to migration studies and, not least, to what, for lack of a better term, one still refers to as 'Lusophone' studies.

The volume contains eleven individual chapters as well as an Introduction by the editors and a brief filmography. The Introduction is very clear and, even though it still reads a bit programmatically, it will be very useful for a large number of scholars in film studies who might lack a point of entry to the situation in Portugal and Brazil. The first chapter seems designed to carry this on and provide an even larger overview of the field, yet, as its title already shows, it is actually both a 'Panoramic View of Lusophone Film' and a specific case study of one individual film, Miguel Gomes's recent and much acclaimed *Tabu* (2012). In a sense this introductory essay already signals a split in the book's conception, a sort of constant slide between the need to provide a generalizing overview and the desire to focus on very concrete examples. In other words, one could say that the introductory essay, like the volume as a whole, does both too much and too little. Perhaps there is an inherent constraint on this project at this moment, as the authors certainly realize that their intended audience might well be ignorant of many specific aspects of the films they refer to. The way that each individual chapter navigates this challenge naturally varies. For instance, the choice of *Tabu* as a case study with which to open the volume can be justified in many ways, taking into consideration the film's widespread reception and the fact that to a great extent it attempts to problematize many of the questions that this volume addresses relating to Portugal's imperial past and its semi-peripheral condition. However, the attention given to plot details can be seen as a sort of fascination that precludes a more detached critical stand. Conversely, the economy of the analysis proffered by Nadia Lie in 'Reverse Migration in Brazilian Transnational Cinema: *Um passaporte húngaro* and *Rapsódia Arménia*' goes a long way towards allowing for a solid anchoring of the two films discussed within debates into transnational and documentary film that transcend the specific case of Brazil.

It might be tempting to see the volume as divided into two parts, one focusing on Portugal, the second, on Brazil; Africa, much less present, would then be seen still under the aegis of the focus on Portuguese film. Besides the introductory chapter which briefly references some African films, I have in mind especially the essays by Nuno Barradas Jorge and Derek Purdue on, respectively, 'Thinking of Portugal, Looking at Cape Verde: Notes on Representation of Immigrants in the Films of Pedro Costa' and '*Outros Bairros* and the Challenges of Place in Postcolonial Portugal'. But to do so would not only be wrong, it would represent a fundamental misunderstanding of the volume's aims: if anything, what this volume makes very clear is how the film production of the various countries considered cannot ever be considered simply within national boundaries: these are all, in multiple ways, transnational films throughout. As such it is not surprising that one of the theoretical leads for the volume is the work of Hamid Naficy in *An Accented Cinema: Exilic and Diasporic Filmmaking* (Princeton, 2001). At the same time, even if this is not something explicitly developed, the examples and issues touched upon in this volume would necessitate a further theoretical development of the terms laid out by Naficy's seminal study.

At the risk of appearing unduly harsh I think it important to note that given the significance, complexity, and political import of the issues debated in this volume, a more directly political engagement would have been welcome, as would a more focused attention to questions of race, gender, and class. Yet, it must also be said that this volume manages exceedingly well to avoid the most common of pitfalls of collected essays: the individual essays represent a multiplicity of voices but the volume holds together and is very coherent. At the same time, even though some essays might appeal more, and others less, to different readers, it is only fair to say that they all subscribe equally well to standards of relevance, clarity and actuality. The individual bibliographies are in themselves a welcome guide to further research, even if in some instances one puzzles as to why references to other published work (on Pedro Costa for instance) are absent. Does the volume raise new questions more than it provides answers? Does it leave some seemingly important areas or specific films untouched? Certainly. But this is not necessarily a fault at all. It is always gratuitously facile to devise a number of unanswered questions and imagine an ideal book instead of the actual one. Important in itself, this volume can be seen as standing at the threshold into a new critical and scholarly engagement with 'Lusophone' cinemas and will be required reading for anyone wanting to engage with the cinemas of the Portuguese-speaking countries.

SUSANA VARELA FLOR and PEDRO FLOR, *Pintores de Lisboa: Séculos XVII–XVIII — A Irmandade de S. Lucas* (Lisbon: Scribe, 2015). 208 pages. Print.

Reviewed by JEREMY ROE (Centro de História d'Aquém e d'Além-Mar, Universidade Nova de Lisboa)

Archival study of painters' guilds and confraternities is a keystone of art history and a resource for cultural studies on themes such as patronage, festivals and urban history. Lisbon's *Irmandade de S. Lucas* has not been subject to the same scrutiny as similar entities elsewhere, and the authors explain that this has been partly due to restricted access to the brotherhood's archive, conserved in the Academia Nacional de Belas Artes. The genesis of this book, then, was due to the authors' gaining access to the archive for a separate project. Their findings prompted the present study, a key motive for which was to update the sparse historiography on this religious-corporate entity, and in particular Garcez Teixeira's landmark 1931 study, *A Irmandade de S. Lucas*.... The result is a book of two distinct parts, firstly a succinct history of the brotherhood, then five appendices of documentary material, which together provide a resource for research and teaching on Lisbon's art and cultural history.

The first part consists of twelve concise chapters covering 48 pages, which open by addressing the historiography on the brotherhood. Attention is then turned to the foundation of the Dominican convent of the Annunciation after 1515 and the chapel of the painters' brotherhood from 1602. The community of nuns included prominent noblewomen, and the authors discuss how their renown, in conjunction with painters' ties to the same noble families, contributed to the brotherhood's choice of location. This book does not undertake a strict chronological survey, in part due to a dearth of documentation for much of the seventeenth century, but instead surveys key episodes and themes: a sermon given on the brotherhood's feast day in 1644, offering insights into the values it espoused; the patronage of the $3^{rd}$ Count of Ericeira; the links to Lisbon's two literary academies, *os singulares* and *os generosos*; and Félix da Costa Meesen, a prominent brotherhood member, and his *Tratado da Antiguidade da Arte da Pintura*. A final chapter offers a brief history of the brotherhood from 1712 until the Napoleonic invasions. The 1755 earthquake marked the start of the brotherhood's gradual demise, and, although the altarpiece and archive were saved, disagreements between the painters on the role of the *Irmandade* would lead to its eventual dissolution.

The final four chapters of this section are devoted to the brotherhood's organization, its finances and how it provided a space for professional collaboration and knowledge exchange. A key issue addressed is how during the seventeenth century the brotherhood fostered painters' professional identity, founded on the notion of painting as a liberal art. Over the course of the eighteenth century in Europe painting academies had fostered both a distinctive cultural identity for painters and models for professional practice. However, efforts to emulate such precedents in Lisbon failed, as Cyrillo Volkmar Machado, one of the brotherhood's last members, recorded, and his reflections on the reasons for this conclude this account of the fraternity's activity.

The appendices form the majority of this book, and they provide a valuable research resource. They record the names and roles of all the painters listed in the various archival sources during the brotherhood's existence. Short biographies are also provided for prominent individuals, further enhancing this documentation. In addition to this the texts of the 1681 and 1706–07 *regimentos* are provided along with information on the funding of the brotherhood. Given the wealth of material discussed in this second section it would seem that there is scope for further study of the *Irmandade* and its cultural significance, whereby this book provides not only a much-needed updated study on the *Irmandade*, but also a foundation for future research.

MARIANA GRAY DE CASTRO, *Fernando Pessoa's Shakespeare: The Invention of the Heteronyms* (London: Critical, Cultural and Communications Press, 2015). 270 pages. Print.

Reviewed by MIGUEL RAMALHETE GOMES (Universidade do Porto | Instituto Politécnico do Porto)

Once a visible star on the Elizabethan and Jacobean stages, Shakespeare later became a black hole, in Gary Taylor's famous formulation of how the sheer amount of work done on and around Shakespeare ultimately trapped him behind his own reputation: 'We find in Shakespeare only what we bring to him or what others have left behind; he gives us back our own values'.[1] The study of Shakespeare's afterlives, which has proved to be one of the most fascinating and fruitful areas within Shakespeare studies, has therefore focused on how and why critics, creative writers, artists, and many others have fashioned Shakespeare for their own purposes and sometimes in their own image.

In *Fernando Pessoa's Shakespeare: The Invention of the Heteronyms* (2015), Mariana Gray de Castro makes a fundamental contribution to this field by proposing to look at 'Shakespeare as Pessoa read, understood, fashioned, cited, assimilated and appropriated him' (p. 17). This monograph, bringing together two such towering figures, might indeed have been considered long due, were it

---

[1] Gary Taylor, *Reinventing Shakespeare: A Cultural History from the Restoration to the Present* (London: The Hogarth Press, 1990), p. 411.

not for the specific circumstances of the publication of Pessoa's works, most of which were left in a fragmentary and unpublished state upon the death of their author in 1935. Their study and ongoing publication has therefore allowed for a continuing discovery of different sides to a figure that is arguably the most many-sided author of Modernism. Castro's book argues precisely that Pessoa's reception of Shakespeare's work and biography was central to the development of his heteronymic project; in Castro's words, 'Pessoa pitched himself against Shakespeare in the impersonal creation of dramatic others' (p. 27). In fact, the book presents a carefully arranged complex of ideas which coalesce into an image of Shakespeare as an imagined *'super-Pessoa'* (p. 223); Pessoa's perhaps disappointing Bardolatry does not however take the form of uncritical admiration, but rather elicits several instances of challenging and sometimes startling pronouncements about his fantasized early modern predecessor.

Opening with a foreword by Helder Macedo, the book is divided into five chapters, each devoted to a specific aspect of Pessoa's hypothesized Shakespeare. Castro begins by tracing Pessoa's interest in Shakespeare's genius as a dramatic poet, which he himself attributes to the playwright's authorial impersonality, in a characteristically Modernist (and autobiographical) argument that is nevertheless deeply rooted in Romantic character criticism and biographical readings. This leads, in the second chapter, to an analysis of Pessoa's fascination with the widely debated authorship controversy, which actually forms the bulk of Pessoa's writings on Shakespeare. Castro persuasively argues that Pessoa was not so much an anti-Stratfordian as someone deeply interested in specific aspects of that debate, namely the perceived discrepancy between Shakespeare's self-effacing life and the immense reputation earned him by his works, which, as we know, he appears not to have been interested in publishing — in both regards, much like Pessoa himself.

In fact, Castro argues, Pessoa seems to have responded best to factual or fictional dimensions of Shakespeare which he could also apply to himself, often using Shakespeare as a testing ground for his autobiographical attempts and heteronymic achievements. This understanding is borne out by her following two chapters: the third chapter, focusing on Shakespeare's alleged madness, shows Pessoa diagnosing Shakespeare as a fellow hystero-neurasthenic; while the fourth chapter, dedicated to Shakespeare's sexuality, discusses how Pessoa confidently projects onto Shakespeare the homosexuality that he himself seemed anxious to reject or explain away in his correspondence with critics about his own work and person. Although exciting in their own right, these two chapters may be of slightly less interest to the Shakespearean reader, since they largely rely on a contextualization of turn-of-the-century culture as a means to give more substance to what are in fact rather brief and repetitive comments by Pessoa on the subject of Shakespeare's supposed madness and sexuality. Indeed, as may be nearly inevitable in comparative studies, the author is evidently much more at ease with the Pessoan critical tradition, whereas her choice of

Shakespearean references, with an emphasis on biographical accounts and on the work of Harold Bloom, may end up seeming somewhat conservative from a Shakespearean standpoint. This is, however, amply compensated by the wealth and range of materials mobilized by Castro, from underlined and annotated passages in Pessoa's library to engagements with Shakespeare in a variety of poems, fragmentary critical essays, and in his correspondence, including an account of Pessoa's 1918 collection of sonnets in English, *35 Sonnets*, which use Shakespeare as a stylistic model. Castro's remarkably thorough research thus allows her to draw an illuminating and nuanced picture of Pessoa's uses of Shakespeare. Her study is further enriched by the inclusion of a substantial part of the Pessoan material pertaining to Shakespeare in a bilingual appendix.

The final chapter of the book ingeniously turns on a possible interpretation of its own argument, namely what the author calls a 'kinship fallacy' — that is, Pessoa's retrospective projection of affinity, which, Castro explains, has been too eagerly taken up in Pessoan criticism. Castro subjects this myth of Pessoa's own creation to a meticulous and thought-provoking deconstruction from which a more complex account emerges, in which the Modernist poet fashions a Shakespeare that, by incorporating several traits that Pessoa identified in himself and in his literary work, would hopefully look like a '*super-Pessoa*', in an inversion of the well-known self-image of Pessoa as a 'super-Camões'. Whereas Pessoa saw himself as surpassing Camões, the picture of Shakespeare as a 'super-Pessoa' is no less flattering to the Modernist poet, in that Shakespeare's genius would evince characteristics easily identifiable as Pessoa's own, at least according to his forceful autobiographical self-fashioning.

Castro's book presents a powerful account of Pessoa's intense and varied engagement with Shakespeare, making a compelling case for the centrality of Shakespeare to the elaboration of Pessoa's heteronymic project. This study will thus be essential reading for anyone working on the presence of Shakespeare in European Modernism and, more specifically, on the reception of his work and biography by Fernando Pessoa. It will also prove an essential contribution to a more complex understanding of Pessoa's myriad-minded invention of the heteronyms.

ANNEMARIE JORDAN-GSCHWEND and K. J. P. LOWE (editors), *The Global City: On the Streets of Renaissance Lisbon* (London: Paul Holberton Publishing, 2015). 296 pages, 250 colour illustrations. Print.

Reviewed by JEREMY ROE (Centro de História d'Aquém e d'Além-Mar, Universidade Nova de Lisboa)

The point of departure for this book was the rediscovery of a painting, albeit regrettably cut into two. Painted by a Netherlandish artist between 1570 and 1619, the *View of the Rua Nova dos Mercadores...*, provides an intriguing visual account of daily life on one of Lisbon's busiest commercial streets and the task admirably accomplished by this book is to recount the entwined social, cultural, visual and material histories for which this street, and Lisbon more generally, was the location. The book's interdisciplinary scope is explored in three sections, 'The Maritime City', 'Bringing a Street back to Life' and 'Material Culture: Case Studies from West Africa and Portuguese Asia'; these cover a range of themes from archaeology to literature and carved rock crystal to lacquered shields. The editors, Annemarie Jordan-Gschwend and K. J. P. Lowe, contribute to each of these sections, where they are accompanied by essays from a range of other specialists. The volume contains eight appendices of documentary evidence and two hundred and fifty colour illustrations, whereby it provides a valuable resource for researchers and lecturers alike.

The volume opens with an introductory essay on visual representations of Lisbon and its streets produced during the sixteenth century, when Lisbon first emerged as a 'global city'. In the book's first section Kate Lowe elaborates on this epithet, discussing descriptions of the city written by foreign visitors that document the commercial impact of Lisbon's international empire. These sources record how their authors frequented the *Rua Nova* and their fascination with the array of exotic items on sale. Lowe then goes on to address another facet of the impact of Lisbon's trade, which was its demographic transformation: Lisbon became a hub for European traders and also the home to large populations of Jews and Africans, and Lowe focuses on visual and textual sources for this latter group. The next two chapters turn from urban Lisbon to the maritime activity it depended upon. Firstly, Rui Manuel Loureiro discusses the India trading route and the movement of Chinese goods. In so doing he seeks to redress the dearth of documentary evidence with other sources on Portuguese trade such as Namban screens. Bruno Werz's final essay complements this endeavour by addressing the archaeological finds from a 1533 shipwreck.

The second section opens with a consideration of the significance of Lisbon's urban culture from a Portuguese literary perspective. The positive enthusiasm of foreign visitors for Lisbon is not reflected in Portuguese poetry and plays, and Tom Earle discusses how their writers betrayed moral concerns about the city's worldly pursuits. Evidently, though, as Jordan-Gschwend and Hugo Miguel Crespo discuss, their warnings went unheeded. Jordan-Gschwend offers a historical reconstruction of the *Rua Nova* and its commerce, accompanied by 3-D reconstructions of its architecture. Crespo then turns his attention to the luxury items that could be purchased there. He identifies a distinctly Portuguese attitude to such items, arguing that purchasers used on a daily basis items considered rare, precious and collectable across Europe. Looking towards the final section Jordan-Gschwend offers a wider survey of the international range of commodities on sale, which included a variety of animals.

The final section offers a series of case studies on the products shipped into Lisbon. Lowe discusses ivories and other items brought from West Africa, Shepard Krech considers the contribution from the New World and Turkey, while the final three essays focus on Asian material culture: Crespo discusses rock crystal carving, Ulrike Körber discusses Indo-Muslim shields and Carla Alferes Pinto discusses Indian Ivory carving. By the end of this survey, then, the somewhat subdued *View of the Rua Nova* painting is brought to life in a new manner. Nevertheless, it is the painting that is the final focus of this book, which concludes with a discussion of how Dante Gabriele Rossetti purchased it in 1866 and how sixteenth-century Lisbon's appeal persisted in nineteenth-century London.

# Abstracts

*'Oh, what words can do!': Rhetoric and the Moral Ambiguities of António Ferreira's 'Castro'*
SIMON PARK

ABSTRACT. The counsellors in António Ferreira's tragedy, *Castro*, have often been regarded as scheming and corrupt. This article argues, however, that their arguments echo debates around the virtues of severity and clemency found in Seneca's *De clementia* and in many Renaissance treatises on kingship. Considering how two different, but equally valid, notions of what a ruler should do push against each other in the stichomythic battles of the play, I show that key terms of moral evaluation end up in flux, thereby rendering the ethical decisions in *Castro* much more fraught. A renewed focus on rhetoric and on Renaissance treatises on kingship also opens up a new approach to the character Prince Pedro, whose angry and uncontrolled speeches might have led early modern audiences to consider him the most wayward in the play.

KEYWORDS. António Ferreira, *Castro*, Portuguese drama, tragedy, clemency, rhetoric, ethics, Seneca, *De clementia*.

RESUMO. Os conselheiros na tragédia de António Ferreira *Castro* têm frequentemente sido vistos como personagens maquiavélicas e corruptas. Este artigo propõe, contudo, que os argumentos destas personagens são revisitações de debates em torno das virtudes da severidade e da clemência encontrados em *De clementia* de Séneca bem como em numerosos tratados renascentistas sobre a realeza. Considerando como as duas noções, diferentes mas igualmente válidas, sobre a conduta de um governante se enfrentam nas batalhas esticomíticas da peça, procuro chamar a atenção para como termos chave de avaliação moral se problematizam, assim tornando as decisões éticas em *Castro* muito mais complexas. Uma nova atenção à retórica e a tratados do Renascimento sobre o exercício do poder real permite também uma nova abordagem à personagem do Príncipe Pedro, cujos discursos furiosos e descontrolados poderão ter levado um público contemporâneo a considerá-la a mais instável da peça.

PALAVRAS-CHAVE. António Ferreira, *Castro*, drama portuguesa, tragédia, clemência, retórica, ética, Séneca, *De clementia*.

*The 'Papel Volante': A Marginalized Genre in Eighteenth-Century Portuguese Culture?*
PEDRO MARQUES

ABSTRACT. Commonly designated as *literatura de cordel*, the eighteenth-century editorial genre *papel volante* has traditionally been associated with popular culture and outmoded rhetorical models and topics. The twentieth century saw the rehabilitation of these pamphlets as publications that disseminated new ideas at the margins of the literary, cultural and political establishments. An analysis of how the *papel volante* reorganized the relation between authorship, target audience and content provides a description of an effective medium that took advantage of a wide social reach and a tension between legitimization and marginality. Authors and publishers of *papéis volantes* used their in-depth knowledge of eighteenth-century patterns of discourse production to subvert its rules, and disseminate marginal topics in early modern Portuguese culture.

KEYWORDS. *Cordel* literature, eighteenth century, marginal literature, *papel volante*, Woman Question.

RESUMO. Normalmente chamado de literatura de cordel, o género editorial setecentista papel volante tem sido tradicionalmente associado à cultura popular e a temas e modelos retóricos ultrapassados. No século XX, estas publicações foram reabilitadas como um meio de difusão de novas ideias que funcionava à margem dos poderes literários, culturais e políticos. A análise de como o género reorganizava a relação entre autoria, público-alvo e conteúdo oferece-nos a descrição de um meio eficaz que tirava partido de um alcance social alargado e de uma tensão entre legitimação e marginalidade. Autores e editores de papéis faziam uso do conhecimento aprofundado dos padrões de produção de discursos no século XVIII para subverter as regras estabelecidas, e disseminar temas marginais na cultura portuguesa setecentista.

PALAVRAS-CHAVE. Literatura de cordel, literatura marginal, papel volante, *querelle des femmes*, século XVIII.

*Landscapes of Portugal in Two Hundred Years of Narratives*
ANA ISABEL QUEIROZ

ABSTRACT. Whether as a romantic depiction or with a pretension to realism, rural life was a classic topic throughout the nineteenth and the twentieth centuries. A few writers represented the impending threats to the natural environment as a consequence of human actions, such as deforestation and poaching. More recently, literary landscape incorporates the profound changes the country has undergone in the last decades, and a global environmental reality at a European and worldwide level. Settings are mostly urban, though some nostalgia for the rural and the 'return to nature' can be seen, in line with the current culture of our days.

From examples of landscape descriptions in fiction and non-fiction, this article focuses on the way in which Portuguese writers have valued the natural and cultural elements according to their literary skills and motives, and the cultural framework of their times. Excerpts from canonical writers and respected current authors are analysed: Alexandre Herculano, Júlio Dinis, Eça de Queiroz, Fialho de Almeida, Raul Brandão, Aquilino Ribeiro, Miguel Torga, José Saramago, Lídia Jorge, Mário de Carvalho and Rui Cardoso Martins.

KEYWORDS. Landscape, Portuguese literature, ecocriticism.

RESUMO. Como uma descrição romântica ou com uma pretensão de realismo, a vida rural era um tema clássico durante todo o século XIX e XX. Alguns escritores representaram as ameaças iminentes sobre o ambiente natural como consequência de ações humanas, como desmatamento e caça furtiva. Recentemente, a paisagem literária incorporou as profundas mudanças que o país atravessou nas últimas décadas e uma realidade ambiental global, a nível europeu e mundial. As configurações são principalmente urbanas, embora alguma nostalgia para o rural e o 'regresso à natureza' possa ser interpretado, em consonância com a cultura atual.

A partir de exemplos de descrições de paisagens em ficção e não-ficção, este artigo trata da forma como os escritores portugueses valorizam os elementos naturais e culturais de acordo com suas competências literárias e motivações e no quadro cultural do seu tempo. São analisados excertos de escritores canónicos e respeitados autores atuais: Alexandre Herculano, Júlio Dinis, Eça de Queiroz, Fialho de Almeida, Raul Brandão, Aquilino Ribeiro, Miguel Torga, José Saramago, Lídia Jorge, Mário de Carvalho e Rui Cardoso Martins.

PALAVRAS-CHAVE. Paisagem, literatura portuguesa, ecocriticismo.

*How to Construct a Master: Pessoa and Caeiro*
JERÓNIMO PIZARRO

ABSTRACT. Fernando Pessoa described Alberto Caeiro as his teacher, despite the fact that Caeiro was a poetic creation. This article studies the construction of that teacher, from a diachronic approach. Rather than a rounded and defined figure, Caeiro is presented as an author who became more and more real, up until and after his fictitious death, in 1915, and indeed was still being constructed in 1935, the year in which Pessoa himself died. It also aims to explain how it was only in 2008 that Caeiro's genetic dossier became much more complete and to stress the fact that the Caeiro revealed by Pessoa in 1925, in *Athena* magazine, actually hides aspects of his heteronym.

KEYWORDS. Fernando Pessoa, Alberto Caeiro, *The Keeper of Flocks*, The Sick Shepherd, The Amorous Shepherd, Walt Whitman, diachronic approach.

RESUMO. Fernando Pessoa descreveu Alberto Caeiro como o seu mestre, embora Caeiro tenha sido uma criação poética. Este artigo estuda a construção desse mestre, procurando uma leitura diacrónica do mesmo. Mais do que estudar uma figura una, redonda e definida, interessa apresentar Caeiro como um autor que antes e depois da sua morte fictícia, em 1915, foi ganhando realidade e que ainda em 1935, aquando da morte real de Pessoa, estava a ser construído. Propõe-se também explicar porque ficou o dossier genético de Caeiro mais completo apenas em 2008 e frisar que o Caeiro revelado por Pessoa em 1925, na revista *Athena*, oculta aspetos do seu heterónimo.

PALAVRAS-CHAVE. Fernando Pessoa, Alberto Caeiro, *O Guardador de Rebanhos*, O pastor adoentado, O pastor amoroso, Walt Whitman, abordagem diacrónica.

*A Life Framed: Serafim Alves de Carvalho's 'Emigrar... Emigrar: as contas do meu rosário' (1986)*
CARMEN RAMOS VILLAR

ABSTRACT. Published in Portugal in December 1986, by the Secretaria de Estado das Comunidades Portuguesas/Centro de estudos, as part of the series 'Portugueses de Longe Escrevem' series, Serafim Alves de Carvalho's *Emigrar... Emigrar: as contas do meu rosário* (1986) emerges at a particularly significant moment in Portuguese history. By focusing its close reading of Carvalho's account on four areas of analytical 'framing', to use the term proposed by Paul Longley Arthur, the article will contribute to existing critical studies of this autobiography by nuancing how Carvalho's self is constructed in the final, published text. In so doing, the article argues that the construction of Carvalho's self, and the content in Carvalho's account, including the contradictions and inconsistencies present in the final text, was constrained by publication aims.

KEYWORDS. Alves de Carvalho, autobiography, photography, ghost-writer, emigration.

RESUMO. A publicação de *Emigrar... Emigrar: as contas do meu rosário* (1986) por Serafim Alves de Carvalho pela Secretaria de Estado das Comunidades Portuguesas/Centro de estudos sob a série 'Portugueses de Longe Escrevem' emerge num período significativo na história portuguesa. Mediante uma focalização analítica seguindo os parâmetros de 'framing' propostos por Paul Longley Arthur, este artigo contribui a trabalhos existentes que analisam esta autobiografia ao matizar a forma como o 'eu' de Alves de Carvalho é construído textualmente. Desta forma, o artigo exporá que a construção do 'eu' de Alves de Carvalho e o conteúdo do texto, inclusive as contradições e incoerências nele, foram condicionados pelas aspirações editoriais às quais o texto foi sujeito.

PALAVRAS-CHAVE. Alves de Carvalho, autobiografia, fotografias, compositor, emigração.

*Writing on Behalf of Those Women 'Que Não [?] Têm Escrita': Gendered Boundaries inside and outside the Fiction of Mia Couto*
TOM STENNETT

ABSTRACT. This article will discuss the relationship between gender and boundaries inside and outside three novels by Mozambican writer Mia Couto: *Jesusalém* (2009), *A Confissão da Leoa* (2012) and *Mulheres de Cinza* (2015). Whereas men and women are forced to occupy separate spaces inside the texts' settings, outside the novels a blurring between masculinity and femininity threatens to occur as Couto aligns his idiosyncratic writing style with that of his fictional women narrators. In subtly fashioning a gender-ambiguous identity on an extra-diegetic level and claiming to speak, through the voice of the female narrator of *Mulheres de Cinza*, for Mozambicans denied access to the written word, Couto encroaches on the limited space afforded to Mozambican women writers.

KEYWORDS. Mia Couto, gender, boundaries, women's writing.

RESUMO. Pretende-se com o presente trabalho examinar a relação entre o género e as fronteiras dentro e fora de três romances do escritor moçambicano Mia Couto: *Jesusalém* (2009), *A Confissão da Leoa* (2012) e *Mulheres de Cinza* (2015). Enquanto que as personagens masculinas e femininas destes romances são forçadas a ocupar espaços separados dentro dos cenários textuais, fora dos textos a fronteira entre a masculinidade e a feminilidade ameaça diluir-se ao passo que Couto alinha a sua escrita idiossincrática com a escrita das suas narradoras ficcionais. Assim, Couto estaria a invadir o pouco espaço concedido a escritoras moçambicanas uma vez que o autor cria subtilmente uma identidade de género ambíguo num nível extradiegético e pretende, através da voz da narradora de *Mulheres de Cinza*, escrever em nome das pessoas que não têm acesso à escrita.

PALAVRAS-CHAVE. Mia Couto, género, fronteiras, escrita feminina.

*Six Crônicas on Slavery and Abolition, by Machado de Assis*
Translated and edited by ROBERT PATRICK NEWCOMB

ABSTRACT. One of the perennial questions surrounding the great Brazilian writer Machado de Assis (1839–1908) is the degree to which he addressed slavery and abolition in his work. The defence of Machado as a writer who, while not a militant, nonetheless opposed slavery has been bolstered by the increased attention paid in recent years to his *crônicas* (newspaper chronicles), several of which reflected on slavery and abolition. In the six *crônicas* presented here in English translation, Machado approaches these themes in ways that are consistent with his literary and philosophical worldview, and he presents slavery as a logical outgrowth of society's underlying brutality.

KEYWORDS. Machado de Assis, slavery, abolition, Brazil, *crônica*.

RESUMO. Um dos problemas mais debatidos em torno do grande escritor brasileiro Machado de Assis (1839–1908) é a questão da proeminência na sua obra dos temas de escravidão e abolição. O estudo das crônicas machadianas, cada vez mais valorizadas pela crítica, serve para defender a hipótese de um Machado que, não obstante sua falta de militância, favoreceu a abolição. Nas seis crônicas apresentadas aqui, traduzidas para inglês, a escravidão e a abolição se descrevem conforme a visão literária e filosófica do autor, segundo a qual a escravidão seria o resultado lógico da brutalidade que é inerente à sociedade.

PALAVRAS-CHAVE. Machado de Assis, escravidão, abolição, Brasil, crônica.